BRITISH FORCES MOTORCYCLES
1925-1945

BRITISH FORCES MOTORCYCLES
1925-1945

Chris Orchard and Steve Madden

This edition is dedicated to the memory of our close friend and fellow enthusiast Clive Curryer who passed away in 2014.

Ariel W/NG in mud.

Cover illustration: Riders training on Matchless G3s. (RLC Museum)

First published 1995
This edition, 2017

The History Press
The Mill, Brimscombe Port
Stroud, Gloucestershire, GL5 2QG
www.thehistorypress.co.uk

© Chris Orchard & Steve Madden 1995, 2017

The right of Chris Orchard & Steve Madden to be identified as the Authors of this work has been asserted in accordance with the Copyright, Designs and Patents Act 1988.

All rights reserved. No part of this book may be reprinted or reproduced or utilised in any form or by any electronic, mechanical or other means, now known or hereafter invented, including photocopying and recording, or in any information storage or retrieval system, without the permission in writing from the Publishers.

British Library Cataloguing in Publication Data.
A catalogue record for this book is available from the British Library.

ISBN 978 0 7509 7023 5

Typesetting and origination by The History Press
Printed and bound by TJ International Ltd

Contents

	Acknowledgements	7
	Abbreviations	11
1	Suitable for WD Requirements?	13
2	Standardisation in the Second World War	28
3	Dealing with Defects	34
4	Raw Material Shortages in the Second World War Affecting Motorcycle Production	40
5	Motorcycle Disposals	44
6	Motorcycles with Provenance	47
7	War Department Manufacturers	50

AJS	50	Moto-Chenille	131
Ariel	53	New Hudson	132
Aveling Barford	61	New Imperial	133
BMW	62	Norman	135
BSA	64	Norton	135
Douglas	87	OEC	145
Excelsior	91	Panther	148
Francis Barnett	98	Royal Enfield	150
Gillet-Herstal	101	Rudge Whitworth	167
Harley-Davidson	101	Stewart-Ehrlich	170
Indian	104	S.O.S.	170
James	110	Sunbeam	171
Levis	115	Triumph	173
Matchless	117	Velocette	190

8	Sidecars	195
9	Miscellaneous Motorcycles	197
10	The VAOS Spare Parts System	201
11	Colour Schemes	207
	Appendix 1: Contract Notes	212
	Appendix 2: Production Tables	213

Acknowledgements

The origins of this book date back to the late 1970s when Chris Orchard's interest in military motorcycles of the Second World War period started, and he contacted John Marchant of the Military Vehicle Trust (MVT; formerly the Military Vehicle Conservation Group), who was kind enough to supply him with motorcycle contract information from a 1944–45 census record. This material, together with the information from original parts lists, drivers' handbooks, ledgers formerly held by the Science Museum Library, contract details in various volumes held by The National Archives at Kew (TNA), records held by the Army Museum of Transport at Beverley (now elsewhere), and additional census details obtained in 1990 from the REME Museum (missing from the original census details obtained), constitute the tabular information at the end of the book.

Help must also be acknowledged from all the private individuals who have sent in details to both authors over the years and who are too numerous to mention individually by name. (If anyone can help with any missing information, the authors would be pleased to hear from you.)

In about 1988 Chris met Steve for the first time when he contacted him for details on his BSA M20. Many months later, Steve persuaded Chris to use this information as the basis for a book and turn it into a 'bible' and reference source for WD motorcycle enthusiasts. Steve then added further information to the details that had already been collected over the years.

The following clubs, individuals and museums are to be thanked for their help in providing substantial information for the original book:

AJS John Allen of the AJS and Matchless Owners' Club, Science Museum Library, John Tinley; **ARIEL** Ralph Hawkins of the Ariel Owners' Motor Cycle Club, Roger and Mick of Draganfly Motorcycles, Bungay, TNA, Science Museum Library; **AVELING BARFORD** TNA; **BMW** John Lawes of the VMCC; **BSA** Steve Foden of the BSA Owners' Club, N.W. Lewis of the VMCC, TNA, Science Museum Library, A.G. Jeal; **DOUGLAS** Reg Holmes of the London Douglas Owners' Club, David Fletcher of the Tank Museum, TNA, F.L. Dolman of the VMCC; **EXCELSIOR** A.D. Mellor; **FRANCIS BARNETT** TNA, John Harding of Francis Barnett Owners' Club; **GILLET-HERSTAL** Bart Vanderveen, TNA; **HARLEY-DAVIDSON** Iain Cottrell of the MVT, D. Sarafan; **INDIAN** J. Reed of the VMCC, M. Hitchens, Lex Schmidt; **JAMES** C.P. Penny; **LEVIS** TNA and David Fletcher of the Tank Museum; **MATCHLESS** (see AJS); **MOTO-CHENILLE** TNA; **NEW HUDSON** Eric Londesborough of the VMCC; **NEW IMPERIAL** Fred Pateman of the New Imperial Owners' Association; **NORMAN** J. Sampson of the British Two Stroke Club; **NORTON** W. Flew of the VMCC, Science Museum Library, N. Hinton of the Norton Owners' Club, Richard Payne and Rob van den Brink; **OEC** M. Shelley of the VMCC; **PANTHER** Barry Jones of the Panther Owners' Club, Imperial War Museum; **ROYAL ENFIELD** Steve Mayhew and Doug Young of the Royal Enfield Owners Club, A.D. Mellor, MoD Boscombe Down, Jan Vandevelde; **RUDGE WHITWORTH** Dave McMahon of the Rudge Enthusiasts' Club; **S.O.S.** Lex Schmidt; **STEWART-EHRLICH** TNA, Dr J. Ehrlich; **SUNBEAM** Derek Beddows of the Marston Sunbeam Register; **TRIUMPH** Martin Jones of the Triumph Owners' Motor Cycle Club; **VELOCETTE** R. Franklin of the Velocette Owners' Club, J. Clew of the VMCC; **SIDECARS** various sources; **MISCELLANEOUS MOTORCYCLES** various sources; **COLOUR SCHEMES** various sources.

Particular thanks must also be given to Peter Watson, our close friend at the offices of EMAP; Brian Baxter and David Ross (photographer) of the REME Museum at Arborfield, Berkshire; Michael Ware and Jonathan Day of the National Motor Museum at Beaulieu, Hampshire; Nick Nicholson of the Aircraft & Armament Evaluation Establishment (now Julie Bromilow at MoD Boscombe Down); members of the MVT (PO Box 6, Fleet, Hants, GU13 9PE); David Fletcher of the Tank Museum, Bovington Camp, Dorset; G. Blewett of the Museum of Army Transport, Beverley, North Humberside; Bill Phelps of the VMCC; Bob Whistler (photo reproduction), Diane Andrews, Alan Brown and others at the Airborne Forces Museum, Aldershot, Hampshire; Bart Vanderveen; C.P. Penny; the Trustees of the Imperial War Museum, London, and of the Public Record Office, Kew, Surrey; and John Underwood of the Science Museum Library. To all, a big thank you for their help on many matters.

Special thanks go to Chris's wife, Gill Orchard, and Ms Jamie Madden, for putting up with us during the writing of the first edition book. Thanks also to Gill's mother, Mrs Paula Smith, for typing numerous letters and chapter drafts over the past few years.

For help with the second edition we would particularly like to mention Peter Cornelius, who updated our information on the pre-war Triumph models, and Clive Elliott, whose articles on spares in the Military Vehicle Trust's publication, *Windscreen*, have been especially enlightening.

ACKNOWLEDGEMENTS

The Museum of Army Flying
Middle Wallop, Stockbridge, Hampshire, SO20 8DY
Tel: 01264 784421
enquiries@flying-museum.org.uk
www.armyflying.com

The Royal Military Police Museum
DSPG PP38, Southwick Park, Southwick, Hants, PO17 6EJ
Tel: 023 9228 4372
museum_rhqrmp@btconnect.com

Royal Signals Museum
Blandford, Dorset, DT11 8RH
Tim Stankus, Archivist,
Tel: 01258 482413
Fax: 01258 482084
archivist@royalsignalsmuseum.com
www.royalsignalsmuseum.com

The Royal Logistics Corps Museum
The Princess Royal Barracks, Blackdown Road, Deepcut, Camberley, Surrey, GU16 6RW
Tel: 01252 833371
Fax: 01252 833484
information@rlcmuseum.com

The Royal Green Jackets (Rifles) Museum
Peninsula Barracks, Romsey Road, Winchester, SO23 8TS
Tel: 01962 828549
curator@rgjmuseum.co.uk
www.rgjmuseum.co.uk

REME Museum
Prince Philip Barracks, Lyneham, Chippenham, SN15 4XX
Tel: 01249 894869
enquiries@rememuseum.org.uk

Royal Enfield Owners Club
www.royalenfield.org.uk

For this third edition special thanks must go to Gareth Mears at the RLC Museum, Richard Callaghan and Matthew Wood at the RMP Museum, Peter Capon at The Museum of Army Flying, Hampshire Records Office/The Royal Green Jackets Museum (Christine Pullen), Henk Joore, John Forsey, Mark Shemilt, Jan Vandevelde and John Tinley for the new photographs used.

Thanks are also due to the various museums, owners' clubs and individuals (see above) for allowing the reuse of the photographs from previous editions in this new edition.

Further mention must be made to John Tinley (AJS), Mick Holmes of Draganfly Motorcycles (Ariel), Henk Joore (BSA), Lex Schmidt (Indian & S.O.S.), Richard Payne and Rob van den Brink (Norton) and Jan Vandevelde (Royal Enfield) for the table updates.

Thanks are also due for the additional information on motorcycle use from RLC Museum, RMP Museum and The National Archives.

Abbreviations

AD	Admiralty Department (government office for the Navy)
AFEE	Airborne Forces Experimental Establishment
AM	Air Ministry (government office for the RAF)
AMC	Associated Motor Cycles
CMP	Corps of Military Police
DME	Director of Mechanical Engineering
IWM	Imperial War Museum
JAP	J.A. Prestwich
LP	Local Purchase
MEE	Mechanisation Experimental Establishment
MoA	Ministry of Agriculture
MoS	Ministry of Supply (government office for provision and demand of military, government and war produce)
MVT	Military Vehicle Trust
MWEE	Mechanical Warfare Experimental Establishment
OHV	Overhead Valve
PRO	Public Record Office (now The National Archives (TNA))
RAF	Royal Air Force
RAOC	Royal Army Ordnance Corps (principally in control of supply and distribution of motorcycles from manufacturers. MoS did the initial ordering)
RASC	Royal Army Service Corps
REME	Royal Electrical & Mechanical Engineers (formed mid 1942)
RN	Royal Navy
SV	Side Valve
SWD	Sidecar Wheel Drive
VAOS	Vocabulary of Army Ordnance Stores
VMCC	Vintage Motor Cycle Club
VRD	Vehicle Receiving Depot
WD	War Department ⎫ government office for the Army
WO	War Office ⎭

1

Suitable for WD Requirements?

The First World War witnessed the first large-scale employment of vehicles and other forms of mechanised transport in the history of conflict. Acting as a proving ground for mechanisation, the war highlighted the advantages and disadvantages of machines and, in some instances, their total unsuitability for military use. Drawing on the experiences of the First World War, the long-term aim in the interwar period was towards the total mechanisation of the armed services and the ultimate replacement of horse-drawn transport. To this end the military authorities created the Mechanical Warfare Experimental Establishment in 1926 (to become the Mechanisation Experimental Establishment in 1934, and referred to hereafter as the MWEE and MEE respectively) located at Cove, near Farnborough in Hampshire. In 1940 the MEE underwent a further change of name to TT2.

The purpose of this establishment was to test and assess the suitability of all forms of mechanised transport, including motorcycles, offered to or acquired by the military authorities for potential service use. Each class of equipment had a standardised evaluation period applied to it. In the case of the motorcycle, the establishment considered that all models should be subjected to a comprehensive 10,000-mile test period consisting of both on- and off-road mileages, the initial 500 miles of the test mileage being a running-in period. During the course of the test period an interim inspection of the motorcycle was carried out, usually following the completion of at least 5,000 miles, in order to note the degree of wear and endurance of individual components. A variety of performance checks were also carried out, but which generally employed ¼-mile standing-start times and fuel consumption figures over 100-mile distances. The machine's off-road ability was also reviewed, including its ability to travel across rough ploughed fields, wet clay, bogs, sandy ditches and loose stone surfaces. Its ability to successfully stop and start on a gradient was also assessed.

Following completion of the 10,000-mile test period, the motorcycle was completely stripped down to measure all components for wear and damage. All the relevant details were added to the interim 5,000-mile report, together with any notable points of concern that had arisen during the entire test period, principally mechanical and electrical faults. The final stage of the test period involved the collation of all the information that had been gathered, resulting in a detailed report on the motorcycle concerned. It noted whether the machine was considered suitable, or unsuitable, for War Office requirements and the completed report was then sealed and classified 'Top Secret'.

Military thinking towards both the type and specification of motorcycles required for service use, together with their intended role and applications, was to vary considerably during the interwar period. This was particularly so during the 1930s, although policy changes were to continue throughout the Second World War and beyond. These revisions in thinking were caused by various factors, not least the changes in hierarchy at the War Office, improvements and advances in motorcycle design, operational experience and the necessary economies arising in wartime.

The situation concerning motorcycle combinations can be used to illustrate some of the above points. Proved to be of considerable military value during the First World War, the motorcycle combination was initially thought to be an ideal step towards the concept of a mechanised army, principally as a lightly armed scouting or reconnaissance vehicle. Design limitations, such as the lack of protection from the elements, inadequate equipment stowage and doubtful cross-country abilities became apparent during the late 1920s after the introduction of the Austin Seven 2-seater car.

This vehicle successfully addressed many of the motorcycle combination's deficiencies and, as a result, the Austin Seven began to take over the role previously the sole domain of the combination. However, it was not entirely superseded, for in the late 1930s the motorcycle combination once again attracted War Office interest in the form of the Norton Big 4. This machine incorporated a driven sidecar wheel and proved to be a major improvement across country over previous sidecar designs.

However, by 1942 the sidecar machine was once again declared to be obsolete, thanks to the arrival of American-manufactured light-utility 4x4 cars supplied under Lend-Lease arrangements. Produced by both Willys-Overland and the Ford Motor Company, these vehicles became known universally as the Jeep. They were vastly superior to extant motorcycle combinations in virtually every aspect, being more rugged and with a greatly increased carrying capability, a superior performance and a better off-road capability among other things. Anyone who could drive a car would have little difficulty

SUITABLE FOR WD REQUIREMENTS?

No. 1 Workshop Group (REME), Chilwell, busy repairing forks and frames. The completed forks in the foreground are Matchless, Triumph and Indian. (REME Museum)

in driving the Jeep, whereas the Norton Big 4 combination, in particular, took an experienced sidecar rider to competently drive the combination across country, more so over difficult terrain. Yet again, the motorcycle combination was downgraded by the military.

No longer required for off-road duties, the War Office still regarded the motorcycle combination as a useful and cheap form of passenger and stores transportation. It therefore continued to order under contract small quantities of machines fitted with sidecars, primarily BSA M20 and Norton 16H models, until shortly before the end of the Second World War. Principal recipients were the Royal Air Force (RAF), where the combination was a useful mode of transport on airfields with far-flung dispersals, and civil defence organisations including some units of the Home Guard where the machines were frequently employed on road patrol duties in rural areas.

The situation concerning solo motorcycles and the War Office was a very different matter, however, with the MWEE/MEE constantly looking for better machines than the examples of the time. It is not widely realised that from its formation in 1926 up to the Second World War and beyond, the MWEE/MEE tested and evaluated countless motorcycles. Almost every machine produced during this period, even if not ultimately tested by the War Office for military suitability, was invariably considered for possible testing.

Solo motorcycles were judged by the War Office to have distinct advantages over most other forms of mechanised wheeled transport of the period. These advantages were of considerable value and included: small overall size, which favoured manoeuvrability and concealment; a good overall performance from the engine; a limited off-road capability and the ability to proceed across, through and around obstacles that impeded larger vehicles; overall value for money and economical running costs; and, in the main, ease of maintenance. The First World War and the years that followed revealed that certain motorcycles were more suited to military requirements than others. With the War Office looking towards the mechanisation of the British Army, motorcycles for the military was one of the many areas to be assessed. The search for the most suitable solo motorcycle for War Office requirements was put in the hands of the MWEE during 1927, a year after the establishment had been formed. At this time, the British Army was still using a number of mechanised vehicles dating from the First World War some nine years earlier, including some motorcycles.

The MWEE was charged with looking at every possible feature of a motorcycle, and testing commenced with experiments using lightweight 2-stroke motorcycles and 3-wheels-in-line machines. Initial results of these first tests tended to reveal that a machine's lightness in weight was important for cross-country use, but this appeared to be at the expense of robustness. Speed on the road was also poor with the 2-stroke engines often showing a tendency to seize. Experiments with the 3-wheel machines showed the type to be extremely heavy and complex in design. The additional expense incurred by the design outweighed the moderate gain in cross-country ability, particularly so as by now conventional solo machines fitted with bigger section tyres were displaying considerably improved off-road performance. Other problems arising with the heavy 3-wheel machines included poor reliability and ride quality that made them tiring for the riders.

Still attempting to find a suitable motorcycle for the military, a committee of War Office representatives visited the 1928 Olympia Motorcycle Show with the objective of finding the most suitable machine of standard design for military purposes. However, no single machine at the show appeared to meet all of the stringent service requirements, particularly at a weight appreciably less than 300lb. In December of that year it was decided to obtain detailed particulars of machines manufactured by leading British companies, with those showing most promise to be submitted for testing by the MWEE and/or in the hands of selected units within the Army's Royal Corps of Signals. The result of this decision saw seven different makes of motorcycle purchased during 1929 for comparative trials against one another, these being the products of OEC, Francis Barnett, BSA, AJS, New Hudson, Matchless and Douglas. Every one of the motorcycles supplied was of 350cc engine capacity (or 2¾hp), the maximum engine size the military authorities deemed necessary for solo use at the time.

However, before the tests had been completed the need for a new type of motorcycle for the War Office became so urgent that the authorities stepped in, ordering an irregular and hasty comparison test between the products of Douglas and Triumph, both companies having held considerable favour with the War Office up to then. Ultimately, the Douglas machine, the model L29, was to be chosen in preference to the Triumph machine, the model NL3. Interestingly, the Triumph NL3 was not even part of the seven-make trial, although later on it was to be tested overseas in Egypt in company with an OEC 3-wheel machine and the Levis.

By November 1929 the trials were concluded and the MWEE had formed the opinion that the heavier machines should be dropped because of the considerable difficulty in riding them across country. The lightweight machines fared little better and they too were dropped owing to their poor performance and susceptibility to damage. This decision left the War Office with three models available for further testing – the AJS model M6, the Matchless T/4, and the Douglas L29, although even these were heavier

Frame jigs for rebuilding motorcycles at No. 1 Workshop, Chilwell. Being worked on is an Ariel W/NG frame. (REME Museum)

than the preferred upper limit set by the authorities. Further testing of these machines resulted in little progress and led to a hardening of the viewpoint that no commercial motorcycle then available could meet all necessary military requirements without drastic modification. In order to meet all these requirements it would be more practical if a dedicated military machine was designed and built, specifically with an upper weight limit of 300lb or less, yet still retaining performance and durability.

Other points of desirability to arise from the testing of machines for military use included such features as enclosed valve operating mechanisms, dry-sump lubrication, general weatherproofing of vulnerable components and twin exhaust ports with dual silencing. Also deemed a necessary feature in all future military motorcycle contracts was a standardised pattern of controls, as proposed by the British Cycle and Motor Cycle Manufacturers and Traders Union in February 1929, and endorsed and supported by the authorities.

However, the War Office had still not given up entirely on the idea of using a commercial production motorcycle of the time, suitably modified of course, although a visit by a group of representatives to the 1929 Motorcycle Show once again proved unsuccessful in establishing a model suitable

No. 1 Workshop Group, Chilwell, overhauling BSA, Norton and Matchless. Note the Matchless (third one in on the right) has two racks fitted for some reason. (REME Museum)

for military use. Certain motorcycles at the show, though, did incorporate various features as required by the authorities, although not sufficient to justify purchase. In the following year thinking changed at the War Office in favour of twin-cylinder motorcycles, which it was thought were generally quieter than single-cylinder versions. The recently acquired Douglas machines remained in service throughout this period, although they were subjected to modification at various intervals. The other remaining machines were quietly, and conveniently, forgotten.

With twins now in favour, Matchless was to supply the War Office with its Silver Arrow model and BSA was to supply its new 500cc overhead-valve (OHV) V-twin model. In due course, the authorities were to favour the BSA twin over the Matchless, and were to purchase quantities of the type at various stages throughout the 1930s. However, the model was prone to excessive cylinder wear throughout its service life, a problem that was never fully corrected.

Another requirement for military motorcycles was an efficient silencing system. During this period the MWEE evaluated a number of different silencers in an attempt to establish the most effective example – the products of Howarth, Premier and Woodvan were investigated but ultimately none proved effective. (In later years, notably during 1938, the War Office was to work with Norton Motors on the silencing problem, only to conclude that it was difficult to silence motorcycles!) By now, attention was also being focused on mechanical noise and some improvements were made in this area. Even by 1934 it was realised that twin-cylinder machines were actually no quieter than single-cylinder variants and considerably more expensive, notably on running costs.

Still seeking motorcycles suitable for military purposes, by 1935 the War Office was once again looking at single-cylinder machines. The basic requirements were for a machine of 350cc or more and of either side valve (SV) or OHV configuration. Accordingly, a trial period was arranged and seven makes of machine were purchased for evaluation purposes, these being the products of Ariel, BSA, Matchless, New Imperial, Norton, Royal Enfield and Triumph. Once the trial was under way, the Ariel machine, which up until then had proved the best both in terms of performance and reliability, became obsolete and was dropped from the testing programme. For the remaining models the New Imperial and Royal Enfield machines showed poorly throughout the test period while the BSA, Matchless, Norton and Triumph models all showed well – initially, that is. All testing was completed within six months, unlike the previous trials of 1929 which ran on for many months more.

In 1936 BSA replaced its model W35/6, which had shown poor reliability during the War Office 10,000-mile test, with a new model, the ubiquitous M20.

Motorcycle wheel rebuilding at No. 1 Workshop, Chilwell. (REME Museum)

Following the company's reorganisation, initially preceded by a name change, Triumph was also to replace the previously tested model 3/1 within its range with a new model, the 3S. Those machines remaining from the military trials of 1935 were now just two in number, the original 16H Norton model and the Matchless G3, small orders for both of which were to follow. Other manufacturers at this time attempted to arouse War Office interest in their products, namely newcomers Rudge and Sunbeam, along with Douglas and Ariel with new machines, but ultimately only Rudge was to succeed modestly in gaining contract status. The Sunbeam model offered was subsequently withdrawn from testing due to the Matchless buy-out of the company, while both the Douglas and Ariel machines ultimately proved unsuitable for service requirements.

During 1936, a need was identified for motorcycles suitable for training purposes and light communication duties. The War Office purchased a quantity of 250cc Matchless models without the type first having been evaluated for suitability by the MEE.

With development continuing, the next official trials took place during 1939, when the various manufacturers were asked to submit a design of a machine not exceeding 250lb in weight, but retaining the performance of a standard 500cc military motorcycle. Norton, Royal Enfield and Triumph were first to submit their respective designs, followed later by those of BSA and Matchless. In the end, only the BSA and Triumph designs were to reach production stage, yet neither was to survive. The bombing of the Triumph factory during November 1940 destroyed that company's model, and BSA's design was cancelled at the last minute by the War Office, most probably for concern over spares for yet another different model of machine from those then in service.

During the build-up to the Second World War military motorcycle production was indeed stepped up and by early 1940 supply was beginning to meet demand. Even so, many of the larger manufacturers were still producing models for the civilian market but could not guarantee immediate delivery because of the pressures of war. By May 1940, however, this was to change following the invasions of France and the Low Countries by Germany and the evacuation of the British Expeditionary Force from Dunkirk. The vast proportion of the British Army's most modern and newest equipment, including motorcycles, had been lost during the evacuation. With the threat of an invasion of Great Britain itself now a very real possibility, the War Office found itself chronically short of virtually every kind of item imaginable, including motorcycles that would be vital for the defence of mainland Britain.

Accordingly, all major manufacturers were inundated with huge orders for motorcycles from the War Office, fresh contracts being placed before the completion of existing ones in some cases. To meet demand, emergency purchases were also made that principally involved the authorities impressing all suitable civilian-destined machines awaiting either completion or delivery from the factories and also from dealers' showrooms. Other machines were delivered to the War Office in the form of 'gifts' – typically suitable machines in good, serviceable condition donated by their patriotic civilian owners. Some 8,000 motorcycles of both impressed and gift status were to be accepted by the authorities at the time, the vast proportion being employed by second-line formations, training units and civil defence organisations.

To further boost the War Office's stocks, machines from Harley-Davidson and Indian, manufactured in America, were delivered to the authorities under the war-aid scheme of Lend-Lease. The first to arrive were combination machines, soon to be followed by solo versions. Generally, the War Office disliked the American motorcycles due in the main to their size and weight; also, the rider's controls in most cases were arranged in a completely different configuration to those on conventional British military machines. This, of course, required good familiarity from a rider before one could be ridden competently and with safety. Many of these Lend-Lease machines were sent to far-flung outposts of the British Empire or issued to UK-based second-line civil defence formations, not to mention sizeable quantities, particularly the Indian model 741B, going to the Royal Air Force.

As the Second World War progressed, the major manufacturers continued to churn out the same basic models for the authorities that they had first supplied during 1940 or earlier. Certain manufacturers even changed from SV to OHV designs during the mid-war period in an attempt to standardise War Office motorcycles as 350cc OHV designs and 500cc SV machines. Motorcycle production settled into a steady, high-volume turnout of machines.

Despite this, the authorities were still concerned about the wide range of different spares required for each type of machine held on inventory, and the possible production and distribution problems that might arise. Even so, some rationalisation had already taken place with the standardisation of certain universal fittings, such as handlebar control levers, saddles, pillion and pannier equipment. Number plates disappeared from military machines from about 1941; rubber fittings, apart from essential items, were deleted from about 1943 onwards owing to rubber shortages caused by the Japanese conquests in South East Asia. Early wartime machines were often updated during the war by fitting newer components, such as the pannier frames; yet others often lost fittings, such as lights, seat covers and front mudguards, either owing to damage or in an effort to lighten the machine. This practice was most common in North Africa, and was probably due to a shortage of spares and attendant maintenance difficulties in the region.

The supply of spare parts was always a problem throughout most of the Second World War: the more isolated the theatre of operations, the more acute the problem became. In many such instances, cannibalisation of damaged machines was necessary in order to produce one serviceable example. Frequently, the popular teledraulic front forks of the Matchless G3/L can be seen adorning the front of a more mundane, girder-forked machine in an attempt to improve handling and comfort. Other noted home-made modifications in the desert included an air filter made from an old mess tin strapped to the top of the fuel tank and sump shields, to name but a couple.

The use of motorcycles in the Indian jungle was raised as a concern in February 1944. A report condemned them as unsatisfactory because of the roads there, so much so that many units were using 15cwts, Jeeps or horses to do what DRs used to do. The rough roads frequently caused 'Barrel springs'

No. 21 Advanced Base Workshop, REME, Belgium, 1945. Note the manufacturers' names hanging above the motorcycles, showing how REME divided its workshops to cope with all the different motorcycle brands. BSA, Norton and Ariel can be seen here. (REME Museum)

to fail on the forks, monsoon time made riding unsafe, spares shortages hindered training, units usually only had 50 per cent of their motorcycles in a useable state and therefore could not be risked for training (they were damaged too easily compared to other vehicle types) and there were not enough trained mechanics. It was thought that only a few should be kept to use on good condition roads. Interestingly, in the report a Military Policeman is quoted as saying 'any poor gentleman who rides one of these excellent machines on this road earns his wife's pension'. The report makes no mention of telescopic-forked motorcycles, so it can only be presumed Matchless G3Ls were not used there, which would have coped so much better.

Captured enemy machines were also used whenever available. Later in the war the authorities actually reserved a series of serial numbers for allocation to such types, and they issued blocks of numbers for REME-rebuilt machines, those impressed, and of local purchase and gift status.

The continuing concern about spares resulted in the establishment of a standardisation committee in 1944 to advise the authorities on a single motorcycle design required for future universal military service. Yet again, models were built by the various manufacturers – Triumph, BSA, Douglas, Norton and Royal Enfield – all of which submitted their designs for evaluation. Progress by the authorities was slow, however, and with the end of the war in sight the need for new machines was considerably lessened. Subsequently all the models offered were dropped except the Triumph design, which lingered on for long enough to evolve into the post-war TRW model.

Following the end of the Second World War, military motorcycle development came to a virtual standstill. New designs were something of white elephants in the austere post-war years, with the country short of money, saddled with huge war debts, and overwhelmed with enormous stocks of now redundant motorcycles to sort out. Practicality and economy were the two main concerns of the period, and the machines retained were typically late or rebuilt examples, with those disposed of by the authorities usually being early production, worn-out, non-preferred or obsolete types. The latter category included the Royal Enfield WD/C, virtually all Triumph models, all Velocettes, the James ML, combinations, and all Lend-Lease American machines alongside all other small quantity makes, everything being disposed of through the trade or returned to the manufacturer by the end of the 1940s. By the early 1950s, the post-war armed forces accepted the BSA M20 as the standard service machine of the period alongside the Matchless G3/L. Small numbers of other wartime types could also be seen, although all had been retired by the end of the decade. As well as disposal to the trade, public or return to the manufacturer, large quantities of surplus War Office machines were disposed of to the governments of the liberated Allied countries. This

Fork jigs for straightening girder forks, at No. 1 Workshop Group, Chilwell. (REME Museum)

was to aid the rebuilding of their armed forces, with such machines filling the gap until newer designs could be purchased.

Military motorcycles retained by the services for post-war use were either nearly new or had been subjected to at least one, if not several, full workshop overhauls. This was particularly so in the case of the BSA M20 and Matchless G3/L, where the machines would be completely stripped down and rebuilt using any serviceable parts available, either reconditioned or new, followed by a repaint. In virtually all instances the engine originally fitted would be replaced by a service-exchange unit. The War Office's primary object was a serviceable machine at minimum cost and it was none too concerned about the correct correlation between frame and engine numbers, nor the fitting of non-original parts. To the War Office, a motorcycle was a motorcycle and identified in the inventory by the serial number (later, registration number) alone. Little wonder, then, that most wartime machines still in service during the late 1950s and early 1960s bore scant resemblance to their original wartime factory specification.

BSA M20 engine under test in the motorcycle repair shop, No. 1 Workshop, Chilwell. (REME Museum)

As previously mentioned, the MWEE/MEE not only tested complete motorcycles (as well as countless other categories of machinery), but also component parts thereof and proprietary fitting too. Such items tested included exhausts, air filters, crash bars, saddles, tyres and twist grips. One of the many oddities tested during the period under scrutiny included the fitting of Framo skis to either side of a motorcycle. When in use they were supposed to enable the rider to transfer part of his body weight to the ground, to provide the machine with greater stability on soft sand or loose gravel when cornering. When not in use they acted as a pair of leg shields for the rider. Testing of this design was carried out in Egypt, only to culminate in failure! Other ideas experimented with included special sidecars for specific applications, and spring frames for motorcycles. Experimental machines were also tested at various times and these oddities included the Triumph

Royal Signals Ariel W/NGs at MT Workshop with a note for REME – 'Any work taken on if you have the money'. (Royal Signals Museum)

and OEC 3-wheeler machines, the Aveling Barford minibike, the Swiss-built Moto-Chenille Mercier model and the well-known Excelsior Welbike, to name but a few. Certain Axis captured machines were also investigated during the wartime period.

2

Standardisation in the Second World War

After the Coventry Blitz of November 1940 and the elimination of the 'standard' 3TW Triumph, the military continued for a time to experiment with the other lightweight machines that it had been looking at since 1939 to try to identify a 'substitute' standardised machine for service use. This experimentation continued from early 1941 through to the autumn of that year.

Also following the bombing of Coventry, it was thought that a standardised engine might be worth pursuing as an alternative and the War Office ordered a number of Ariels, Nortons and Royal Enfields that were to be fitted with the preferred 350cc OHV engines from AMC and BSA. (Interestingly a W/NG Ariel fitted with a G3/G3L engine still exists and the contract plate on the rear mudguard, where the catalogue reference number should be, does not have a number but shows an 'X' instead.)

Eventually nothing came of either idea because of the demand for high volumes of motorcycles at the time. With the delivery requirements there was no time to wait for field trials and an eventual conclusion and then to re-tool all the manufacturers to make the chosen motorcycle. The upshot was that all the manufacturers were left to continue building their various models to meet the high demand. However, something had to be done regarding parts procurement because this was starting to cause a major headache owing to the wide range of different models and types in use and being supplied.

Due to this confusion, in about 1940 small brass contract plates were introduced to motorcycles, giving the contract number and catalogue reference number. Three years later the brass was changed to pressed and plated steel. These helped identify the motorcycle such that the correct manufacturers' parts list would be used when parts were needed for it. All manufacturers' parts list were stamped on the cover and sometimes on the first page with the contract and catalogue reference number in purple ink. An example would be 9841/16/1, which is a Matchless G3L contract (see photo in Chapter 10).

Although some common parts were stocked by the military and noted in some of the various manufacturers' parts lists from about 1940 onwards, specific proprietary parts lists for each manufacturer's models were available to help the repair workshops for all the usual common types of WD motorcycles.

In about 1941 a decision was taken to only order certain models and to cease production of some 500cc models, and all 350cc and 250cc side valves, because the authorities favoured only 350cc OHV and certain 500cc SV motorcycles. This left only six motorcycles in production in the UK of 350cc and over: Ariel W/NG, BSA M20, Matchless G3L, Norton 16H, Royal Enfield WD/CO and Triumph 3HW. As the chosen six became available the non-preferred and remaining impressed motorcycles were replaced in the front line and passed to rear-guard formations such as the Home Guard. Lend-Lease motorcycles generally went to Free Forces, overseas dependencies or to the RAF. Efforts were also made to distribute the six models among the services and their forces on a logical basis to ease problems for the REME workshops.

With the chosen six models also came the first signs of some form of standardisation of parts. The standard headlamp became the Lucas type DU42R fitted with a type CZ27 ammeter and a Lucas RS-39 four-position lighting switch in a panel and a mask, and the tail light became the Lucas MCT 1, this coinciding with the deletion of rear number plates. (Alternative Miller items were the type 72M headlamp fitted with a type 72M/75V ammeter and a 72M/125 four-position lighting switch and a mask, and tail light type 31 WD). Until then at least two diameters of headlamp had been used, with the switch and ammeter fitted either in the headlamp or in a panel in the tank.

Other parts such as dipswitches, horns (Lucas and Clearhooter), regulators (Lucas MCR1 or Miller CV1WD), detachable wire connectors for the rear lamp and speedometers were probably adopted at this time or soon after.

In 1942 pannier bag racks were added to all 350cc and larger motorcycles to a design established by Norton. Contracts were also issued for parts to update older models of the 'chosen six' with these racks. Raw materials shortages forced other changes such as the deletion of a number of rubber parts, which in turn helped out with the procurement issues.

However, further rationalisation was still required. Therefore in 1944 the Standardisation Committee imposed an extra standardised range of parts to cut down its inventory for the 'six'. From that year onward the manufacturers' parts lists started noting these new 'universal' parts as 'standardised'. The parts chosen to be standardised were saddles, handlebars (LV7/BC/91–111) and controls, a new universal air cleaner (MT12/NC11783), and headlamp (push-button).

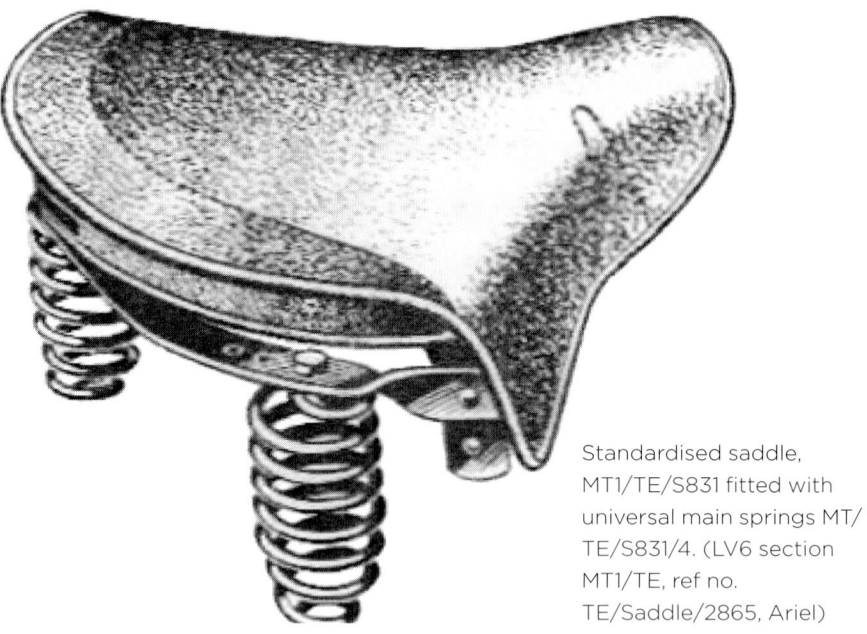

Standardised saddle, MT1/TE/S831 fitted with universal main springs MT/TE/S831/4. (LV6 section MT1/TE, ref no. TE/Saddle/2865, Ariel)

These saddles were produced both by Terry and Lycett (the latter originally having a saddle with aero-elastic mattressing rather than springs) and were specified to replace all other saddle designs used on the 'six'. Only the nose brackets and mounting points for the main springs to the frame varied. When ordered as a spare, supplied separate to the saddle was a 'kit, parts, universal saddle', which came in a square box and comprised loose front and rear brackets and various bolts and fixings to mount the saddle on any of the WD machines then in service.

A further variety of saddle occasionally seen comprised the cover only; this was made from khaki-green-coloured waterproofed canvas. It is believed that this cover, which would fit both Terry and Lycett saddles, was introduced for hot-weather (tropical and desert) areas. It had been found that the heat and sunlight in these areas could soften or even melt the standard rexine covers, not to mention making sitting on the thing (in shorts) an uncomfortable, painful experience. Some of these covers turn up today on wartime machines and are mistakenly thought to be an 'economy' version.

A new handlebar and controls layout was introduced in mid-to-late 1944. These were listed as BSA standard parts in some of their rival manufacturers' parts lists. All very late contracts such as Triumph 3HW S5340, RE WD/CO S1546, BSA M20 S7218, and Ariel W/NG S6287 used these parts, although

STANDARDISATION IN THE SECOND WORLD WAR

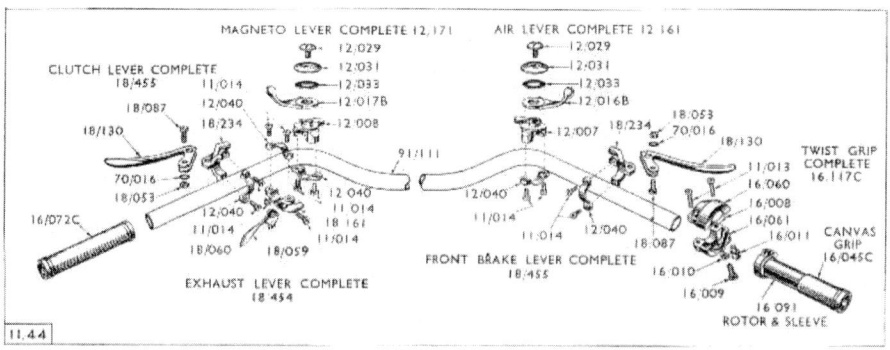

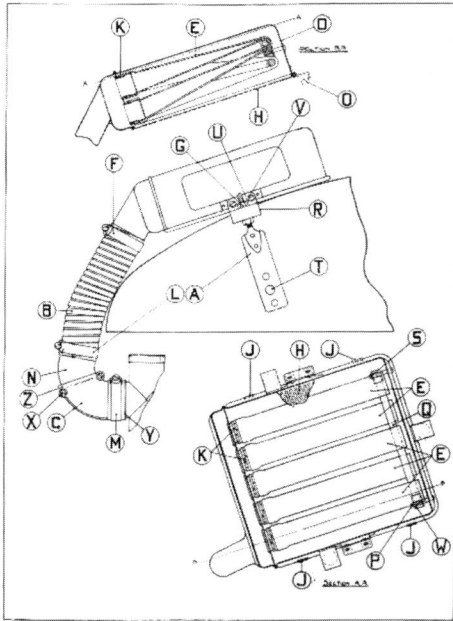

Handlebar illustration and parts list (from a late Ariel W/NG spare parts list).

Vokes air cleaner (from a late Ariel W/NG spare parts list).

Push-button headlamp (from a late Ariel W/NG spare parts list).

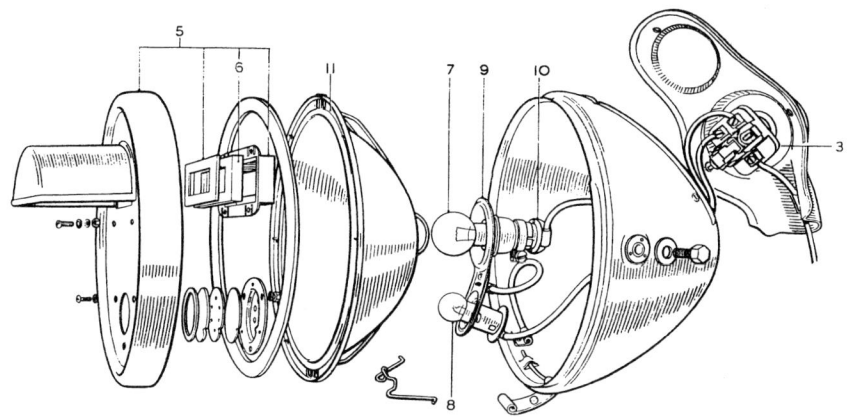

A new old stock switch on its mounting plate for under-seat fitment. (Authors' collection)

studying preceding contracts it seems that some of the parts, notably the handlebars, may have had an earlier phased-in introduction.

All the handlebar controls were based on Amal patterns (both the twist grip and decompressor lever were identical to earlier Amal patterns). Both Amal and Bowden produced these controls. No manufacturer's name was stamped on these parts. The air and mag levers were different from earlier Amal parts in that, apart from the lack of embossed name, the clamp was now a separate one-piece screw-on item, rather than the twin 'hinged clamps' of the earlier pattern.

Another standardised item was the universal air cleaner as made by Vokes. It had been in limited service since 1941, but in late 1944 it became a specified part for all new motorcycles after hot-weather experience in Italy and north-west Europe between 1943 and summer 1944 had shown that conditions were extremely dusty. Mounting parts for the 'six' varied; for example, Matchless models seem to have employed a filter that had a 3-point, rather than a 2-point attachment, having an additional attachment point at the front of the filter that hooked on to the front of the fuel tank bridge as well as the sides. There also appears to have been some variation in the angle of the filter hose piece connection port. Again, Matchless machines appear to have used a different filter hose on some models than other manufacturers.

Three manufacturers modified their fuel tanks to accommodate the Vokes filter hose, namely BSA, Triumph and Norton.

This illustration is taken from an Ariel W/NG parts list and judging by the part numbers it would seem that Norton developed these filters for use.

The last major change in the Second World War was the adoption of the 'push-button' headlamp (MT3/LU/50073). The dipswitch and ammeter disappeared and the lighting switch (Lucas U39-L15) was repositioned on the motorcycle below the saddle. It was introduced to simplify the wiring of a machine between the headlight and the main frame. Heavy field use of bikes had shown wiring looms to be at their most vulnerable against the constant movement of the forks, resulting in frequent electrical failures that were difficult to repair in the field. The new arrangement reduced the number of wires between the headlight and mainframe, thus helping reduce the problem. Introduced into service on new machines, the idea was simply too late in the war to have any positive effect or reduction. Peacetime reduced the incidence of headlight failure due to lack of field or combat use, and a reversion was made to the previous arrangement.

3

Dealing with Defects

Before the war the War Office had about 4,000 approved motorcycles in service and by August 1940 this had risen to around 68,000, which were largely unapproved. By September 1942 this figure had increased to 157,000, and by May 1945 to 250,000. RAOC had been dealing solely with repairs and maintenance before the war, and REME from mid 1942. However, it was becoming clear by 1940 that some of the new equipment in service (not just motorcycles) needed modifications to overcome defects from design or manufacture because of inadequate testing before production, and this additional workload had now to be placed on its field workshops for delivered equipment.

Reporting of a defect on a motorcycle started with a report from the unit concerned being sent through the normal RAOC/REME channels up to the General Headquarters if in the field, or to the War Office if the unit was based in the UK. From there it was circulated to the Ministry of Supply (MoS), which ensured the Director of Mechanical Engineering (DME) saw a copy, as did the appropriate inspection department of the MoS , which in the case of 'B' vehicles was headed by the Chief Inspector of Electrical and Mechanical Engineering. On receipt of the report the DME's specialist branch would check for other similar reports of the defect, and based on the findings the DME would issue a recommendation as to the necessity of carrying out a change, with an appreciation of the defect and suggestions for the solution, all of which were forwarded to the MoS. A solution to the defect was generally issued after the discussions between the MoS, the manufacturers and the technical branch of the DME. In the case of major defects the Ministry of Supply would stop the production line and thus prevent large quantities of faulty components getting into the field.

When the modification had reached the stage of manufacturing drawings with details and requirements for stores, a draft of the change was forwarded by the MoS to the DME (at the War Office) where full instructions to units and REME for carrying out the modification was embodied in a circular to all concerned. All modifications were subjected to General Staff approval and also needed financial approval when new stores items were required.

With US-built motorcycles the defect-reporting route was different. In this case REME findings were submitted to the US War Department (Ordnance Department, Signal Corps or Engineering Corps) with a recommendation for action to be taken to incorporate a remedy in production, and also for modification to existing equipment.

There follows a listing of motorcycle-related defects from 1940 onwards that RAOC/REME had to deal with on top of its usual work in the Second World War.

LIST OF DME CIRCULARS

Immediate Action

Circular Number	Date	Detail	Motorcycle
B.40	28/10/40	Fitting of security bolts to prevent damage to valves (see also B.345)	Norton
B.54	5/04/41	Throttle handlebar control	Matchless
B.71	3/02/41	Fitting of security bolts to prevent damage to valves (see also B.345)	BSA, Matchless, Ariel, R. Enfield
B.71/1	31/05/41	Amendment to B.71	–
B.80	3/12/40	Substitution of separate horn push for combined horn push and dipper switch	All M/Cs
B.116	29/04/41	Fitting compression plate	Matchless
B.116/1	27/03/42	Amendment to B.116. Delete 5/8" before TDC and insert 3/8" before TDC	Matchless
B.118	30/10/41	Washer, rear brake drum flange to hub fixing bolts	BSA
B.118/1	23/02/42	Spring washer, rear brake drum flange bolts (cancelled by B.608)	BSA
B.125	21/07/41	Provision for immobilising	All M/Cs
B.133	14/06/41	Modification to oil scavenging pump	R. Enfield
B.140	9/06/41	Lamp, instrument panel and inspection	Matchless
B.141	12/05/41	Fitting of new headlamp mask and removal of dipper switch	All M/Cs
B.147	8/11/41	Bolt, rear stand. Lock-nut for bolt	BSA
B.155	31/03/42	Fitting pannier bags and pillion seat conversion sets	Norton
B.158	6/07/41	1. Saddle front mounting. 2. Battery fixing bolt	BSA
B.173	8/04/42	Carburettor: adjustment for petrol economy	BSA and Norton
B.182	15/04/42	Kick starter: safety spring clip	Matchless

Circular Number	Date	Detail	Motorcycle
B.195	10/09/41	Fork springs: shock absorber adjustment hand control	BSA
B.214	16/07/42	Locking plate for valve rocker box caps	Ariel
B.259	31/01/42	Engine lubrication. Dipstick	R. Enfield
B.272	23/02/43	Fitting pannier bags and pillion seat conversion sets	R. Enfield
B.273	12/06/42	Fitting pannier bags and pillion seat conversion sets	Ariel
B.274	10/05/42	Fitting pannier bags and pillion seat conversion sets	BSA
B.278	17/05/42	Modification to clutch, gearbox and back stand. New lock washers and alteration to pinch bolt	Ariel
B.289	29/07/42	Kick starter: safety spring clip	Ariel
B.301	21/05/42	Spanner for dynamo securing strap	All M/Cs
B.305	21/11/42	Carburettor jets and chokes	R. Enfield
B.321	18/07/42	Lucas magdyno, dynamo end cover; lubrication	All M/Cs
B.365	12/01/43	Electrical cables: risk of fire	R. Enfield
B.417	31/03/43	Dynamo bracket screw at driving pinion end of Lucas magdyno	Norton, BSA, Ariel, R. Enfield
B.417/1	1/08/44	Amendment to B.417	Norton, BSA, Ariel, R. Enfield
B.305/1	21/01/43	Amendment to B.305. Feltham	R. Enfield
B.459	10/05/44	Fitting of pannier bag conversion sets	Matchless
B.609	14/12/43	Ignition HT lead, procedure on replacement	All M/Cs
B.345	11/05/43	Security bolt. Removal from front wheels	All M/Cs
B.608	16/12/43	Rear hub and brake drum flange bolts	BSA

Where Necessary

Circular Number	Date	Detail	Motorcycle
B.18	10/09/40	Modification: front forks, rear tank bracket and rear brake cover plates	R. Enfield
B.18/1	22/09/42	Front forks: welded type	R. Enfield
B.19	1/10/40	Petrol tank lugs (fracturing)	Norton
B.41	24/02/41	Fitting flexible petrol and oil pipes	Norton
B.46	19/11/40	Rear stand and mudguard	Norton
B.101	19/05/41	Fitting of WD panel air cleaner for Middle East	BSA
B.210	15/05/42	Rear stand, method of repair	Norton
B.212	16/11/41	Modification to horn bracket	Norton

DEALING WITH DEFECTS

Circular Number	Date	Detail	Motorcycle
B.212/1	16/07/42	Amendment No. 1. Cancels B.212	Norton
B.224	25/03/42	Rear wheel studs. Rear wheel sleeve nuts	Norton
B.257	12/05/42	Fitting panel air cleaner in Middle East	Norton
B.304	7/09/42	Change speed mechanism – bushes fitted to cam plate and spring cover plate	Norton

Pillion Seat and Pannier Bag Conversion Set for B.S.A. W.D. M 20 Model 500 c.c. S.V. Solo Motor Cycle

SET "A"   PART No. 66-7000.

Suitable for W.D. M20 Model machines up to Frame No. WM20–44212 comprising:—

Component Number.	Description.
66-6915	Pannier carrier, complete (2 off).
66-6916	Pannier bag (right-hand).
66-6917	Pannier bag (left-hand).
66-6918	Pannier bag strap (long).
66-6919	Pannier bag strap (short).
K132A	Pannier carrier fixing bolt (4 off).
M263	Pannier carrier fixing bolt nut (4 off).
29-541	Pannier carrier fixing bolt washer (4 off).
66-6955	Carrier.
K132A	Carrier support lug bolt (2 off).
M263	Carrier support lug bolt nut (2 off).
29-541	Carrier support lug bolt washer (2 off).
28-2338	Carrier and mudguard stud bolt (2 off).
36-382	Carrier and mudguard stud washer (2 off).
65-6794	Lifting stay and mudguard support stud (2 off).
36-382	Lifting stay and mudguard support shakeproof washer (2 off).
EA80	Lifting stay and mudguard support nut (2 off).
24-5207	Lifting stay bottom stud (left-hand).
24-5205	Lifting stay bottom stud (right-hand).
EA80	Lifting stay bottom stud nut (2 off).
36-382	Lifting stay bottom stud shakeproof washer (2 off).
66-6886	Mudguard bottom stay (right-hand).
66-6887	Mudguard bottom stay (left-hand).
EA80	Bottom stay stud nut (2 off).
36-382	Bottom stay stud shakeproof washer (2 off).
66-6750	Pannier steady tube (left-hand).
66-6748	Pannier steady tube (right-hand).
K132A	Pannier fixing bolt (6 off).
29-541	Pannier fixing bolt shakeproof washer (6 off).
M263	Pannier fixing bolt nut (6 off).
66-9180	Pillion seat.
K132A	Pillion seat fixing bolt (4 off).
M263	Pillion seat fixing bolt nut (4 off).
29-541	Pillion seat fixing bolt washer (4 off).
66-4942	Pillion footrest clamp assembly, complete (right hand), comprising:—
66-4945	Footrest lug (right-hand).
66-4707	Footrest lug stud washer (3 off).
E19	Footrest lug stud nut (3 off).
66-4948	Clamp.
66-4940	Spindle.
27-6312	Spindle bolt.
EA80	Spindle bolt nut.
66-4943	Pillion footrest clamp assembly, complete (left-hand), comprising:—
66-4946	Footrest lug (left-hand).
66-4707	Footrest lug stud washer (3 off).
E19	Footrest lug stud nut (3 off).
66-4947	Clamp.
66-4940	Spindle.
27-6312	Spindle bolt.
EA80	Spindle bolt nut.
66-4718	Rear prop tube.
66-4722	Rear prop locating sleeve.
66-4721	Prop stand clip plate.
3-938	Prop stand clip plate bolt.
66-4707	Prop stand clip plate bolt washer.
EA82	Prop stand clip plate bolt nut.

SET "B"   PART No. 66-7001.

Suitable for W.D. M20 Model machines bearing Frame Nos. WM20–30907 to WM20–42000, WM20–44213 to WM20–44712.

Comprising:—All components as Set "A" with the following additional items:

Component Number	Description.
15-6045	Side prop stand backstay clip (right-hand).
15-6046	Side prop stand backstay clip (left-hand).
EB144	Side prop stand backstay clip bolt.
EB201	Side prop stand backstay clip bolt nut.

Front page of BSA's instructions for adding pannier frames for bags. (B.274, BSA)

Circular Number	Date	Detail	Motorcycle
B.323	31/07/42	Dynamo and regulator wiring	All M/Cs
B.324	16/10/42	Clutch control cable and chain wheel centre	Ariel
B.343	24/11/42	Gearbox camshaft bearing: kick-starter end	Ariel, Matchless
B.343/1	31/12/42	Gearbox camshaft bearing: kick-starter end	Ariel, Matchless
B.356	12/05/43	Speedometer head and drive cable (Smith manufacture) modifications to improve reliability	All M/Cs
B.390	20/01/43	Horn: revised design and location	BSA
B.413	17/02/43	Petrol pipes	Norton
B.433	1/07/43	Road wheel hubs and spokes	R. Enfield

Another page from BSA's instructions for adding pannier frames for bags. (B.274, BSA)

General Instructions

Circular Number	Date	Detail	Motorcycle
B.81	31/12/40	Revision of spares lists consequent on modification to handlebar controls and cables	BSA
B.81/1	24/04/41	Amendment No. 1	BSA
B.106	26/04/41	Dublchek Schrader valve caps	All M/Cs

DEALING WITH DEFECTS

Circular Number	Date	Detail	Motorcycle
B.127	16/05/42	Method of fitting chevron tyres	All M/Cs
B.168	20/01/42	Carburettor float needles. Test for defective needles before replacement	All M/Cs
B.174	8/08/41	Ignition timing	All M/Cs
B.200	20/03/42	Tyre pressures (cancelled by B.400)	All M/Cs
B.211	14/10/41	Procedure for reporting faults on AF G.889	All M/Cs
B.217	31/10/41	Maintenance of spark plugs	All M/Cs
B.231	28/11/41	Sparking plugs oiling up. Adjustment of oil feed to inlet valve	Matchless
B.238	20/12/41	Crankshaft-timing pinion. Correct fitting of key	Matchless
B.260	31/10/41	Kick-starter ratchet gears	All M/Cs
B.268	12/06/42	Replacement of Tecalemit grease nipples	All M/Cs
B.288	7/04/43	Pannier bags, earlier type. Addition of rubbing strips	All M/Cs
B.307	26/05/42	Teledraulic forks. Maintenance by w/shops. Alteration to task book	Matchless
B.307/1	17/07/44	Teledraulic forks. Maintenance by w/shops. Cancels B.307	Matchless
B.310	10/06/42	Clutch adjustment and controls	BSA
B.313	8/07/42	Initial inspection	All M/Cs
B.325	8/08/42	Limit of wear, outer covers	All M/Cs
B.340	12/09/42	Engine lubrication. Method of checking oil level, etc.	Norton
B.345	11/05/43	Security bolt (front wheel)	All M/Cs
B.357	22/09/42	Gearbox lubrication: correction to task books. C.600 instead of grease GS	Ariel
B.388	22/12/43	Fitting of modified fork crown and handlebar lug	Matchless
B.400	21/01/43	List of tyre pressures (cancels B.200)	All M/Cs
B.400/1	12/05/43	Amendment to B.400	All M/Cs
B.402	21/11/42	Handlebar grips: rubber substitute, method of fixing to handlebars, and twist grip rotors	All M/Cs
B.407	4/02/43	Target fuel consumption figures	All M/Cs
B.432	27/01/43	Dynamo: method for removal or replacement	Matchless
B.456	25/02/43	New range of lubricants WD 'B' vehicles	All M/Cs
B.492	17/11/43	Precautions when using MT 80 fuel	All M/Cs
B.517	16/07/43	Defects, rendition of AF G889 in accordance with AC 2240/42 (cancels B.211)	All M/Cs
B.608	16/12/43	Rear hub and brake drum flange bolts	BSA
B.754	5/07/44	Front and rear hub bearing seals	Matchless

4

Raw Material Shortages in the Second World War Affecting Motorcycle Production

As the Second World War broke out in September 1939, it was inevitable that rationing would be introduced at some point, and ultimately just about everything in the UK was affected. This led to a 'black' market for all sorts of goods thereinafter.

Industry was also hit by many shortages mainly due to shipping losses of imported raw materials and other finished goods. Aircraft production was high up on the list of priorities and aluminium was its main material. The government at the time took to collecting scrap metal of all sorts to recycle and be made into items for the war effort. The high-quality material was used in aircraft production and the poorer quality for other less important requirements. This meant that many industries had to look at using other materials in its place and the motorcycle industry starting making some of its less critical parts in steel or cast iron (i.e. chain cases, brake plates, timing covers, tappet covers, and rocker covers). Of course, this made the motorcycle heavier, which is something the War Office had always been keen to reduce, but needs must. (In Germany, shortages got worse as the war went on and DKW ended up making motorcycles in the latter years of the war with cast iron crank cases and gearboxes.)

Besides these redesigned parts, other items such as front and rear number plates were deleted altogether, steering dampers on some motorcycle models went too, dipswitches, and perhaps headlamps were reduced in size to save glass, steel or silver plate – why make a big headlamp that only gets shrouded? Similarly, the tail lamp was redesigned and made smaller in size, and it replaced all the various civilian-style lamps that had been supplied and became a standardised part. Plated finishes were also dispensed with on

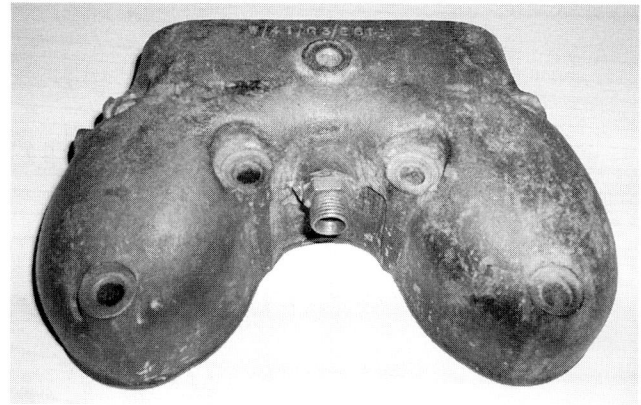

Matchless rocker cover made in cast steel with the part number 'W/41/G3/E61 2' stamped on top – heavy! (Authors' collection)

many items or changed to a plating material that was more readily available, or just simply painted.

Many pre-war motorcycles were equipped with solid brass handlebar levers. These were altered to be made of pressed steel to save brass for other uses. These redesigns were changed again when standardisation became an issue.

Again, a number of pre-war and very early war motorcycles used by the War Office were equipped with alkaline batteries from new, instead of the more common lead-acid variety. These batteries were made up of plates of nickel and iron (or of nickel and cadmium), with an alkali electrolyte. Visually these 6V batteries had five cells instead of the three with a lead-acid battery, and had to be used with a different regulator marked NiFe. It appears that from about 1940 these were phased out to save the nickel and cadmium for other uses.

However, when the USA joined the war in 1941 and the Lend-Lease agreement started, some of these material shortages, particularly those for aluminium, finished steel, forgings, plus various other chemicals, eased some of British manufacturing's problems and helped boost output. In time this supply of materials also enabled the manufacturers to go back to supplying some parts in their original materials.

Also, by early 1941 a chronic shortage of chromium oxide chemical had become apparent, which obliged the re-evaluation of camouflage paints in use with the armed forces on large vehicles and buildings. However, the impact on the motorcycle industry was only minimal, they just continued with colour changes from Deep Bronze Green No. 24 (pre-war), to Khaki Green No. 3 (outbreak of war), to Standard Camouflage Colour No. 2 (brown, in 1943), and then Standard Camouflage Colour 15 (olive drab, from 1944 onward) as per Army Council Instructions.

December 23, 1943.   Motor Cycling

MINISTRY OF SUPPLY

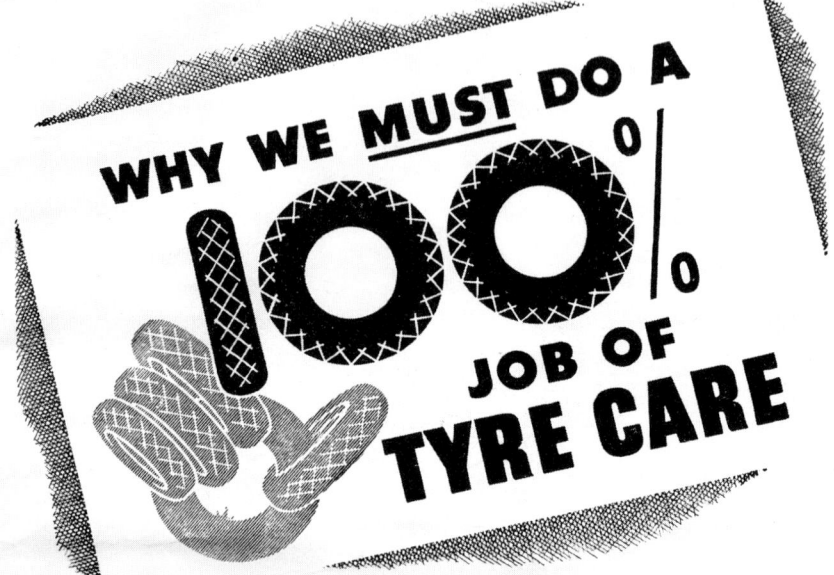

It is important to remember that synthetic rubber cannot entirely replace "crude" (i.e. natural rubber). Supplies of crude are required in varying degree to mix with synthetic.

The Allied Nations reserve of crude must, therefore, be more jealously guarded than ever. Heavy duty tyres already in service — those fitted to lorries, buses, etc. — represent by far the greatest bulk of that reserve. The manufacture of new heavy duty tyres consumes by far the greatest amount of rubber.

100% TYRE CARE INCLUDES:

WATCH YOUR SPEED — not exceeding the legal limit for a commercial vehicle: not over 40 m.p.h. for a car.

NEVER accelerate fiercely: never brake hard: never bump or scrape the kerb: never drive on a flat tyre.

AVOID overloading. Always "spread" the load.

DIG OUT flints, glass, nails, etc., daily.

CHECK air pressures regularly and often.

CHECK wheel alignment regularly.

CHECK brake adjustment regularly.

CHANGE round wheels and tyres (including spares) properly and regularly.

PAIR, space and change round twin tyres properly.

REMOVE stones trapped between twin tyres after every journey.

WIPE OFF oil, grease and paint.

KEEP tyres and tubes in good repair.

TAKE expert advice regularly on tyre care and maintenance.

SUBMIT TYRES FOR REPLACEMENT WHEN SMOOTH

Government tyre care notice. Great health and safety advice – replace when smooth! (Authors' collection)

The supply of rubber was also an issue from 1942 with the Japanese occupying the Dutch East Indies, so superfluous parts such as knee grips, footrest rubbers, gear-change rubbers and kick-start rubbers ceased to be specified and supplied, with the relevant parts redesigned to accommodate the loss of rubber. However, not all parts could be dispensed with, so handlebar grips were changed for canvas items, and rubber-mounted handlebars redesigned for solid mounting. Inner tubes (for all vehicle types) were to be made of a synthetic rubber (using butadiene), to save rubber for mainly tyre production. Butadiene was made from oil, but oil was needed for fuel too and for making many other products – toluene for making TNT, and also as a lubricant for engines, machinery and equipment of all sorts. To provide the oil for Allied needs the industry in America upped its production, thus avoiding a shortage of rubber and fuel. Pre-war British oil supplies had been imported from the Far East (Sumatra and Borneo) and the Middle East (primarily Iran) but surface raiders, aircraft, and submarines sunk a lot of merchant shipping in the early war years, limiting supplies until America stepped in. Interestingly, there was oil already being extracted in Nottingham by BP, although not in massive quantities, and in the war this extraction was increased but not made known about.

5

Motorcycle Disposals

In April 1944 a decision on disposal of certain makes and models had been made when their condition had got to Class IV or lower. This affected all 350cc makes except Ariel and Matchless, and all 500cc makes except BSA and Norton, but Triumph's 5SW was excluded this unless it needed a new engine. These instructions applied to those 'at Home' with exclusion for motorcycles used by the Home Guard, and those in VRDs. Condemned WD contract types were sent to MoS storage depots for disposal and non-WD types to command vehicle parks.

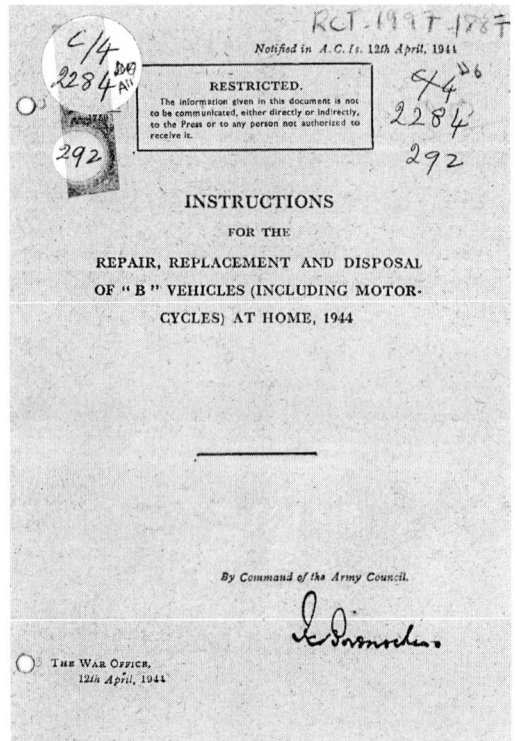

Instructions for the Repair, Replacement and Disposal of 'B' Vehicles (Including Motorcycles) at Home, 1944. (Authors' collection)

1960 Ruddington catalogue cover. (Authors' collection)

Towards the end of November 1944, a survey cataloguing all types of 'B' vehicles was published by the War Office. This list also noted that certain models were already deemed obsolete, those being:

- Excelsior Welbike
- Norton combination with box body
- Norton combination with sidecar
- Indian combination with sidecar
- BSA combination with sidecar

Those motorcycles still deemed to be in use in 1945 by this record are:

- Royal Enfield 125
- James 125
- Ariel 350
- BSA 350
- Royal Enfield 350
- Matchless 350
- Triumph 350

Lot No.	Description	W.D. No.	W.D. No.	W.D. No.	Remarks
5111	**TEN ITEMS**				
	B.S.A. SOLO MOTOR CYCLES, 500 c.c., s.v.	A 69YD53	E 80YC51	I 65YD61	
		B 81ZB91	F 79YC20	J 97YC73	
		C 75YD19	G 81ZB85		
		D 65YD69	H 79YC24		
5112	**TWELVE ITEMS**				
	B.S.A. SOLO MOTOR CYCLES, 500 c.c., s.v.	A 96YC44	E 49YD91	I 75YD45	
		B 91YC89	F 98YC59	J 67YD14	
		C 85YC88	G 94YC39	K 77YC91	
		D 96YC84	H 73YD68	L 60YD96	

Lot No.	Description	Service or Reg. No.	Capacity		Remarks
5113	MATCHLESS SOLO MOTOR CYCLE	24YA10	350 c.c.	o.h.v.	
5114	B.S.A. SOLO MOTOR CYCLE	70YD04	500 c.c.	s.v.	
5115	**THREE ITEMS**				
A	B.S.A. SOLO MOTOR CYCLE	85YC75	500 c.c.	s.v.	
B	Ditto	57YD65	500 c.c.	s.v.	
C	Ditto	60YD02	500 c.c.	s.v.	
5116	B.S.A. SOLO MOTOR CYCLE	59YD00	500 c.c.	s.v.	
5117	Ditto	77YC74	500 c.c.	s.v.	
5118	Ditto	86YC52	500 c.c.	s.v.	
5119	Ditto	94YC82	500 c.c.	s.v.	
5120	**FIVE ITEMS**				
A	B.S.A. SOLO MOTOR CYCLE	63YD90	500 c.c.	s.v.	
B	Ditto	65YC11	500 c.c.	s.v.	
C	Ditto	81ZB19	500 c.c.	s.v.	
D	MATCHLESS SOLO MOTOR CYCLE	23YA95	350 c.c.	o.h.v.	
E	Ditto	33YB46	350 c.c.	o.h.v.	

25% CASH DEPOSIT IS PAYABLE ON THE FALL OF THE HAMMER

Inner page of the sales catalogue. (Authors' collection)

- Velocette 350
- Ariel 500
- BSA 500
- Indian 500
- Norton 500

(Note. This other list conflicts with the 'at Home' directive, so it probably refers to overseas.)

However, in the years following the Second World War many of these makes/models of motorcycles were to be sold off at a number of venues in the UK (Ruddington, Byram Park, etc.) and overseas very shortly after the war ended, and regularly for many years after the war to reduce the amount on charge and latterly because of new approved replacement models.

It was quite usual for sales to have lots with quantities from two to twelve, and even to be hidden in the backs of lorries, much to the surprise of the buyer. Motorcycle dealers often attended these sales and repainted and reconditioned them for sale.

6

Motorcycles with Provenance

1. During some research at the RMP Museum for this edition, this interesting document was found dated 2 June 1944. The paperwork, as you can see overleaf, lists the riders and their BSA M20 motorcycles that actually went over to France for D-Day. This is the best document we have ever come across giving some wartime details on a motorcycle's history. (Did they survive the war?)

   From the list we can see that most of the BSA M20s are from contract S1048. At the bottom of the list are two more M20s from contract S2603 (C5210873 and C5211311) and both would have been very new at the time. At the top of the list there is one M20 from contract C11101 that would have been a couple of years old.

This CMP BSA M20 could be C5116995, which is on the list. The CMP motorcyclists are demonstrating how a metal rod fitted to a motorcycle can prevent the rider from being killed by a wire stretched across the road, 25 October 1944. (B11247, IWM)

List of Corps of Military Police (CMP) motorcycles heading for France, dated 2 June 1944. (RMP Museum)

2. The Transport Work Ticket (opposite) was given to us by Edward Thorne many years ago. It is dated 23 September 1940 and it seems he was based at Hadera (in the then country of Palestine), doing round trips to places such as Haifa, Nazareth, Jerusalem and Nablus.

MOTORCYCLES WITH PROVENANCE

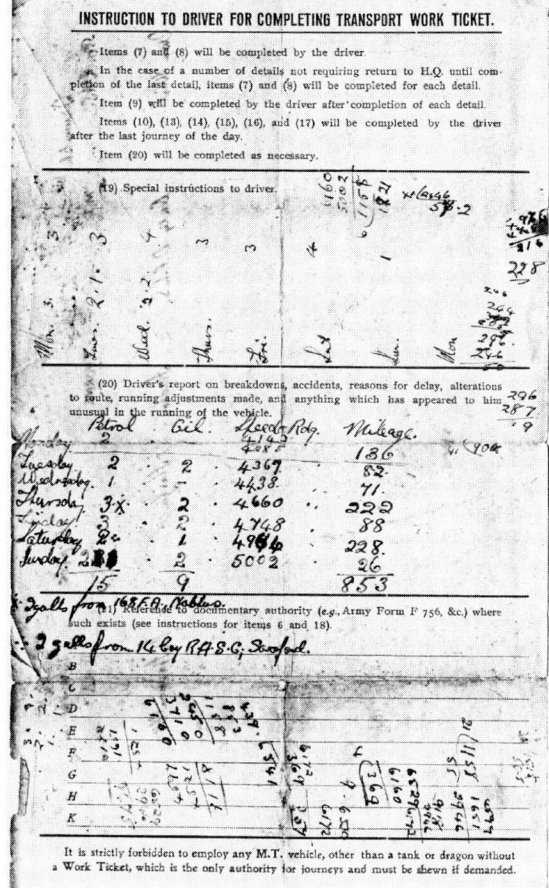

Front of Transport Work Ticket issued to Edward Thorne, who rode a Triumph 3SW at the time. (E. Thorne)

Reverse side of Transport Work Ticket issued to Edward Thorne. (E. Thorne)

7

War Department Manufacturers

AJS

As an independent concern, A.J. Stevens & Co. Ltd (AJS) supplied few motorcycles to the War Office and a smaller number still after the company became part of the Associated Motor Cycles (AMC) empire in 1931. During 1929 the company was involved in the seven-make trials of that year, submitting its 350cc OHV Model M6 for War Office evaluation. Having survived the initial trial period, the model was deemed successful enough to be submitted for further testing alongside the Douglas- and Matchless-produced machines, but ultimately only a handful of examples of each company's models were to be procured.

At the same time the M6 was being looked at, the India Office was purchasing the side valve M5. How it faired in India is unknown.

It is interesting to note that, following the purchase of AJS by the Matchless concern in the 1930s, the products and designs of the former company generally disappeared, though the AJS name was kept alive by carefully planned 'badge engineering' by the AMC concern. Fully aware of the loyalty of riders to individual marques, AMC discovered that some customers would not buy a Matchless model unless it carried the AJS logo, and vice versa. Thus AMC could supply one basic model in a particular class under two different marques with, apart from the insignia, only minor differences between the two. Perhaps the most manifest of these differences was the engine's magneto-mounting position, ahead of the cylinder barrel on the AJS and to the rear on the Matchless, which noticeably altered the shape and position of the engine's timing cover.

After the outbreak of the Second World War it made sense to produce one named model for various reasons and the Matchless name was upheld, the AJS name disappearing from use after 1940 until the end of the war. However, substantial numbers of various AJS 1940 civilian-specification models were impressed for service use in 1939–40, militarised only by the overall khaki paint finish.

AJS M5 349cc SV Single-Cylinder – Late 1920s
The AJS M5 was supplied to the India Office in the late 1920s. How it coped with India's roads and climate is unknown. Likewise, the numbers used are unknown.

AJS M6 349cc OHV Single-Cylinder – 1929–31
The AJS Model M6 was to be submitted for War Office testing alongside the products of six other manufacturers during the trials of 1929. The type was to prove reasonably successful throughout the initial trial period and was thus selected to continue with further evaluation, along with the Matchless Model T/4 and the Douglas L29.

After collating the results of these evaluations, the MWEE was indecisive as to which of the three machines was most suitable for military use. Ultimately, the Douglas company was to receive the principal orders for supply of its product, most probably because its machine was the lightest of the three. AJS, however, was to supply a handful of the Model M6 to the War Office up to and including 1931, although the military authorities were never really satisfied with the type and the total number supplied barely entered double figures.

The primary fault with the Model M6 in comparison with the Matchless and Douglas products was its overall weight (295lb), some 26lb heavier than the Douglas. The weight problem was noted during testing in the desert in 1931 when it was compared against a Levis 6-port, Triumph, and the Douglas L29. The M6 was described as heavy, unmanageable and unsuitably tyred for its weight, which in turn made the machine's performance seem poor and prevented comparisons with the other models.

Official photograph of a 1929 AJS M6, as used in the 1929 trial. (RLC Museum)

AJS Model 8SS 498cc OHV Single-Cylinder – 1940

Purchased under contract in mid 1940, only two of these machines were officially supplied to the War Office. They were procured following the losses at Dunkirk, when demand by the War Office for any remotely suitable machine was paramount, and were presumably available for immediate delivery from the AMC factory.

AJS model 8 498cc OHV Single-Cylinder – 1940

Purchased by the War Office under contract at the same time as the Model 26, the Model 8SS and the Model 9, the Model 8 was purchased presumably for the same reasons; namely, that it was available for immediate delivery at a time of great need.

Only one example was supplied and, apart from the colouring, it was of standard civilian specification, although whether this was 'standard' or 'de-luxe' is not known.

AJS Model 9 498cc SV Single-Cylinder – 1940

The AJS Model 9 and Matchless G5 were the only SVs from the AMC company to be supplied during the war. Only two examples were officially supplied, at the same time and for the same reasons as the Model 8SS, the Model 8 and the Model 26.

It is presumed that both were of standard 1940 civilian specification, apart from the military paintwork.

Catalogue picture of a Model 9. (AJS)

Impressed AJS twinport with panel tank and high-level exhausts. (Ed Abbott)

AJS Model 26 347cc OHV Single-Cylinder – 1940

Only one Model 26 was officially supplied to the War Office, at the same time and under the same conditions as the AJS Model 8SS, the Model 8 and the Model 9, although with a different contract catalogue reference number.

The Model 26 was generally the AJS-badged variant of the Matchless Model G3 and the example supplied was delivered at the time when the AMC factory was in full production with the Model G3 for the War Office.

ARIEL

Ariel's first connections with the War Office after the First World War was during 1935, when the it purchased one of the company's VA3 models for evaluation for potential military service, along with machines from six other manufacturers. The test results were mainly favourable for Ariel's offering, although the model was not chosen because it was due for replacement.

The following year saw some key personnel at the War Office remaining in favour of twin- or multi-cylinder machines, principally because they were still considered noticeably quieter than single-cylinder models. Ariel therefore supplied two of its model Square Four machines for evaluation purposes, one of 1000cc and the other of 600cc engine capacity. Performing well in general, both models were ultimately rejected as unsuitable because of poor ground clearance and excessive weight.

In September 1939 Ariel's VA was tested for suitability against a War Department 16H Norton. This was followed in mid 1940 by a demonstration of the company's Model W/NG prototype, witnessed by officials for the War Office and the French government. The testing of the model suitably impressed the French officials, the Ariel factory ledgers detailing a quantity supplied to their government during 1940. The British, however, only considered the W/NG suitable as an emergency purchase, should it become necessary.

In late 1939, following the outbreak of war, Ariel supplied a quantity of the 500cc model VA to the War Office. This was presumably because the demand for service machines had dramatically increased following the outbreak of hostilities. Further orders arrived for other models produced by the company, and yet more following the Dunkirk evacuation to compensate for the huge losses of equipment. Thereafter the War Office settled with the W/NG model, as supplied by the company, for the remainder of the Second World War.

During the later stages many of the early W/NG models supplied at the beginning of the war, along with smaller quantities of NH and VH models, were modified to bring them up to the same standard as the current models then being supplied. The principal modification involved fitting pannier and pillion equipment, although smaller modifications were also carried out.

Following the end of the Second World War, Ariel, along with other major manufacturers, saw the bulk of its motorcycles disposed of by the War Office as surplus to peacetime requirements, according to official policy. Many went to civilian dealerships for reconditioning to civilian specifications, while others were supplied to overseas governments for use by their post-war forces.

Ariel VA3 557cc SV Single-Cylinder – 1935 Evaluation Model

Ariel's Model VA3 was procured as one of the seven manufacturers' models evaluated for military suitability during the tests of 1935. The model supplied was of standard civilian specification of the time, but with the addition of a service-specified crankcase shield, a Dunlop sports rear tyre and a carrying rack on top of the rear mudguard.

During the course of the tests, the MEE noted that, although the cross-country performance of the model was good, the machine was difficult to ride across specific obstacles such as logs. Defects noted were few and an interim inspection of the test model at 5,565 miles showed the only real wear to be at the top of the cylinder bore and on the piston, indicating that it was top heavy.

Official photograph of the 1935 VA3 test model. (138/D6, The Tank Museum)

After the conclusion of the tests, the MEE expressed a liking for the model. Ultimately, however, the VA3 was not procured for service use as Ariel was intending to replace it with a new model.

Ariel 4F (Square Four) 597cc Overhead-Cam Four-Cylinder – 1936 Test Model

Loaned to the War Office and tested by the MEE during October 1936, this was a completely standard civilian-specification model. The particular machine concerned was supplied directly from Ariel and was considered for testing because, at the time, the War Office favoured the quietness and performance of twin- or multi-cylinder machines.

The results of the testing found the model extremely powerful and well able to negotiate difficult country within the limits of its ground clearance, although its considerable weight led to the conclusion that the type would be unsuitable for War Office use.

Catalogue picture of a civilian Model 4F Square Four. (Ariel)

Ariel 4G (Square Four) 997cc OHV Four-Cylinder – 1936 Test Model

Supplied along with the 600cc Model 4F Square Four on loan to the War Office for evaluation purposes, the larger 1000cc Model 4G Square Four was likewise evaluated by the MEE for military service suitability during October 1936.

Following the completion of the tests, the results were more or less identical to those of the 600cc 4F model.

Ariel VA 497cc SV Single-Cylinder – 1939 Prototype

Just before the outbreak of war Ariel offered the War Office its Model VA for testing, as it was similar to the current BSA M20s and Norton 16Hs in service.

Performance tested against a standard War Department Norton 16H and one fitted with a spring frame, it performed well enough for a contract to be issued soon afterwards.

Ariel W/VA (Lightened) 497cc SV Single-Cylinder – 1939

Only one Model W/VA (XG10208) was produced, in request for a lighter machine, but how the lighter weight was achieved is not known.

Testing was carried out at Farnborough against a standard W/VA and standard Norton 16H, where the lighter model proved the easiest to handle. The project was probably shelved because the War Office had decided on the W/NG by this stage.

Ariel W/NG 349cc OHV Single-Cylinder – 1940 Prototype

The forerunner of the company's standard wartime service Model W/NG, the prototype was based on Ariel's winning machine of the 1938 Scottish six-day trial. The prototype was prepared ready for demonstration to War Office and foreign officials by mid 1940, the result of the demonstration obviously impressing the French government as orders followed.

The British testing of this on-loan machine (XG12179) in July 1940 showed up a number of faults. The machine's condition was described as merely fair on the customary strip-down and inspection, and it was noted as suitable only for emergency purchase. By the time the test had ended and the reports were finished in August 1940, however, a British order had already been issued.

Ariel W/VA 497cc SV Single-Cylinder – 1939–40

The Model W/VA was supplied by Ariel in limited quantities during the early part of the Second World War, probably because it had similar characteristics to the War Office Norton 16H and BSA M20 machines that had been in service since the outbreak of the war.

Official photograph of an Ariel W/VA. (KID 5699, IWM)

Basically a militarised civilian model, the W/VA model served principally with the War Department (Army) in a variety of second-line roles, which probably involved fitting a sidecar to a number of examples.

Small quantities were also supplied to the Air Ministry (RAF) and the Ministry of Agriculture (MoA), no doubt for use in conjunction with the efforts on the home front by the Women's Land Army at various farming locations throughout the country.

Ariel VH (Red Hunter) 497cc OHV Single-Cylinder – 1940
The 497cc Red Hunter model supplied to the War Office following the Dunkirk evacuation of May 1940 was principally a civilian-specification model, and the small quantity of machines supplied were either readily available for delivery or available for construction without delay from stocks of parts available. Accordingly, the batch supplied contained machines fitted with either the single- or the twin-port cylinder heads; the Ariel factory ledgers note the various VH models supplied to the War Office as either 'VH' or 'VH2', indicating these two versions.

The Model VH was Ariel's competition/sporting model of the time and all are believed to have served with the War Department (Army).

Ariel NH (Red Hunter) 347cc OHV Single-Cylinder – 1940
Along with the larger 500cc Model VH, the 350cc Model NH was also a competition/sporting model of the Ariel range. It was purchased by the War

Catalogue picture of a 1940 civilian VG. (Ariel)

Office along with the contract for the batch of VH models. All are believed to have served with the War Department (Army).

Ariel VG (De-Luxe) 497cc OHV Single-Cylinder – 1940–41
The Model VG De-Luxe was a civilian-specification machine supplied to the War Office at irregular intervals between April 1940 and January 1941. It is presumed that the type was supplied to satisfy the demands of the time or to employ stocks of completed machines or parts otherwise lying redundant; all are believed to have served with the War Department (Army).

Ariel NG (De-Luxe) 347cc OHV Single-Cylinder – 1940
The Ariel NG De-Luxe model was the civilian-specification lower capacity version of the 500cc VG model. Purchased at the same time as the small batches of VH, NH and VG models, and presumably for the same reasons, all are believed to have served with the War Department (Army).

Ariel VB (De-Luxe) 598cc SV Single-Cylinder – 1940
This was a civilian-specification model, and only two machines were supplied during August 1940. Following this delivery, no further Model VB De-Luxes were supplied. Primarily because of their size and type of engine unit fitted, it is presumed that these two machines were ultimately to have sidecars fitted at some stage of their service life.

Ariel W/NG 347cc OHV Single-Cylinder – 1940–45
The Ariel W/NG model became the company's principal and, after 1941, the sole model supplied to the services. Between 1940 and 1945 some 40,000

Catalogue picture of a 1940 civilian VB. (Ariel)

plus W/NG models were produced for primarily the British War Department (Army), with smaller quantities also being supplied to both the Air Ministry (RAF) and the Admiralty Department (Navy), as well as several second-line formations, including some civil defence organisations, and orders from foreign governments. Indeed, the first service order for the W/NG model was placed by the French government.

Based on a pre-war competition model, the production model W/NG Ariel was subjected to various minor alterations and modifications over the course of its five-year production run between 1940 and 1945. The first production quantities of W/NG models still retained civilian pattern front and rear number plates, even if no number was carried on them, but these were no longer fitted after 1940. A top-feed float chamber was also specified for the carburettor on most early models as opposed to the bottom feed of later production models. The two triangular toolboxes were fitted on the offside and initially had the screw knobs to secure the lids positioned in the centre-face of each box. This design was modified during 1941 for toolboxes incorporating a revised pattern lid, the top fitting having a half-hinged lid and the bottom box the fastening knob repositioned to the more common location in the top upper corner of the lid.

All model W/NGs produced up to the end of 1941 were still fitted with gear change, kick-start and footrest rubbers, along with tank knee grips and celluloid or rubber handlebar grips. All of these fittings had to be withdrawn from production models from 1943 onwards owing to the rubber shortages arising because of the Japanese conquests in Burma and other areas of the Far East. To compensate, cast-steel patterned footrests were fitted to offer some element of grip to the rider, and standard military pattern canvas webbing handlebar grips were fitted in place of the rubber ones. Further modifications to the W/NG model included replacing the previously employed rubber-mounted handlebar with a solid clamp. (Service usage had shown instances of the handlebars actually turning in the rubber mounts during heavy cross-country use and so, in 1942, rubber mounting was stopped at engine number BH 23937.) That same year the universally introduced military pannier frames, bags and new rear carriers in which to accommodate the latter were also fitted. Pillion facilities were now specified as standard, and all these components were fitted to the model during the production stage. It should be noted that many earlier W/NG models were updated after 1942 by fitting the then current pannier and pillion fittings, with Ariel frequently supplying complete sets of equipment for such purposes. Later models were fitted with a pressed steel primary chaincase and engine-timing cover, in a drive to conserve supplies of aluminium alloy, and the removal of the steering damper on the forks. In late 1944 the last batches of machines were produced with a revised lighting system, which incorporated an updated headlight and switch-panel position, plus universal pattern Vokes air filter fitted to the top of the fuel tank as standard.

The W/NG model was fairly popular with the services during the Second World War, and particularly so with troops on the front line, who found its

A 1941 W/NG in No. 4 Base Workshop, Cairo, September 1942, with Bren gun attachment. (REME Museum)

Early RAF W/NG with a few parts missing. Serial number reads RAF 94335. (John Tinley)

performance, ground clearance and competition ancestry a bonus in forward rough terrain areas. The model retained its popularity for the remainder of the war and continued in service in forward and second-line areas in much the same way as before.

The type also served in limited numbers with both the Air Ministry (RAF) and the Admiralty Department (Navy), and probably with certain other bodies as well.

Surprisingly, the W/NG model is not at all common today when compared to surviving examples of other manufacturers' models; this is particularly unusual when the total production figures of the model are considered. It is known that many war surplus W/NGs were sold to other countries for use by their forces after the end of the war and several ex-military W/NG models exist that were dealer-reconditioned to a civilian specification.

AVELING BARFORD

Aveling Barford Experimental Lightweight 125cc Single-Cylinder 2-Stroke – 1938

Aveling Barford built only one experimental prototype lightweight, which was a mini-motorcycle weighing 154lb. It had several unorthodox features, most notably its drilled angle iron sprung frame.

First delivered on 24 November 1938, the machine was returned twice (first on 25 November 1938 and then on 29 July 1939) for modifications between trials. It was thoroughly tested in July 1939, when it completed 206 road miles and 151 cross-country. After testing, the riders criticised the cramped riding

The 1938 Aveling Barford prototype mini-motorcycle. Note the crude construction and wheelbarrow wheels. (WO 194 [33]-481, The National Archives)

position (even though the motorcycle height was adjustable), which threw a lot of weight on to the rider's wrists, and the foot brake was considered to be badly positioned. Generally it was considered to perform very well across country and on loose surfaces with its tracks fitted, and was also easy to handle, but the top road speed of 25mph was thought too slow; as the test progressed, this decreased further still as the engine bearings wore, letting air into the crankcases of the machine's Villiers engine.

Although not judged suitable for use by the War Office, the general design was regarded as a potential basis for a future War Department lightweight.

A second machine was built later in 1939 by one of the same two craftsmen (who were both called Henderson and worked at Aveling Barford in Glasgow) and it featured in *The Motor Cycle* on 14 November 1940. It was different from the first model and was scooter-like in appearance, but still had an angle iron frame and trolley-type wheels.

On a slightly sad note, the first motorcycle appears not to have survived the war; it is listed in a November 1944 census record as being converted to an air compressor!

BMW

Two motorcycles were registered in 1940, but it is unclear which models they were. It is possible that they were either captured models or motorcycles straight out of a showroom, purchased in an attempt to evaluate quickly the opposition's equipment.

BMW R12s captured in the desert and being used by British troops. (E. Thorne)

A BMW R75 undergoing evaluation after being captured in the desert. Note the applied British registration on the petrol tank. (STT 6996N IWM)

If captured they are likely to have been models R35, R75 or R12 (in combination or solo form) and, if bought from a showroom, models R51, R66 and R71 are possibilities.

BSA

Birmingham Small Arms Company (BSA) was the largest motorcycle manufacturer in Britain at the outbreak of the Second World War, and perhaps naturally the largest supplier of motorcycles to the armed services, its involvement with the military having started during the First World War.

During 1929, three BSA S29 De-Luxe models were purchased from the company by the War Office for participation in the seven-make trials of the time, but the testing was cancelled before completion because of hasty decisions within the higher echelons of the War Office at the time. During the early 1930s the War Office began to favour multi-cylinder engines, believing them to be quieter than single-cylinder versions, and BSA supplied sizeable quantities of its 498cc War Office V-twin model to both the War Office and the Air Ministry between 1933 and 1937, with minor changes to each contract.

By 1935, War Office opinion about machine suitability had changed yet again, and it now came out in favour of either 350cc or 500cc capacity single-cylinder machines of either SV or OHV configuration – twin-cylinder machines had proved to be no quieter after all. BSA was thus to submit its current W35-6 model for War Office evaluation, alongside products from six other principal motorcycle manufacturers of the time.

After completion of the 1935 trials, however, the W35-6 model failed to meet with War Office approval. In 1936, BSA submitted another of its products for testing – its first 496cc SV single-cylinder motorcycle, the first M20. Completion of the testing this time, however, showed the machine's engine to have suffered unacceptable wear and it was thus declared unsuitable for War Office procurement.

Undefeated, BSA was to submit a further three improved versions for War Office evaluation during 1937 and two of these were subjected to the standard military 10,000-mile reliability trial. After the trial the MEE considered the reliability of the model as only 'fair', although it did note the type as 'suitable for WD requirements'. Thus commenced a near thirty-year love–hate relationship between the British military and the BSA M20 model, an affair that was to continue in certain isolated instances until 1971.

In 1937 the War Department (Army) received a batch of BSA's B20 model for employment as military training machines. A second order followed, and was delivered during early 1938.

Also in 1938 the first sizeable War Office order was placed with BSA for the M20 model, along with a small order for some of the company's 'Gold Star' competition machines.

In 1939 further quantities of M20 models were ordered, as well as a number of military specification C10 lightweight models, principally intended for military training. After the outbreak of war in September of that year orders for the M20 model continued, although after France collapsed in mid 1940 BSA, along with most other manufacturers, was inundated with War Office demands for machines of all types and that year supplied quantities of M20s, M21s, C11s, C12s, B29s, M22s, M23s and M24s, many simply militarised versions of models originally intended for the civilian market.

By 1939 military thinking had concluded that any purpose-built military motorcycle had to be of lightweight design, with a specified upper-weight limit, a reasonable performance and other stated qualities necessary for service use. So, following several prototypes in 1940 and one production batch in 1941, the W-B30 350cc lightweight service model was suddenly cancelled by the War Office during late 1941, just as mass production was about to commence. As a result the service rider was to be sentenced to the M20 model for the remainder of the war and beyond.

During 1944 a War Office standardisation committee was established to assess the possibility of a new universal motorcycle for the services. Yet again military opinion changed, now back in favour of twin-cylinder machines. BSA offered a twin-cylinder SV machine of 500cc capacity for War Office consideration. The proposed new requirement and the establishment of a standardisation committee were the result of the Ministry of Supply becoming increasingly concerned about the numerous types of machines then employed throughout the services and the subsequent heavy demands for spares and repair facilities – a complicated situation to administer if nothing else.

Development of the twin-cylinder machine, however, was slow and lacked the urgency of earlier years, particularly as the end of the war was now in sight. It was not until well after the end of the Second World War, during the late 1940s, that the results of the 'twins' trials were available. The motorcycle eventually chosen was Triumph's 500cc SV-twin TRW model. In many ways BSA was to have the last laugh as its M20 model was to continue in service as the standard military model right up to the end of the 1950s, and then remain serving in limited numbers, notably overseas and with Territorial units, until the end of the following decade. In British military service, the M20 model actually outlived the TRW Triumph, a supposed replacement for the ancient BSA. The M20 further served alongside the 350cc OHV unit-construction BSA W-B40 service model, which was introduced during the early 1960s and served in limited numbers up to the mid 1980s. The last M20 model was not retired from military service until the beginning of the 1970s!

BSA Model S29 De-Luxe 499cc SV Single-Cylinder – 1929

Three of BSA's Model S29 De-Luxes were purchased by the War Office for evaluation purposes for the seven-make trial of 1929 and were all of standard civilian specification of the time, although fitted with the then optional electric lighting.

The War Office trials, conducted by the MWEE, were never completed satisfactorily and the results never properly assessed nor collated. As the War Office was impatient to receive a replacement for its ageing Triumph Model H machines, it did not want to wait for the results of the trials, which were therefore cancelled, and it went ahead of its own accord, purchasing machines manufactured by Douglas.

BSA War Office Twin 498cc OHV V-twin (Experimental) – 1932

According to surviving official documentation, this motorcycle was not actually purchased by the War Office but was loaned by BSA for evaluation purposes and remained the property of the company for the duration of the assessment period.

This motorcycle evolved as a result of the War Office's desire for quieter machines. In the 1930s its opinion was that twin-cylinder bikes were generally quieter than single-cylinder models.

The War Office Twin was tested against contemporary products from rival manufacturers, the Douglas L29 and the Matchless Silver Arrow. Following

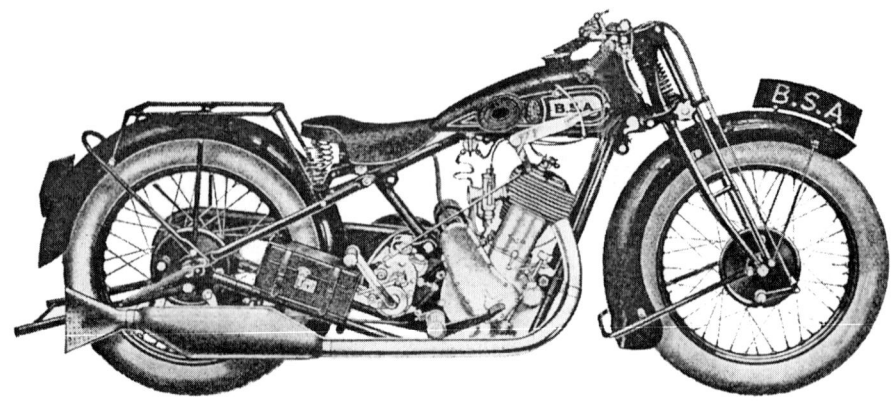

Catalogue picture of a 1929 S29 De-Luxe, as bought for use in the 1929 trial. (BSA)

completion of the standard War Office 10,000-mile test, it proved to be the most reliable of the three machines. However, although ultimately recommended as a model suitable for military service, concern was expressed over the considerable wear to the pistons and cylinders of the machine.

BSA War Office Twin 498cc OHV V-Twin – 1933–37

After the largely successful testing of BSA's experimental War Office twin-cylinder machine during 1932, the company duly began to receive orders for production models of the type during the following year from the War Office, delivery of the first examples probably being made in late 1933.

As the model settled into military service it was obvious that the problem of piston and cylinder wear that had afflicted the experimental model of 1932 had not been fully resolved with the production machines. It was generally thought that lubrication problems in the cylinder areas were the root cause. BSA itself specified the use of a high-quality lubricating oil for use in the machine. Once in service use, however, even in peacetime, machines were frequently lubricated by an inferior quality product, which the War Office had purchased in bulk and which was intended for general use in everything from tanks to stationary engines. During 1935 the MEE tested examples of the BSA War Office Twin using Wakefield Castrol XL and the results indicated that this

Official photograph of a 1933 BSA War Office Twin. (RLC Museum)

CMPs with a 1935 BSA War Office Twin with pre-war Norton 16Hs, Aldershot, April 1939. (RMP Museum)

or similar offered far better protection against wear than the standard War Office bulk M265 grade oil.

Various minor changes affected the model during the span of its production and supply to the War Office, the majority of these concerning different contracts as opposed to individual machines. Notable changes in 1935 included the installation of cast-iron pistons, a modified lube system, and air-hardened cylinders being fitted on some machines. Late machines probably all had pillion equipment fitted and certainly foot-change gearboxes.

It is interesting to note that on the outbreak of the Second World War in 1939, the War Office and the Air Ministry still had numbers of the Twins 'on the books' and some still in first-line use, particularly in situations where the Norton 16H and BSA M20 models had not yet been delivered as replacements.

BSA 249cc OHV Single-Cylinder – 1936

This machine was tested and rejected on the same day, although the reasons for its rejection remain unknown. Information on this model's performance during testing unfortunately no longer exists, and neither is it certain which model was tested, because BSA had three listed that year – the B-2, the B-18 Light De-Luxe, and the B-3 De-Luxe.

BSA B23 348cc SV Single-Cylinder – 1936

Tested over one day, this motorcycle was returned, presumably because it was deemed unsuitable.

Trials were also carried out with a BSA 249cc OHV, a 500cc OHV and a 348cc OHV during the same day, and it seems that these too were rejected by the War Office.

BSA B26 348cc OHV Single-Cylinder – 1936

This machine was tested and returned on the same day as the three other models supplied by BSA. Archive details on this model's performance during testing unfortunately no longer exist.

BSA M22 496cc OHV Single-Cylinder – 1936

This motorcycle was brought in along with three other BSA models for a one-day test, the outcome of which is unknown.

BSA War Office Twin (Lightened) 498cc OHV V-Twin – 1934

The problem of piston and cylinder wear on the production War Office Twin was not the only concern of the service authorities of the time. It had also been tentatively suggested that the standard production model was not lightweight, and very heavy to manoeuvre, particularly off-road. A lighter version, coupled with less power and thus easier to ride, was suggested, with a maximum speed of 50mph.

BSA set about reducing the weight of the machine by taking a standard model and fitting a lighter saddle, an Elektron gearbox shell, lighter flywheels, a smaller fuel tank and wheel rims and tyres of a smaller width while removing the steering damper and the rear rack. It also lightened the crankcase shield, mildly retuned the engine and modified the top of the frame. However, after the modifications were completed the machine was a mere 22lb lighter than the standard model.

Testing concluded that the weight saving was so small as not to matter and the detuning of the engine, coupled with the still heavy weight of the machine (380lb), impaired the overall performance notably (46mph compared with the standard version's 53.4mph), particularly in cross-country use and on fuel consumption. The end result was that no further action was taken in respect of lightening the War Office Twin, the project remaining a one-off, with the War Office now looking towards a new design of machine as an alternative to the BSA Twin.

It is also worth noting that the Army thought that the steering damper was essential for cross-country use and it did not like the deletion of the rear rack for obvious reasons.

Official photograph of the 1934 War Office Twin (lightened). (162/B1, The Tank Museum)

BSA W35-6 499cc SV Single-Cylinder – 1935 Evaluation Model

In 1935 the War Office instigated a trial involving the motorcycle products from seven different manufacturers including BSA, with all of them supplying 4-stroke single-cylinder machines of either SV or OHV engine configuration. BSA's model was its 499cc single-cylinder SV Model W35-6, which was subsequently purchased.

The model was ultimately to fail the MEE 10,000-mile test with several faults noted throughout the course of the 8,000 miles the test example actually completed. At 339 miles the engine seized because the piston stuck in the cylinder bore through lack of lubrication due to loss of oil. A further problem occurred at 2,498 miles when the fuel tank started to leak. Other notable defects were a broken oil gauge and a slight knock from the engine, plus the machine's brakes were considered to be rather poor in the wet. At 6,237 miles the test model was fitted with a new engine that was carefully run-in, but by the time 7,563 miles had been completed a cracked cylinder barrel was noted between the cylinder bore and the exhaust port. Other modifications and alterations included converting the test model from a hand-change to a foot-change gearbox at 2,498 recorded test miles, modifying the lube system to overcome the seizure fault and, at some stage, fitting another frame.

BSA M20 496cc SV Single-Cylinder – 1936 Evaluation Test Model

After the failure of the company's W35-6 model during the 1935 trials, BSA submitted a new model for War Office evaluation in 1936 in a further bid to win another government contract.

Official photograph of the 1935 W35-6, as used in the 1935 trial. (138/F5, The Tank Museum)

Official photograph of the 1936 M20 prototype (the first military version). Note the lack of an engine head steady and the 20in wheels. (KID 5608, IWM)

The M20 test model was initially evaluated by the MEE at Farnborough, Hampshire, where it showed itself to be at least comparable to Norton's similar 16H model. In light of this, a full reliability trial of the type was initiated.

The result of the trial was not as successful as had been hoped, although the model did improve on the performance of the previously tested W35-6 by at the least completing the trial programme.

The old BSA curse of cylinder bore and piston wear was again highlighted during the course of the test, a new cylinder, piston and other engine components having to be fitted at the 6,538-mile stage.

The result was that the MEE considered the reliability of the model as 'fair' and thus not entirely suitable for military service.

BSA M20 496cc SV Single-Cylinder – 1937 (Improved Version)
Having noted the comments of the MEE about the W35-6 model of 1935 and the original M20 model of the following year, BSA supplied a further three M20 models to the War Office under contract 294/C.991 during 1937. These three had been fitted with improved components to offset the previously noted reliability and wear problems.

Two of the three examples purchased were delivered to the MEE for use in the standard War Office 10,000-mile reliability trial, while the third was delivered to a normal service unit for general use and assessment.

The two examples tested showed improved reliability figures on completion of the trials, although they were still only considered 'fair' as opposed to 'good'. That said, however, the military authorities did note the model as suitable for their requirements. Thereafter, the military model M20, as it was known to literally thousands of British servicemen and others, was born.

It should be noted that these pre-production M20 models differed to a considerable degree from the later, more commonly encountered wartime production version. Differences were to include mechanical as well as cycle components, although the model was not generally altered in design to the version familiar to many until midway through the 1939 production year.

1937 M20 prototype (modified). Note the added head steady and air filter. (KID 5738, IWM)

1937 BSA M20 prototype with rubber seat, revised air cleaner, pannier-style toolboxes, and panel tank. (RLC Museum)

BSA B20 249cc SV Single-Cylinder – 1937–38 (H–B20 and J–B20)

The BSA B20 model was primarily a civilian-specification motorcycle that was purchased by the War Office principally for use as a learner-rider training machine and also for light communication duties.

The first contract was placed with BSA and delivered to the War Office in 1937; the machines supplied were therefore built to the specification laid down by BSA for that year. The second, larger contract was placed and mostly completed within the same year, the last deliveries being made to the War Office during early 1938. However, the second contract was placed after the commencement of production for the 1938 season, so these machines were constructed to the specification for the 1938 model, prefixed by the letter 'J' rather than the first contract's letter 'H'.

A final point to note is that the B20 model was purchased without prior testing and evaluation by the MEE, as was standard practice.

BSA M24 (Gold Star) 496cc OHV Single-Cylinder – 1938 (J-M24)

In a shrewd attempt to make its motorcycle products even more appealing to the War Office, BSA persuaded the Army to purchase some of its 500cc Gold Star models for trials and competitions of both a national and international nature during 1938. A major competition win would provide the country, the War Office and BSA itself with considerable publicity. To gain further favour with the War Office BSA sent one of its own competition riders to coach the British Army teams.

Official photograph of the 1938 B20. (KID5696, IWM)

Official photograph of the 1938 M24 Gold Star in its very non-military finish. (KID 5613, IWM)

Following War Office approval and the coaching of the Army trials teams by the BSA rider, they competed in all the leading events of the time, giving a particularly good performance at the 1938 International Six-Day Trial in Wales. It has been suggested that this success led to the War Office's first order for a large batch of M20 models, the request coming only days after the successes at the trials.

BSA C10 249cc SV Single-Cylinder – 1939–40 (K–C10 and W–C10)

The BSA C10 model supplied to the War Office was basically a standard civilian specification with a few minor alterations. These included the use of WM2 wheel rims so that the wider War Department tyre could be used, and the addition of an ignition warning light and a small carrier on top of the rear mudguard.

The model was supplied under two contracts, with some 1,935 machines being provided in total. The initial pre-war contract was for 585 machines of the 'K' specification of 1939, while the second contract was for the 'W' type of 1940. As between the civilian and the military versions of the motorcycle, there were also slight differences between the 1939 and the 1940 models. These included the toolbox, the speedometer drive, the engine-tappet cover, the rear light, the number plate and the front fork damping, which was repositioned.

The C10 model was purchased with the primary intention of providing a cheap, lightweight utility machine for training duties and light communication work – basically the same requirements for which its predecessor, the B20 model, had been employed. The C10 models, however, were a distinct improvement on the B20s, having a foot-change gearbox for a start.

Unlike the B20 model, the BSA C10 was tested for suitability by the MEE, although this was of no real value since the first batch of the type had already been purchased and put into service before the testing. The model was compared with Royal Enfield's then similar offering, the 250cc SV Model D, also purchased by the War Office in similar quantities and for a similar purpose. The officials considered the Royal Enfield Model D to

BSA C10 with its rider J. Stratfull of the Royal Corps of Signals in 1939. (Royal Signals Museum)

A pair of BSA C10s in 1939, with riders Jim Smith and J. Stratfull. Note the made up windscreen. (Royal Signals Museum)

have a slightly better performance than the BSA C10 model, although the BSA product was considered more dependable. Although neither type was considered to be outstandingly reliable, on inspection at the 5,000-mile point of testing neither displayed any real wear to the mechanical components, and both models were noted as suitable for the War Office, for training and light communication duties.

The C10 model was thus used by the War Office until at least 1942. Thereafter many were transferred to other government departments for the remainder of the war. As far as the training role of the C10 model was concerned, it was replaced by early production, larger-capacity machines, themselves withdrawn from first-line service following replacement by newer or improved types.

BSA C12 348cc SV Single-Cylinder – 1940 (W–C12)
The BSA C12 model of 1940 was the final model of the 'C' group of lightweight utilities, having a larger engine capacity (348cc) than the 249cc SV C10 model and the 249cc OHV C11 model. Both the C10 and C11 models continued in production after the war in much the same basic mechanical format, although when the pre-unit construction C12 model reappeared during the 1950s it had an engine capacity of 249cc and not 348cc, as its predecessor had in 1940. Perhaps rather strangely, the War Office did not pursue any contracts for the supply of the BSA C12 model despite the engine being comparable in performance with both the Royal Enfield Model C and the Triumph Model 3SW, both SV 350cc machines then in current production and use.

However, the model was not entirely rejected for service use. In September 1940 the Admiralty Department (Navy) received some sixteen examples of the type to order.

BSA M22 496cc OHV Single-Cylinder – 1939 (K–M22)

According to the BSA factory ledgers, six M22 models were supplied to the War Office direct from the factory in September 1939. The contract number is not known and neither are the precise details relating to specification of the models supplied. It can be presumed, however, that the six examples supplied were civilian models, militarised as far as paintwork was concerned, and immediately available for delivery.

BSA M23 (Silver Sports) 496cc OHV Single-Cylinder – 1939 (K–M23)

Due to the immediate demands for machines of all types following the outbreak of war, as well as the six model M22s, a slightly larger quantity of the similar M23 Silver Sports was also supplied. According to the factory ledgers, nineteen examples of the 1939 specification M23 model were provided, probably standard civilian models finished in the usual military paint scheme.

BSA M24 (Gold Star) 496cc OHV Single-Cylinder – 1939 (K–M24)

One of BSA's top of the range models, the 1939 specification M24 Gold Star model was again ready for immediate delivery from the factory's stock of completed machines, a total of eight being supplied directly to the War Office. It can be presumed that they were close to standard civilian specification and fitted with full road equipment, again being militarised only to the extent of the paintwork. It is probable that the supplied examples were used for general Army duties, along with all the other hurriedly requisitioned models, rather than for competition use, despite the type being a powerful competition model.

BSA M21 591cc SV Single-Cylinder – 1939 (K–M21)

These machines were the last of the 'M' group BSA models to be supplied to the War Office direct from the factory in October 1939, only a few weeks after the outbreak of war. As with the similar M22, M23 and M24 models, the type was a civilian-specification model and available for immediate delivery, although only one machine was actually supplied, rather than the several examples of other types, all of which may have been impressed into service.

BSA C11 249cc OHV Single-Cylinder – 1940 (W–C11)

Some 530 C11s were supplied during early 1940 to the Office of the High Commission of India, London, presumably for service overseas. Although the machine was based on the 1940 civilian-specification C11 model and shared many parts with its C10 stablemate, the following alterations were incorporated into the government contract: a rear carrier above the mudguard; a tank-top-mounted air filter (not the later military Vokes universal

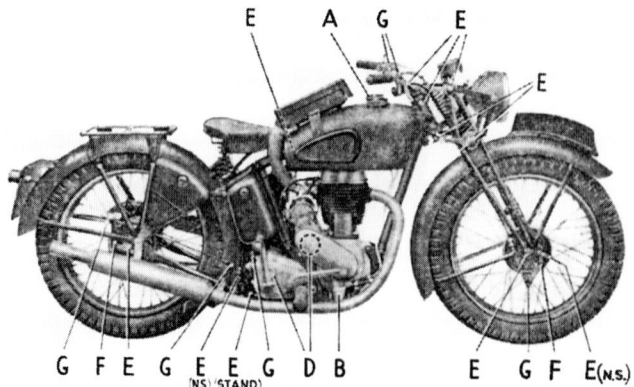

Period illustration of the 1940 W-C11 to military specification. Note the unusual magdyno ignition for the type, plus the early tank-top-mounted air cleaner. (BSA)

type, however), indicating possible use in a hot, dusty climate; an additional toolbox; a standard magdyno unit in place of the usual coil and car type distributor components; a standard pattern saddle in place of the rubber Dunlop type; and different oil and petrol filler caps, similar to those fitted to the M20 model but of a smaller size.

BSA B29 (Silver Sports) 348cc OHV Single-Cylinder – 1940 (W-B29)

The BSA B29 model with its sporting performance and single-cylinder engine fitted with hairpin valve springs was a new model introduced during late 1939 for the 1940 production range. Not originally intended for military service, few of the type had been sold to the civilian market of the time before a contract was issued by the War Office for immediate supply of the model.

Probably militarised only to the extent of its overall service paintwork, an estimated 167 examples were supplied to the War Office during the latter half of 1940. Smaller quantities of impressed machines from dealers' stocks may also have been made available.

BSA M21 591cc SV Single-Cylinder – 1940 (W-M21)

The BSA M21 model supplied to the War Office held both the same demand date and the same contract number as the comparatively small quantity of B29 models supplied. The demand date followed the evacuation of the British Army at Dunkirk and the loss of much equipment.

It is possible that these M21 models were originally destined for Holland, but had not been delivered before that country fell to the Germans. It is therefore not confirmed whether the machines were militarised civilian-specification models or purpose-built military types.

The M21 was not generally a faster machine than the M20 model. Although it had a larger capacity engine, this was designed primarily to provide a greater degree of flexibility for pulling a sidecar, in the nature of low-speed, high-gear engine torque, rather than additional speed. It is possible that several examples of the military-supplied M21 model were ultimately to be fitted with sidecars for various purposes.

BSA WM21 600cc SV Single-Cylinder SWD Combination – 1940
Tested in August 1940 against a standard Norton Big 4 and also an experimental 596cc OHV Norton combination, this machine was found to perform better than the Big 4, but only comparable to the 596cc combination. However, its top speed (46mph) was thought too low for service use and its petrol consumption unacceptable. On the plus side, it was considered easier to handle than the two Nortons (largely because of its narrower track) and was less affected by the sidecar wheel's drag. Needless to say, it was not recommended for service use and was judged to need redesigning.

Specification wise, it could carry three men and 1cwt of equipment, weighed 5¾cwt, and had 3.50–19 tyres; how the sidecar wheel drive worked is not known.

BSA Experimental Model 500cc SV – 1940
Few details are known about this model, but it is probable that it was a lightweight M20 and it used an experimental frame (EX315). Other manufacturers at this time (such as Norton) were also looking at lightening their current War Department models as an alternative to the special lightweights currently under development.

BSA 348cc Experimental Lightweight OHV Single-Cylinder – 1940 Prototype
BSA developed a 348cc OHV single-cylinder experimental model during the early part of 1940 as a result of the War Office's considerable interest in a purpose-designed military lightweight machine with the performance of a standard 500cc SV model.

The original War Office requirement was issued in 1939, but at this time BSA, along with Matchless, were not invited to supply a suitable model for evaluation against the three types tested from Norton, Triumph and Royal Enfield.

Tested by the War Office in spring 1940, after it had been developed and supplied under contract, the one example produced proved to be of satisfactory performance, comparing well with Triumph's 3TW. On this basis a second machine was actioned for further testing with a number of amendments incorporated.

It is noteworthy that BSA based this experimental lightweight machine on its 1940 B29 Silver Sports model, although obviously with many modifications and changes, including weight reduction. This machine can generally be considered as the military-designed B30 prototype, a model with considerable potential yet no future, at least not with the military.

BSA B30 348cc OHV Single-Cylinder – 1940 Pre-production Version

Following the success of the pilot version, this second version, incorporating the amendments, had gained 25lb in weight. After 5,000 miles of testing against an Ariel W/NG, the motorcycle was found to be in good condition, and its increase in weight was noted as not seriously affecting its ease of handling. Subsequently, fifty machines were ordered to the same specification, although these were some 15lb heavier because of restrictions on the amount of aluminium that could be used.

BSA B30 348cc OHV Single-Cylinder – 1941 (W–B30) Production Models

A production batch of fifty B30s was supplied under contract during the spring of 1941 and distributed among units and formations in order to further assess the type's suitability for military service. Although the majority were to be received by British Army units, it is interesting to note that three of the fifty examples were allocated to the United States, two to Canada and a further one to AMC, a company that would fit teledraulic front forks.

Official photograph of the production WB30. (REME Museum)

The modifications incorporated in the fifty pre-production examples over the original 1940 prototypes included: a smaller front brake; a different headlight and stays, the former containing a dry-cell battery; a direct lighting system, the usual dynamo replaced by an alternator situated atop the magneto; the removal of the standard battery and carrier; a repositioned field-stand; a different chain guard; a different fuel tank that had no knee-grip rubbers; and many other details too numerous to list.

The War Office was extremely pleased with the overall performance and suitability of the B30 model, placing a larger order with BSA for the supply of the first of supposedly many, under contract number 294/C.13290. Without prior warning, however, the War Office abruptly changed the contract's specification to the supply of 10,000 standard M20 SV models. The likely explanation seems to be last-minute concern over the potential difficulties of calling yet another model into military service, together with all the necessary spares and servicing requirements.

BSA M20 496cc SV Single-Cylinder – 1939–45 (K–M20 and W–M20)

Viewed as a near failure in the eyes of the War Office in 1936, this was ultimately to evolve into perhaps the most illustrious and longest-serving model in the history of British military motorcycling, not to mention becoming the most numerous type produced for the War Office itself.

The military model M20 was produced by BSA in several variations until 1942, when the type was largely standardised, undergoing only minor modifications thereafter until the end of the Second World War. The very earliest examples supplied, the K–M20 models from the 1939 production year, were generally a type constructed from a combination of standard and de-luxe model components with the addition of certain military-specified fittings. (However, it is interesting to note that, principally from contract number 294/C.3655 onwards, the factory ledgers detail the type as 'de-luxe'.)

The military-specified additional fittings included the large 8in Lucas DU142 headlight, complete with the switch panel and ammeter, a timing-gear cover incorporating a screw-in plug permitting access to the magneto drive-pinion nut, and 'winged' filler caps for both petrol and oil tanks. Other points of interest, concerning certain early W–M20 examples as well as the War Department K–M20 models, include the presence of a semi-rod-operated front brake, a screw-in speedometer drive box on the front wheel brake-plate face, a rather bulbous 3½-gallon fuel tank, and an alloy tappet cover carrying the BSA 'piled-arms' emblem, and the lack of a cylinder-head engine-steady bracket, pillion seat and footrests. Both front and rear number plates were fitted as standard, and some models also had an oil-pressure button indicator

Official photograph of the 1938 M20, RME367, C389369. (KID 5727, IWM)

incorporated in the timing cover. The early military M20 models were fitted with a long field-stand on the rear nearside of the machine, attached to, and pivoted from, a lug brazed on to the upper nearside rear-frame tube (deleted on later models). When not in use this stand was secured horizontally along the rear nearside of the model by means of a spring clip attached to a stud affixed to the central rear mudguard stay-cum-lifting handle (also deleted on later versions).

According to the factory ledgers, a number of the later K–M20 models within contract 294/C.3655 were originally destined for customers in Sweden, South Africa and India, despite the war having started, and that even after some six months of hostilities BSA, along with several other manufacturers, was still selling its products to overseas governments and commissions including Holland, Ireland, India and South Africa as well as civilian dealers and distributors.

From October 1939 detail changes were made to the W–M20, as the former K–M20 was now known. These included a new less bulbous 3-gallon fuel tank and girder forks minus the hand-adjusted damper knob, which was replaced by a simple locknut impossible to adjust while riding. The speedometer driver was relocated to the nearside of the front wheel, the valanced rear mudguard was removed, and finally Jaeger speedometers were fitted to some models.

During late 1940 certain numbers of civilian-specification M20 models were purchased by the War Office direct from the BSA factory, mainly to de-luxe specification as applicable to the civilian market of the time, although a few standard examples were also supplied, probably militarised only to the extent of the colour scheme.

The 1941 model differed only slightly from the 1940 model, both front and rear number plates being removed, and the alloy tappet cover replaced by a plain steel version.

Official photograph of an India Office M20. (Henk Joore)

George Forsey doing his D/R course at Blandford camp in about 1941/42 and on his left arm the good conduct stripes, above them the yellow and red RAC arms of service stripes. Above that is the shield-shaped badge, half red, half yellow with stars on for RAC Southern Command. (John Forsey)

Between 1941 and 1942 further changes to the M20 were made, including the reinstallation of the offside hand-adjusted damper knob. Service experience of the model, particularly in North Africa where proper roads were few, had shown the need for readily adjustable fork damping in order to offset wear and possible failure of the fork. The first damper knobs were made of Bakelite, and later of pressed steel. Other changes included the use of a 6in Lucas DU42 headlight, complete with the hooded, slotted blackout shield, instead of the 8in DU142 type, and the fitting of the universal War Department pattern L-WD-MCT1 tail light. By early 1942 a new full-size rear carrier had been fitted to accommodate the newly introduced universal War Department pattern steel pannier frames and bags, together with a pair of lower support stays for the frames. Pillion equipment was also now standardised and a pillion seat and footrests were fitted to all production machines. To accommodate the new equipment it was necessary to alter the design and mounting position of the long nearside field-stand, which was now much longer than before. The securing clip was repositioned to sit just above and forward of the nearside rear wheel spindle nut, the stand sitting at an angle of approximately 45 degrees as opposed to near horizontally as before.

Late 1942 saw the deletion of rubber fittings on all new machines, the replacement of the handlebar grips with universal War Department canvas items and the relocation of the horn to the nearside front engine plate on many machines. Further modifications include the removal of the rib-centred rear mudguard in favour of a simplified plain item, although the front mudguard continued to retain the ribbed centre until the end of the war.

During the latter half of 1943 the girder fork steering damper was removed from all new machines, the crankcase sump shield was redesigned to incorporate additional protection at the sides for both the engine and frame rails, and the fuel tank was altered by having the rear offside corner removed to accommodate the substantial hose section leading from the tank-top-mounted universal War Department pattern Vokes air filter to the carburettor air intake. This last modification was carried out on a large proportion of machines destined for service in hot, dusty climates. By early 1945 the Vokes filter was fitted as standard to the fuel tank of all new models irrespective of where they were destined to serve, the filter being secured to the tank by mounting strips attached to the previously redundant knee-grip locating holes on either side of the fuel tank. The last notable change to affect the model during the war occurred in early 1945, when the lighting system

A mid-war M20 in service in Algiers early 1945. Rider is Peter Sharpe. (Peter Sharpe)

was altered by removing the ammeter and installing a simple push-button 'change-over' switch for the headlight, the main lighting switch now being of a different pattern, located on a simple bracket beneath the offside of the saddle.

The vast majority of BSA M20 models delivered were employed by the War Department (Army), although smaller quantities were also used by both the Admiralty (Navy) and the Air Ministry (RAF). It is interesting to note that the Air Ministry used quantities of the model fitted with a Swallow-manufactured sidecar, and that a great number of the smaller M20 model contracts throughout the Second World War specified sidecar lugs for the frame, generally removed from all the larger contracts, which were specifically solo only.

Although intended as a general-purpose motorcycle for convoy escort and long-distance communications duties, because of the sheer number supplied the model was employed ultimately in every theatre of war and for virtually every purpose imaginable, whether suitable or not. It is perhaps for this reason that the model is the one best remembered by and familiar to most ex-servicemen and other individuals when military motorcycles are mentioned. The post-war service of the BSA M20 model further increased its renown, the type being retained in service as the standard War Department motorcycle throughout the National Service period of the 1950s and onwards in limited numbers until the end of the next decade. This was despite the fact that it was never totally suitable, and was most probably retained only because of the huge quantities of machines and parts available after the end of the war.

Admittedly, by the end of the Second World War the model's reliability was reasonably good, having served through six years of harsh conflict without any major failing. The M20's clutch had always been a problem, especially if contaminated by oil, and would drag or slip when hot, not to mention not fully releasing on occasions (even when new!) due to the limitations of the single-spring, multi-plate design. The post-war service authorities were so concerned about the problem that a modification directive was eventually issued in 1958, permitting the installation of four small screws to the central spring-nut in an attempt to effect some adjustment to the non-adjustable design! Another M20 idiosyncrasy, never fully resolved, was a tendency for the machine to refuse to start when hot, largely because the heat from the cylinder evaporated the fuel in the carburettor before it could enter the engine. The model was also prone to backfire through the carburettor causing a fire, and post-war regulations invariably specified the carriage of a fire extinguisher somewhere on the machine.

With so many examples produced, the BSA M20 is a common machine today, although few retain their correct original factory specification, especially the early wartime or pre-war examples. During the course of the Second World War and throughout the post-war period, virtually all M20s were rebuilt by the military at least once, if not several times. Engines were changed around under service-exchange schemes and rebuilt models were constructed from stocks of parts assembled from all years and contracts. In certain instances, the military authorities would fit a brand new frame or engine unit to a rebuilt machine and not stamp the item fitted with a number, further complicating the task of dating such a machine today.

BSA 495cc SV Parallel Twin-Cylinder – 1944–45 Prototype
This model was developed by the company towards the end of the Second World War as BSA's answer to the War Office's request for a standardised military motorcycle to replace most types in use then. Once again, thinking had changed and was now inclined towards a twin-cylinder machine of 500cc capacity, retaining an SV configuration.

A sole example was built, fitted with telescopic forks, and submitted for evaluation. However, the War Office's testing programme was to become a long, drawn-out affair and interest in the project declined somewhat with the end of the war clearly approaching. With the cessation of hostilities, and faced with the prospect of enormous stocks of now redundant machines and stark post-war economies, the programme was temporarily suspended. When interest recommenced during the late 1940s the War Office in the end favoured Triumph's TRW model.

Official photograph of the 1944–45 prototype parallel twin. (REME Museum)

DOUGLAS

Douglas was the largest manufacturer and supplier of military motorcycles for the Allied forces during the First World War, the company name being as familiar then as perhaps BSA's was to become in the next global conflict. However, during the interwar years the Douglas' business with the War Office gradually diminished and by the outbreak of the Second World War it had ceased supplying any motorcycles to the military, its role during the war being concerned with other forms of mechanical and industrial production.

In 1929 a quantity of the company's 350cc SV flat-twin Model L29 was hastily purchased by the War Office, which was too impatient to wait for the results of the seven-make trials currently being conducted by the MWEE and in which the L29 was involved. During 1931, a Model A31 was tested, but ultimately was not pursued as the MWEE stated a preference for the latest version of the existing L29 model, the L29/4, following comparative testing.

In 1934 Douglas submitted two examples of the company's 500cc Blue Chief model for War Office evaluation, one fitted with a 4-speed gearbox and the other a 3-speed. Following testing, the MEE concluded that the 4-speed version was no better than the 3-speed. Another 3-speed was purchased for further evaluation during 1935, but the model failed to pass approval for service.

After this, Douglas had no further involvement with the War Office in respect of motorcycles until about 1944, when the Ministry of Supply requested the company to produce two prototype machines to the late war design specification for a proposed standard military motorcycle. However, neither of these prototypes met with approval, and Triumph secured the contract with its TRW model. Douglas had one final contact with the War Office in the immediate post-war period, when the company supplied to contract seven machines of 125cc engine capacity with post-war registration numbers of 20 CL 57 to 20 CL 62. Little more is known about these.

Douglas Models L29, L29/2, L29/3, L29/4 348cc SV Flat-Twin – 1929–32

The Douglas Model L29 was procured initially as a hurried replacement for the War Office's fleet of by then ageing and obsolescent machines, the bulk of which were of Triumph origin. By 1929 officials at the War Office were too impatient for a suitable replacement motorcycle to wait for the MWEE to collate the results of the various machines on trial, and instead instigated a much shortened trial between the Douglas L29 and a Triumph Model NL3. The results showed in favour of the Douglas model, it being lighter and easier to handle, and a first contract for supply of the type was placed.

Official photograph of the 1929 Douglas L29 (first version). (WO 194 [45]-5872, The National Archives)

Douglas L29/3 in use with The Royal Green Jackets in 1931. (170A12W_P_4972-1, Hampshire Archives/The Royal Green Jackets Museum)

Although the seven-make trial was concluded during late 1929, principally because of the actions of the War Office, testing continued on a reduced scale and the Douglas, AJS and Matchless machines were chosen for further evaluation. The MWEE report concluded that it had made no decisions as a result of these tests. Relevant or otherwise, the War Office was to purchase more Douglas machines, all Model L29s but with detail changes from contract to contract, hence the designations L29/2, L29/3 and L29/4.

It is worth noting that Douglas listed the Model L29 for 1929 only, the 'L' designation standing for 'lightweight', even though it was only marginally different from a heavyweight model, the B29. The L29 was replaced the

The final version of the Douglas L29, termed the L29/4. Note the totally different frame, which now has a centre stand. (WO 194 [45]-6891, The National Archives)

following year by the Model L3, which was a completely different machine and also a true lightweight. Evidently, after 1930 the L29 was built exclusively to War Office order.

Douglas A31 348cc SV Flat-Twin – 1931

The Model A31 was new to the Douglas range of machines for 1931 and an example was tested by the MWEE for suitability for service usage. Following a period of evaluation, the model was considered to have satisfactory performance despite a defective piston gudgeon pin causing a breakdown at the 4,850-mile stage of testing. To further assess the type's suitability, it was retained at Farnborough for comparative trials against the new Model L29/4 from the company, which itself was claimed to be an improvement over the then current Model L29/3.

Compared to the Model L29/4, the Model A31 was a true lightweight machine, weight reduction having been achieved by the lightening of various

Official photograph of the 1931 Douglas A31 test model. (KID 5432, IWM)

components. The MWEE, however, considered that eventually such lightened components would have to be restored to their original weight if they were to withstand rigorous usage under typical service conditions. Principally on this basis, the Model A31 was discarded in favour of the new Model L29/4.

Douglas Experimental Model – 1932
Although this particular motorcycle is listed as an experimental model of 1931, it was not actually delivered until 1932.

At the time of writing, it has not been possible to establish which Douglas model underwent testing.

Douglas 5Y2 Blue Chief 500cc SV Flat-Twin – 1934–35
Three of these models were to be evaluated by the MEE, with the first two examples being loaned by the Douglas company during 1934. Of these, one was fitted with a 3-speed gearbox and the other with a 4-speed version. Tested during November 1934, both examples were considered to have a good off-road performance, but the MEE found that no advantage could be gained by the 4-speed model. Consequently, another 3-speed model was purchased during 1935 for further testing, during which it completed some 2,930 miles on roads. The MEE reported that the model had a generally unsatisfactory performance with a high consumption of both oil and petrol, and that its mechanical reliability left much to be desired. In light of this, further trials of the model were discontinued.

Official photograph of the 1935 Douglas Blue Chief (military version), as finally purchased with a 3-speed gearbox. (245/D1, The Tank Museum)

Official photograph of the 1944/5 Douglas DV60, which is labelled as No. 2. (MVE 12851/1, IWM)

Douglas DV60 602cc SV Transverse Flat-Twin – 1944–45 Prototype

The only motorcycle produced by the Douglas company during the Second World War, the DV60 was built in response to the War Office request for a standardised model of military motorcycle. The prototype machine constructed to the specifications laid down by the Ministry of Supply was termed the Model DV60 and was submitted to the MEE at Farnborough for evaluation before the end of the war.

Testing was slow, however, and eventually abandoned completely because of the approaching end of hostilities. The entire project was then temporarily shelved. The model was eventually to reappear in early post-war years with a new frame and other minor detail alterations in an attempt to secure the contract, but ultimately this was won by Triumph's TRW model with the Douglas product, along with offerings from both BSA and Norton, fading into obscurity.

EXCELSIOR

The Excelsior company, like several other comparatively small manufacturers of motorcycles, entered the Second World War engaged with other forms of government contract work rather than the supply of motorcycles. With the larger manufacturers able to produce and deliver machines on a grand scale, the engineering facilities of smaller companies were deemed better utilised on other aspects of much-needed war work.

However, the mid-war years saw the Excelsior company once again involved with limited motorcycle manufacturing, which continued alongside all other forms of contract work at the time.

The motorcycles produced included the famous Welbike for the airborne forces, plus a very small quantity of the company's universal model of 125cc capacity.

Prototype Welbike 98cc Single-Cylinder 2-Stroke – 1942

It should be noted that the very first Welbike prototype model was not actually an Excelsior, the company having had no involvement with the original concept or design.

Along with the Royal Enfield WD/RE Flying Flea and the James ML (military lightweight), the Welbike was originally designed to provide the developing British airborne forces with a form of cheap, lightweight, reliable and semi-expendable form of transport for limited front-line use following a parachute or glider landing. With space and weight at a premium within an aircraft, the size and weight of a motorcycle were crucial. A small folding design that could be dropped by parachute from an aircraft into a drop zone was considered the best option, the machine being contained within a modified standard equipment container for the purposes of the drop. Once on the ground, the machine had to be capable of being released from the container and brought into use with the minimum of delay.

This prototype machine was produced at the military research establishment at Welwyn in Hertfordshire by J.R.V. Dolphin. The initial model was rather crude and basic, fitted with a 98cc Villiers 2-stroke engine. The name Welbike

Official photograph of a pre-production prototype suitably modified to tow the container in which it is dropped by parachute. (NB 3383-3, Crown Copyright, MoD Boscombe Down)

was coined a short time later, the first part of the name relating to the town where the machine was created. Following its construction, the prototype was subjected to a certain degree of testing to establish suitability for its intended purpose. It proved to be incredibly tough for such a small machine, and although really harsh treatment bent and distorted the type, it would not actually break apart. Interestingly, the prototype Welbike reflected only a few features of the small Aveling Barford machine on test a few years earlier (see p. 33).

Excelsior Welbike 98cc Single-Cylinder 2-Stroke – 1942 Pre-production Version
Following completion, the prototype machine was delivered to the Excelsior motorcycle company's premises for further development. It was examined in detail and minor development modifications were carried out on paper. New jigs and fixtures were made for the type incorporating these modifications, which included improvements to the fuel tank, tyres, footrests and throttle. A handful of pre-production machines were constructed to further assess the machine's suitability for production and service. How many of these versions were built has not been established, although an estimation would be a minimum of six. Incredibly, at least one survives today in private ownership.

All these pre-production versions were subjected to extremely varied and rigorous testing. Experiments conducted around September 1942 included dropping the suitably packaged machine from an aircraft for it to land with the aid of a parachute. It is likely that at least a couple of these pre-production versions were destroyed or damaged during such testing, although this cannot be firmly established.

A further point that arose from the trials was that the type's Villiers junior de-luxe engine unit needed some slight modification. As standard, it was found that the little 98cc unit was struggling to attain full power across poor, soft terrain with a fully laden soldier sitting astride. Accordingly, the engine unit was 'retuned' to provide a marginally increased performance, and built with generous clearances to the working parts so that it could be driven at full power immediately on starting, without risk of seizing or damaging the power plant.

All the experimentation on the model was carried out by the Airborne Forces Experimental Establishment (AFEE) at Sherburn-in-Elmet, near Leeds, West Yorkshire. Besides the drop tests, the motorcycle was tested for its towing ability, the idea being to ascertain whether the machine could tow its own dropping container, fitted with wheels but loaded to 350lb. This it managed, but only on hard, level surfaces.

Excelsior Welbike 98cc Single-Cylinder 2-Stroke – 1942–45

On completion of the trials and development work on the pre-production versions of the model, production of the type commenced in earnest. A small, simple design, the Welbike proved cheap and fast to produce. This is highlighted by the fact that the model was painted while still on the production line. Following the fitting of the engine but before the fitting of the wheels, saddle and handlebar grips, the machine would be hung on a rail in the paint shop and completely sprayed with the appropriate colour. The wheels, saddle and grips would then be added and the whole put into another area for test and delivery!

The Welbike was the smallest motorcycle to see service with the British military and quite likely the smallest military machine in comparison to the products of other nations as well. Initially, all production was allocated for issue to the expanding airborne forces, particularly for use in parachute assaults, although by late 1943 the type was also in use by assault troops, mainly Army Commandos and Royal Marines (on charge to the Admiralty), on beachheads such as Anzio, Normandy, and so on. By 1944, and into 1945, the Welbike was also being used by the RAF, particularly in the Far East, where the type was considered ideal solo transport around an airfield. Several aircrews 'acquired' examples to stow aboard their aircraft for such times as they might be required.

Three main production versions of the Welbike were built, each subsequent version improving slightly on the previous model, although the modifications were usually very minor. Total wartime Welbike production, excluding the

Official photograph of a Mark 1 towing a container with a revised attachment method. (NB 3383-1, Crown Copyright, MoD Boscombe Down)

pre-production versions, was some 3,923 examples, of which the first 1,183 were of Mark 1 design. The most noticeable difference between this and later versions was the lack of a rear mudguard. The next contract was for 1,400 examples of a lightly modified design; these machines were designated Mark 2, Series 1. The third and final Welbike contract was for 1,340 machines, which were again slightly improved, and designated Mark 2, Series 2. Apart from the lack of a rear mudguard on the Mark 1, other differences between the early and late machines included the saddle-type fuel tanks, which on early versions had a vent screw in the left-hand tank to enable the unobstructed filling of the tank, and the filler cap itself being incorporated with the pump that was used to pressurise the fuel tanks prior to starting the machine. This was a time-consuming operation and on later versions a filler cap was added to the left-hand tank and the vent screw switched over to the right tank, thus avoiding the need to remove the fuel pump. Other modifications affected the mounting of the tanks and the positioning of the fixing straps to the frame. As previously mentioned, all Mark 2 models acquired a small rear mudguard as well as splash shielding between the fuel tanks.

The Mark 1 Excelsior Welbike with a dynamo attached. This conversion was known as a Wel-charger and was a modification carried out by the airborne forces. To ride the motorcycle, the driving chain had to be removed and the dynamo turned 90 degrees clockwise. Note the added centre stand. (Airborne Assault Museum)

Wel-charger in ready-to-ride position. (Airborne Assault Museum)

Contrary to popular belief, the Welbike was perhaps not as widely utilised as had been intended. Ideas for the use of the model, tested and practised in training, frequently proved impractical when it came to actual operations. Having landed in a hostile, exposed area, many parachutists were more concerned with getting under cover as fast as possible and the idea of spending time, even if minimal, setting up a Welbike for riding was often less attractive than getting out of the area on foot. Parachute operations also frequently separated men and equipment, sometimes by miles, and thus much was lost, often to the enemy. Further, at night or in extremely soft, poor terrain, the little Welbike with its small wheels and 98cc engine, carrying a rider and equipment with a total weight of up to 300lb, was simply not up to the job. Because of this, further tests were carried out on an improved container in May 1943, designed to take some of the load off the motorcycle. The Mark 1 versions saw the most use and consequently the loss rate was highest among this version. Many of the later Mark 2, Series 2 models were never actually used and were disposed of after the war still in their original packing.

It is rumoured that eventually the majority of Welbikes were disposed of overseas as, without some modification, the type was unsuitable for civilian use in the United Kingdom – among other features the machine lacked the necessary two brakes required by law. However, some at least were sold off within the UK, probably for 'running about on farms'.

A final twist to the Welbike story was the redesign of the model during the early post-war period by its original designer, J.R.V. Dolphin. He took his ideas to Brockhouse Engineering (trailer manufacturers during the Second World War), whereupon the Corgi was born. Today, one can occasionally see Corgis

Mark 2 Welbike in Singapore. (REME Museum)

at military vehicle shows painted green and termed 'post-war parachutists' scooters', or even on the odd occasion an actual Welbike! The post-war Corgi was never used by the military apart from a few examples bought by the Royal Navy as 'dockyard runabouts', and the authors know of no evidence to substantiate claims to the contrary.

Excelsior Universal 125cc Single-Cylinder 2-Stroke – 1942

Little is known about this particular machine's involvement with the military, although at least one example was supplied to the War Office under contract during early 1942 and there exists the possibility of further small quantities of the type also being supplied.

The universal model was fitted with a Villiers 9D engine unit identical to that fitted to the similar James ML model. In fact, the Excelsior machine was similar to the ML in many other respects. It is likely that the type was originally acquired for assessment for suitability by the airborne forces, along with the

James ML and the Royal Enfield WD/RE, as the machine's contract number is very close to the one issued to James for its ML model.

FRANCIS BARNETT

Like James, Norman and Excelsior, Francis Barnett was a manufacturer that used proprietary 2-stroke engines from Villiers of Wolverhampton. Although 2-stroke engines were generally not favoured by the War Office, the MWEE did start testing one in 1928, choosing Francis Barnett as the supplier of the motorcycle. This one-off was a specially modified Model 9 constructed to meet the requirements of the military. Testing was carried out at the MWEE, which was also testing a lightweight from Levis and a 3-wheeler from Osborn Engineering Company (OEC); the results obtained were inconclusive.

The following year (1929) Francis Barnett was chosen to take part in the MWEE's seven-make trial. For this, it supplied three bored-out Empire Model No. 12 motorcycles, the only 2-stroke models participating. However, before all the testing was finished, the authorities went ahead with a rushed trial between a Douglas and a Triumph, before finally opting to buy the Douglas. Some six months later, when the trial finished in November 1929, the modified Model 12s were rejected (along with several other makes), largely because they were considered not powerful or robust enough to withstand service life.

Following this trial, the authorities abandoned 2-strokes in preference for 4-strokes for the next seven-make trial in 1935, and it was not until 1938 that they looked again at a 2-stroke motorcycle. However, in 1941 Francis Barnett did get an opportunity to supply another motorcycle, as a contract was issued for either one or several 150cc Plovers, but why or for whom they were bought is not known at the time of writing.

Francis Barnett Military Lightweight 172cc Single-Cylinder 2-stroke – 1928

This motorcycle was one of the first military motorcycles developed by the MWEE, the other being the OEC 3-wheeler.

Studying the photograph, the motorcycle appears to be based around a Model 9 Francis Barnett, which had a 172cc twin-port Villiers engine. Modifications carried out on the standard model were larger tyres, special clearance mudguards and special gear ratios.

In 1928 it was tested against a Model M Levis and one of the OEC 3-wheelers, but the test results were regarded as 'inconclusive' and 'tended to show that lightness was of great importance in connection with the development of a cross-country motorcycle and the problem was to reconcile light weight with

Official photograph of the 1928 lightweight that was based on the company's Model 9. (WO 194 [45]-5813, The National Archives)

Francis Barnett Model 12 (Modified) 350cc Single-Cylinder 2-stroke – 1929

Three of these were bought for the 1929 seven-make trial, in which they were the only 2-strokes competing against mainly SV and OHV machines.

Although Francis Barnett's Model 12 was normally a 250cc on the civilian market, these three had enlarged engines to take them out to 350cc and this was achieved by upping the bore from 67mm to 79mm. Quite what else was changed over the standard machine is not known, as in the official War Office photograph the motorcycle looks very standard.

Testing finished in late 1929, when the machine was rejected as unsuitable along with several other makes. It is probable that this was because of its lack of power across country (i.e. no bottom-end power), which was a continuing criticism of all 2-strokes at the time, and also because of its light construction that meant parts were easily damaged in severe use (i.e. cross-country riding).

Official photograph of the 1929 Model 12, as used in the 1929 trials. The engine capacity was increased from its normal 250cc size to 350cc by boring it out from 67mm to 79mm. (WO 194 [45]-5871, The National Archives)

Francis Barnett Plover 150cc Single-Cylinder 2-stroke – 1941

Bought under contract, it is not clear whether one or several of these machines were actually purchased, neither is it known whether the model chosen was a K40 or a K41.

Considering the date it was purchased, it is possible that the Plover was being looked at for the role eventually filled by the Royal Enfield WD/RE and James ML models.

The K41 Plover was fitted with a 148cc Villiers engine and an Albion 3-speed gearbox. Image is from a 1939 advert. (Francis Barnett Motorcycles)

GILLET-HERSTAL

Gillet-Herstal 728cc Parallel Twin-Cylinder 2-Stroke SWD Combination – 1939

This Belgian-made combination was tested and demonstrated in mid 1939 along with a Norton Big 4. Brought over to England by M. Gillet at Norton's request, it was demonstrated by a Belgian driver carrying two passengers. It proved to be a good performer on gravel and sand but suffered a bit in the mud, possibly through its own weight (91/2cwt, compared to the Norton's 61/2cwt). During testing, it failed a few tests that the Big 4 passed, but generally there was little to choose between the two motorcycles, and neither was considered better than the other.

Technically the Gillet had a few advantages over the Norton, as it had a sidecar wheel brake (which made steep descents easier to control) and a reverse gear.

HARLEY-DAVIDSON

Along with Indian, the American company Harley-Davidson was to supply a quantity of its combination and solo motorcycles to British and Commonwealth countries under the Lend-Lease agreement of 1941. To date, the final quantity of Harley-Davidson motorcycles supplied to and used by the British forces has not been established, although it is known that the Air Ministry (RAF) employed a quantity of the WLC solo model and that the War Office (Army) utilised a limited number of the larger-capacity combination machines. The South African forces were also sent a large quantity of machines via the British Supply Council, with other Commonwealth countries, principally Canada, supplied direct from Harley-Davidson. It is of note that most of the combination machines donated had left-hand sidecars fitted, even though normal American practice was to fit a right-hand version. During 1941 a combination model, ELC, plus a solo WLC test model were sent for evaluation purposes via the Canadian forces. Both versions were subjected to a form of suitability test but not the standard 10,000-mile reliability and endurance test, probably because a prompt decision was required.

When it is considered that the British had been looking at the suitability of new lightweight machines of some 260lb in weight at this time, with examples having been supplied from BSA, Triumph and others, and rejected for various reasons including their weight, cost, performance, poor fuel consumption, among others, it is therefore rather surprising that these low-slung, heavy, cumbersome machines with poor fuel consumption and cross-country capabilities and weighing, at the very least, some 550lb (WLC solo), were considered at all for British military use. Indeed, at the time, the War Office was voicing criticism of the weight of its then current machines including the BSA M20, the Norton 16H and the Matchless G3, and these were about 150lb lighter than the WLC. Other disadvantages of using US machines for the British military were the unfamiliar control layout, including a hand-operated gear change (dropped in the mid 1930s by British manufacturers) and foot-operated clutch, all of which required time-consuming practice from the British riders. On the plus side, however, all the American machines were very comfortable to ride, with large leather-topped saddles, wide handlebars and footboards. They were, by virtue of their design, weight and construction, incredibly robust and consequently reliable and extremely well suited to long-distance road use, in which most were ultimately employed.

At the end of the Second World War, virtually all surviving Harley-Davidson machines supplied to the British military were disposed of as surplus on to the public market. In the late 1940s a number of dealerships advertised in the press, offering both new and reconditioned Model U combinations for sale, as well as quantities of the smaller solo WLA/WLC version. However, Harley-Davidsons used by the RAF overseas, in places such as Singapore, are known to have remained in service until the late 1950s.

A 1943 WLC in service with 83 Group, 2nd Tactical Air Force, RAF, in Holland, 1944. Reg Humphries is stood to the front on the left. (Reg Humphries)

A Second World War American 78th Division photo with an RAF-marked Harley-Davidson WLC being ridden past a huge Second World War US Army tank transporter. (Authors' collection)

Harley-Davidson WLC 750cc SV V-Twin – 1941–44

The first example of the Canadian specification WLC was received for evaluation testing in September 1941, and was delivered to a depot in Slough, Berkshire. This machine had almost certainly been acquired via the Canadian authorities and must have been accepted, as it was soon to enter limited service with the British forces, principally with the RAF.

It is likely that the first WLC supplied for testing was to 1942 model specifications, as initial deliveries of the type may also have been. These early versions differed in a number of details from the 1943 (export) specification models, which were supplied later on. The most notable differences were the use of longer front forks, the positioning of the headlamp and horn, the tail lights and the lack of a rear luggage carrier. Apart from these features there are numerous other detail differences between the two models, and more differences still between these and the similar American military specification model, the WLA, which incidentally was never officially used by the British.

Harley-Davidson ELC 1000cc OHV V-Twin Combination – 1941

As with the smaller WLC model, an example of this large combination machine was delivered for evaluation by the War Office during late 1941, again presumably acquired via the Canadian authorities. Although information is unclear, the model appears not to have gained acceptance for British military use.

Harley-Davidson UA/Model US 1200cc SV V-Twin Combination – 1942–43

The Model UA and Model US were basically militarised versions of the company's civilian Model U machine. As with all other Harley-Davidsons, the Model UA and US were really only suitable for long-distance road use and therefore, in consideration of all other factors, only at their best in the hands of an experienced motorcyclist (as was the similar Indian Chief combination).

Most Lend-Lease UAs differed to the ones used by the US Army; they had valanced mudguards, a different silencer and a front wheel stand. Late models had sand pads added to the rear stand, both 16in and 18in wheels are known to have been fitted, and occasionally the sidecar bodies had doors fitted. All Model USs were delivered to South Africa.

INDIAN

Following the withdrawal of the British forces from France at Dunkirk in mid 1940, and the consequent loss of large quantities of much-needed equipment, the British government looked towards the then neutral United States and her industrial might for assistance. This request was to evolve into the Lend-Lease agreement of 11 March 1941, which enabled the United States to supply Britain with a wide variety of industrial and humanitarian aid without invoking a change to the American constitution.

Among the enormous quantities of goods and equipment supplied by the United States to Britain were some 10,000 motorcycles of various types, supplied by both Harley-Davidson and Indian, although Indian was ultimately to supply the bulk of the equipment. The first Indian models to be delivered into the United Kingdom were the large Chief combination machines, namely the Model 340B, which was followed by sizeable quantities of the smaller solo Model 741B. Both models were to see service with 'free' forces within the United Kingdom (e.g. the Dutch, Polish), the Air Ministry (RAF), and with rear echelon troops within the British Army in the UK (such as the Corps of Military Police). The machines also saw limited use with civil defence and fire organisations, and Commonwealth and governmental departments and ministries, some of the latter located in the most remote and far-flung places in the world.

Delivery of the major Indian model, the 741B, was halted by mid 1943 as British motorcycle production had finally caught up with demand, and by 1944 even the British manufacturers were being instructed by the government to slow down production of machines because of stockpiling, supply outstripping demand and the course of the remainder of the war now being firmly in favour of the Allies. Along with examples of Harley-Davidsons, large quantities of surviving Indian machines, primarily 741B models, were disposed of via civilian dealerships following the end of hostilities. These disposals principally concerned machines located within the UK; those that had been sent to numerous overseas locations were usually disposed of *in situ* or simply left there.

Only one other Indian machine was to be evaluated by the War Office for suitability during the Second World War, namely the Model 640, which the Canadian forces were using at the time. Although not established, the type was presumably rejected in favour of the smaller, lighter, and more economical Model 741B.

A point of interest with all the Indian and Harley-Davidson models supplied was the typical American design of the rider's controls. With a hand-change gearbox, a left-hand-operated throttle twist grip and a foot-operated clutch among other peculiarities, the average British military rider was required to retrain his mind in the operation of the machine both prior to and when riding. This persistent state of unfamiliarity with the American types was perhaps one of the main factors that contributed to their unpopularity in the higher echelons of the War Office and their distribution among second-line formations and to some of the more remote outposts of the Empire. As with Harley-Davidson, however, all the machines were built to a high standard and were very sturdy and reliable; furthermore, they were infinitely more comfortable to ride than their British-built counterparts.

Official photograph of an early 340B combination. (REME Museum)

Indian 340B Chief 1200cc SV V-Twin Combination – 1940–41

These large and powerful combinations were originally ordered by the French government, but following the fall of France in mid 1940 it seems that the models not yet delivered were reallocated to the British War Office to be used when such machines were urgently required after Dunkirk.

All the combinations supplied were fitted with right-hand sidecars rather than left-hand, as was usual in the United Kingdom. A number of them were allocated to the free Polish forces, at the time located in Scotland. Many of these machines were to have the overall basic light olive-drab paint finish supplemented by random overpainting of a wavy, curved camouflage pattern in a darker shade of green or brown, similar to an aircraft.

Several subsequent contracts were placed with Indian for further supplies of the Model 340B, with minor differences in the specification of the early and later versions. Early models (French specification) were fitted with a pillion saddle, leg shields, a spare wheel carried on top of the sidecar body, a civilian pattern air cleaner (rather than the later model's military pattern oil-bath type cleaner), plus a civilian pattern rear light rather than the later twin-light arrangement. It also seems that some later specification Model 340Bs were subjected to a tyre size reduction from 450.18 to 400.18, among other detail changes.

When tested in the summer of 1940 by the War Office, it was concluded that the Model 340B held a good performance from the engine. However, the type suffered from poor ground clearance and, compared with the British

Indian 340B with sidecar as used by WO1 Coulson of the Corps of Military Police in Lisburn, Northern Ireland. (RMP Museum)

Norton Model No. 1 Big 4 combination, the lack of sidecar wheel drive, plus the immense weight of the machine, rendered it useless for cross-country work. The brakes were also regarded as poor, making the model unsafe for general roadwork unless it was controlled by specially selected riders, those who possessed considerable motorcycling experience. The overall summary concluded that the type was unsuitable for War Office use except on the road, and then only in experienced hands. That said, the demands of the early war years and the conditions of the Lend-Lease agreement left the British authorities with little alternative at the time other than to accept the model into limited service, suitable or otherwise.

It is of note that some of these machines were disposed of as early as 1943, when numbers of the type were transferred from the military into the hands of the Midlothian post office, presumably to be used for delivering parcels, a task to which it was well suited.

Indian Model 640B 750cc SV V-Twin – 1940

Two examples of the 750cc V-twin Indian Model 640B were subjected to evaluation by the War Office during 1940. They were supplied at a similar time to the two comparable Harley-Davidson models, also subjected to evaluation, and it is presumed that the testing was conducted prior to the possible purchase of a quantity of the type.

Very little is known about the testing of these machines. As with the Harley-Davidson models tested, it can be assumed that those supplied were of Canadian military specification.

Indian Model 741B 500cc SV V-Twin – 1941–43

The Indian Model 741B machine was easily the company's most prolific model of the Second World War. In comparison to most typical American machines, the Model 741B had a considerably smaller engine capacity, although it still retained most of the features and characteristics of its larger stablemates, including bulkiness and weight, which unfortunately only served to restrict further the moderate performance of the 500cc SV V-twin engine.

Virtually from its inception, the Model 741B was produced by Indian specifically for export purposes under the terms of the Lend-Lease agreement, and was delivered worldwide to just about every Allied country, outpost and organisation, in quantities ranging from one solitary example to a few thousand. The type was originally supplied fully assembled and ready for immediate use, although later supplies arrived in crates, only partially assembled for ease of transit and storage. Some of the early examples of the Model 741B to arrive in the United Kingdom had to have their wiring and electrical layout substantially modified by the military authorities in order to

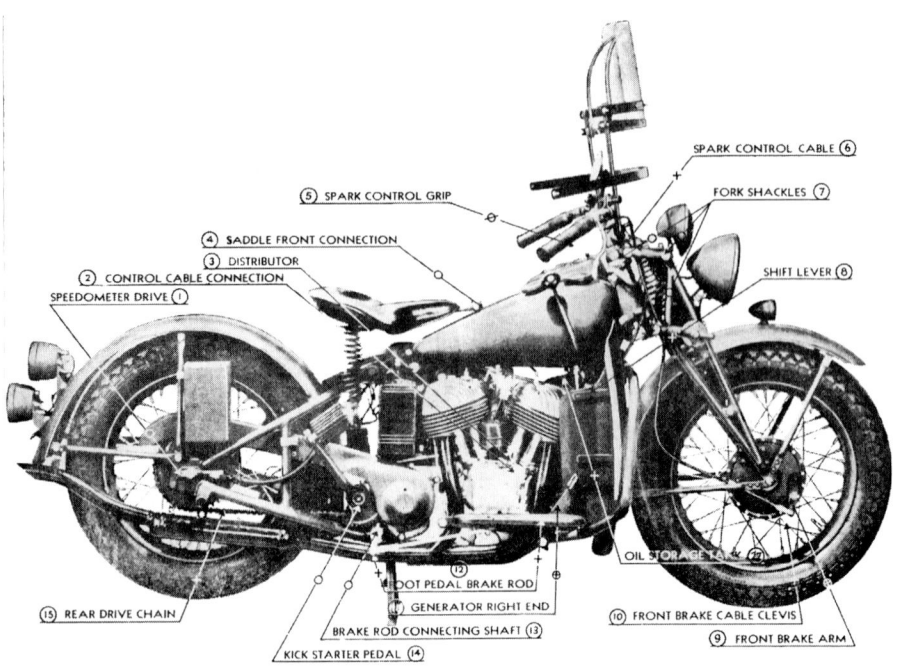

Workshop Manual picture of an Indian 640B. (Indian Motorcycles)

comply with the strict blackout regulations then in force. On 17 December 1941 Indian issued a set of instructions to accompany a standardised kit of parts necessary to complete the modification work. The changes also required the removal of the lower rear light, but interestingly, photographic evidence suggests that this was not always carried out, the light possibly being disconnected rather than removed completely. Other common modifications to the model, though not affecting all machines, included the extending of the foot brake face, and the removal of the toolbox, saddlebags and crash bars, the latter usually painted white if left fitted. Other minor alterations were also implemented. As with Harley-Davidson, there were changes in details between early and late specification machines, including a change of air cleaner from a round to a rectangular pattern, the bolt-on headlight mounting on early versions becoming part of the forks, the primary chain cases still affording access to where the pre-war magneto drive went on some early versions, and rubber-covered footboards changing to ones of perforated steel. Also, incorrect information that appeared in early manuals was corrected in later editions.

Although initially supplied at a time when machines were much needed, the War Office, together with many servicemen and women, generally regarded the Model 741B with suspicion and disdain, principally because of the type's poor overall performance and the unconventional (at least to the British) layout and operation of the machine's controls, which made it initially difficult to ride. One contract set out to alleviate this by ordering fifty machines with Norton handlebars and controls, although whether the clutch and gear change were altered is unknown.

However, the authorities were unable to simply reject the model, the nearest alternative being to allocate the type to second-line units, formations, other services (such as the RAF) and to Commonwealth forces. Other quantities of the type were 'disposed' of by allocating them to every possible overseas outpost, department, ministry or embassy where, after the war, they were quietly forgotten about.

When contracts for the 741B ceased in 1943 the United States was left with surplus stocks of machines that had been awaiting despatch overseas, and in which the American military authorities themselves now had little interest. In 1944 they disposed of the machines, selling them off to the public at substantially discounted costs. This caused the Indian company extreme concern, as the discounted price was far cheaper than one at which it could afford to sell or even manufacture. This matter was only one of a number of unfortunate incidents that effectively culminated in the death of the Indian company a few years later. In the United Kingdom many of the machines previously issued to the Army were transferred to various civilian and governmental organisations during 1943 and 1944. After the war virtually all Model 741B machines in service within the United Kingdom were disposed of through dealerships, for refurbishment and sale on to the civilian market, including stocks of brand-new machines still packed in their shipping crates.

Official photograph of Indian 741B from contract S2220 at Farnborough 1942. (REME Museum)

Workshop Manual picture of an Indian 344 combination. (Indian Motorcycles)

Indian 344 Chief 1200cc SV V-Twin Combination – 1944

Essentially the same machine as the earlier Model 340B, the 1944 specification model 344 Chief combination incorporated a number of modifications over the earlier version. By this time the combination had been superseded by the Jeep light utility car for at least the last two years of the Second World War, and it is believed that these later 1944 Model 344s were ordered for a specific, unestablished purpose and for issue to the military in India.

In comparison to the earlier Model 340B, this later version had the sidecar fitted to the left side of the machine and had standard American military lighting as fitted to the 741B.

JAMES

In the years before the Second World War the James Cycle Company Ltd of Greet, Birmingham, was one of the numerous moderately sized motorcycle manufacturers of the period offering a comprehensive range of machines, from small lightweight utilities through to large capacity 4-strokes. The depression and recession years of the 1930s, however, had considerable effect on the firm, as it did most motorcycle manufacturers. Although James managed to survive and witnessed the outbreak of the Second World War it was, by this time, mainly producing various utility-type machines powered by a variety of proprietary engines manufactured by Villiers. With war under way, the company's engineering and production facilities were redirected towards manufacturing other products for the war effort, notably aircraft components and munitions.

It was not until 1942, three years after the outbreak of war, that James became involved in motorcycle production again. At the time the British airborne forces, comprising parachutists, glider-borne troops and all other conceivable assault and supporting elements, were expanding rapidly, becoming a fully operational force capable of leading the assault on the Axis forces. Equipment for use by the airborne troops was a priority and procurement and development of such happened without delay. One requirement for the airborne and assault formations was a reliable, lightweight motorcycle that would take up minimum space en route to battle, could be delivered and brought into action easily, was capable of being manhandled over impassable obstacles by one man, and yet was cheap enough to be abandoned should the need arise.

Following a similar course to that of Royal Enfield's WD/RE model, the Flying Flea, a small quantity of 1939 civilian-specification 150cc James K15/K16 machines (the exact model is unconfirmed) was procured for evaluation purposes by the War Office. As further testing was conducted with the lighter 125cc K17 model, it is presumed that these 150cc models were simply too heavy for airborne use. The K17 made a reasonable impression with the authorities and the model was developed further into the prototype example of what was to become the ubiquitous James ML (military lightweight) model. Further testing led to the procurement of twelve more modified prototypes for evaluation purposes, the results of which were incorporated into the final production version of the ML. With the company's ML model now approved by the War Office and in production, James spent the final years of the Second World War producing this model along with other types of work for the war effort. The end of the war saw the loss of service contracts for a time but the wartime success and reputation of the ML model secured the company's success in the immediate post-war years.

James K15 Or K16 150cc Single-Cylinder 2-Stroke – 1942

Ten examples of this model were procured under contract by the War Office for evaluation purposes to assess its suitability for possible use by the developing airborne and assault formations. The exact model is unconfirmed. The machines were all built to 1939 specification and it is presumed that they were supplied from unsold stock, or alternatively built up from stocks of spares held at the factory since the outbreak of war.

Little is known about either the results of the testing or the fate of the machines concerned. It is presumed, however, that the model was ultimately rejected by the War Office because of its weight.

Catalogue picture of James models K15 and K16. Similar versions were bought for testing. (James Cycle Co. Ltd)

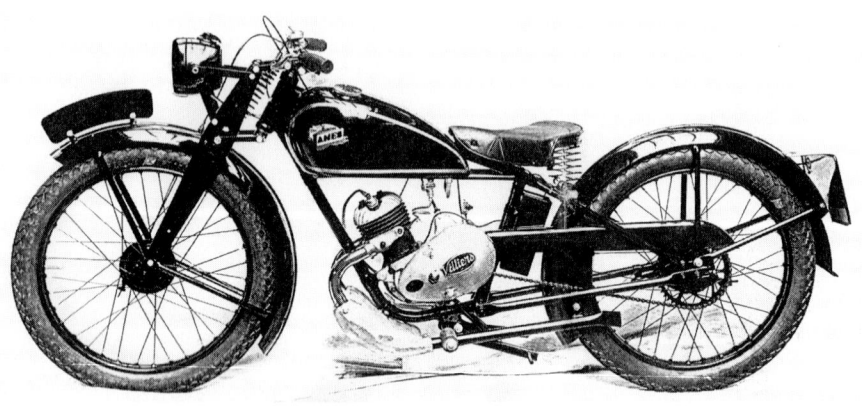

Catalogue picture of James model K17. The War Office bought similar versions for testing. (James Cycle Co. Ltd)

James K17 125cc Single-Cylinder 2-Stroke – 1942

It is presumed that the K17 model was supplied to the War Office for evaluation purposes at the same time as the larger K15 or K16 models, and quite probably caused these two models to be rejected. Two examples of the K17 were supplied, again presumably either from unsold stock or built up from spares held by the factory, and again to 1939 specification.

As for the K15/K16, little is known of the test results but it seems clear that the K17 model performed well enough as James went on to produce a bike based on the K17 model that was to become the ML model prototype machine.

James ML 125cc Single-Cylinder 2-Stroke – 1942–43 Prototype
Development of the K17 model resulted in a prototype machine supplied for War Office testing during late 1942 and early 1943. This machine bore a passing resemblance to the K17 model and was designated the model 'ML' (military lightweight). It was available for testing at around the same time as the Royal Enfield WD/RE model (prototype) and performed reasonably well for the intended role. Further modifications were suggested, which led to a further twelve modified examples of the type being delivered. All were sent to various airborne and assault formations throughout the military and performed well, with only minor modifications proposed for incorporation into the main production versions, one change being a shorter rear mudguard.

James ML 125cc Single-Cylinder 2-Stroke – 1943–45
The production version of the ML model began to be delivered to the British Army during March 1943, about the same time as the equivalent Royal Enfield WD/RE model. All models were initially allocated solely to airborne and assault formations in training, with some later going to the Admiralty.

James ML undergoing trials up a steep hill. (RLC Museum)

James ML with rider's shoulder badge removed by the military photograph censor. (John Tinley)

Ultimately, the James ML model was to see more wartime service with assault and other ground formations than with airborne units, the Royal Enfield WD/RE model taking precedence here. Most period photographs of the ML model in action show the type in the hands of assault or Commando personnel. Indeed, the ML acquired notoriety as a 'mechanical sheep-dog' on the Normandy beachheads during the D-Day landings of June 1944, rounding up and directing columns of troops on the sands and dunes. It is likely that this is where its nickname the 'Clockwork Mouse' was coined.

Compared with the rival WD/RE model, the James ML was at least 26lb heavier, much of the weight probably arising from the use of heavy brass castings and components on the model's Villiers 9D engine unit, principally the exhaust ports and the heavy magneto flywheel assembly. Although not an excessive additional weight under normal conditions, 26lb was considered critical when packing an aircraft, loading a glider, or dropping by parachute. Another disadvantage of the ML model was the fact that no purpose-designed drop cage had been produced to enable it to be dropped by parachute, as the WD/RE could.

However, the James company was evidently pleased to be producing motorcycles again, even if just one particular model, and certainly made sure that everybody could identify its product. In particular, the company capitalised on its past reputation, using the word 'famous' in its advertising campaign, as well as the fact that its ML model with front-line formations was spearheading the war against Germany at the time. In many ways the company had a right to be proud of its ML model, as it was generally considered to be much more reliable than the rival WD/RE both mechanically and in durability, the lighter weight of the WD/RE resulting in marginally greater fragility in both respects.

With the end of the war in 1945, the bulk of the surviving ML models were either disposed of to dealers, or returned to the factory for rebuilding to civilian specification before being released on to the market along with similar new civilian examples of the model. With new machines impossible to find and fuel still rationed, a cheap ex-military ML model was ideal for transport purposes as it could return at least 100mpg.

LEVIS

Levis was one of England's leading 2-stroke manufacturers before the Second World War, although it did fit 4-stroke engines to its motorcycles as well.

The company's first involvement with the War Office came in late 1928 when the MWEE was carrying out comparison tests of lightweight and heavier motorcycles.

The model initially bought for this test was the 250cc Model M, which had a 3-port engine. Weeks later two further models were bought, this time Levis's 6-port models, which were then despatched to Egypt for evaluation. In July 1929 the reports of the testing in Egypt showed that the 6-port had performed well against the OEC 3-wheeler and the Triumph NL3, and indeed was considered to be the best machine.

Based on this, more 6-port models were ordered in August and a further batch in 1930. Ultimately, however, they were dismissed as most officials favoured 4-strokes, and no more 2-strokes were bought until nearer the outbreak of war. Strangely enough, Levis did receive a wartime order for some 350cc machines that ended up being cancelled two months later; it is not known whether any were delivered.

Levis Model M 250cc Single-Cylinder 2-Stroke – 1928
Bought with the idea that a lightweight motorcycle would perform well and meet military requirements, this motorcycle was purchased for comparison testing with other types of motorcycles, one of which was the OEC 3-wheeler.

Testing was carried out by the MWEE at Farnborough, and although the model's lightness proved an asset, its speed on the road and general robustness were not to its liking.

Catalogue picture of a 1928 Model M, similar to the model purchased by the War Office. (Levis Motorcycles)

Levis 6-Port 250cc Single-Cylinder 2-Stroke – 1928–30

This model was supplied presumably to overcome the criticisms of the Model M. They were sent straight to Egypt for testing with other manufacturers' models, namely Triumph's NL3 and OEC's 3-wheeler.

The results of the reports from July 1929 concluded that the Levis was the best machine, and much better than the previous Model M. Following on from this two more orders were received, one in 1929 and the other in 1930.

Interestingly, the 1929 Egypt reports made no note of engine seizures under sustained load, although this was to occur on some machines in the cold UK!

Further testing in Egypt in 1930–31 against a Douglas, Triumph and AJS, showed that the 6-port had sufficient power for normal cross-country work, although it was underpowered for cross-country hill climbing, and that it was a good performer on roads (40mph). Ultimately, although the 6-port appeared promising, it was still considered unreliable (piston scoring due to seizures) and not robust enough for service, probably a rather prejudiced idea as Ministry officials really preferred 4-strokes.

Official photograph of a Levis 6-port in service with the RASC overseas. The British serial number is on the tank, besides carrying a local registration. (RLC Museum)

Levis 350cc – 1941

A demand for 2,000 motorcycles was issued to Levis, only to be cancelled just over two months later. Whether any actually got built or delivered, and even which model they were, is not known at the time of writing.

MATCHLESS

Matchless was the third largest of the major manufacturers to supply military motorcycles during the Second World War with its well-known G3 and G3/L models. The G3/L in particular became perhaps one of the most popular and sought-after machines during the war, principally because of the fitting of the then new teledraulic front forks that, in military usage, were a considerable improvement and advantage over the girder fork designs of the period.

During the First World War, Matchless had been a small, almost insignificant, supplier of motorcycles for military use and it was not until 1929 that the company became involved with service models again when three examples of the company's 350cc SV Model T/4 machines were purchased for evaluation purposes in the seven-make trials of that year. However, before completion of the 1929 trials, War Office impatience for a new military model led to the hurried purchase of Douglas Model L29 machines. This meant that when the reports from the trials became available during November 1929 they were, to a degree, rather pointless.

The 1929 trials reports did, however, designate several motorcycles as unsuitable for military service. The Matchless product, along with the AJS and Douglas models, was retained for further testing, having shown some potential. Ultimately, no further Model T/4 machines were purchased for evaluation, although in the following year, 1930, a 400cc narrow-angle V-twin engine Silver Arrow model was purchased, largely because opinion at the War Office was changing, twin-cylinder motorcycles now considered quieter than single-cylinder machines.

Following evaluation, a small quantity of the Silver Arrow models were purchased for service use in 1931, although the reports received by the War Office from the Armoured Fighting Vehicles (Signals), Southern Command, stated that the machine was unsuitable.

The company next became involved with the military in 1935, when its Model 36/G3 machine showed promise in performance tests, although its overall reliability did not inspire as much confidence.

Also, in 1936 a 250cc G7 was tested and a number were purchased (before the test results were available) for use in instructional purposes. The results finally described the model as only fair, and no further motorcycles of this type were purchased.

Nonetheless, the Model 36/G3 proved itself enough for the War Office to place an order for a quantity of 110 examples and following the testing of a specific machine, serial number C 353544, during late 1937 the type managed to acquire a good report from the MEE. The Model G3, with various modifications, continued to be purchased by the War Office until 1942, the pre-war quantities supplied being varied and small in comparison to the bulk of the type delivered following the outbreak of war in September 1939.

Although Matchless was supplying military motorcycles to War Office order during late 1939 and early 1940, the company, along with most other motorcycle manufacturers, was still producing limited quantities of machines for the civilian markets, including overseas customers. However, this state of affairs was dramatically altered in mid 1940, when the War Office purchased or requisitioned virtually every remotely suitable civilian motorcycle, awaiting despatch or completion at the manufacturers or for sale in showrooms, to replace the quantities of military motorcycles lost at the Dunkirk evacuation. Matchless supplied from factory stock limited quantities of its civilian-specification G80, G90, G5 and G3 models accordingly.

In 1940 Matchless also participated in the War Office lightweight motorcycle project, supplying the MEE with, initially, experimental 250cc and, later, 350cc machines. The 250cc version proved unsuitable because the engine capacity was too small to provide the necessary performance, while the 350cc model was ultimately more successful and the forerunner of the 41/G3/L model of the following year, which was arguably the most popular of the wartime British military models.

The G3/L model, introduced during late 1941, was to remain in volume production until 1945, the quantity produced being the third largest behind BSA with its Model M20 and Norton with its Model 16H. Matchless production from 1942 until the end of the war was entirely devoted to the G3/L model, with minor detail changes and improvements from contract to contract.

Matchless Model T/4 350cc SV Single-Cylinder – 1929

Selected by the War Office for evaluation purposes in the seven-make trials of 1929, the Matchless Model T/4 was to eventually complete the testing. However, prior to completion of the trials and collation of the results of

Official photograph of the 1929 Matchless T/4, as used in the 1929 trials. (WO 194 [45]-5878, The National Archives)

the various machines on test, the War Office, impatient for a new military motorcycle, purchased Douglas machines after a short comparison with the Triumph product then on test.

After the trials, which must have now seemed rather pointless, machines from Matchless, AJS and Douglas were deemed successful. However, further frustration was caused, as the military authorities could not decide which machine would be most suitable. As War Office preference now lay with twin-cylinder machines, which it considered to be quieter than single-cylinder versions, no further Model T/4s were purchased.

Matchless Silver Arrow 400cc SV V-Twin – 1930–31

The War Office's change of preference in the early 1930s for supposedly quieter twin-cylinder machines was a particularly important consideration for military machinery, and Matchless supplied it with an example of its Silver Arrow V-twin engined model for evaluation against the current Model L29 Douglas machine.

Testing, however, showed the Matchless product to be rather unreliable. Having completed a somewhat troublesome 12,200 miles, the example was replaced with an improved 1931 specification example, which incorporated various improvements on the defects that had been noted. After the completion of 1,650 miles, the later model proved satisfactory to the MWEE, although certain minor repairs and adjustments had been necessary.

Official photograph of a Matchless Silver Arrow. (KD 5701 [or KID5701?], IWM)

Further evaluation of the model was carried out by the Armoured Fighting Vehicles (Signals), Southern Command, which, following an extended trial of the type, concluded that 'certain features would prevent this make and type of motorcycle being suitable for signal duties'. Nothing specific was quoted although it is reasonable to assume that the interconnected brakes on the model were a cause for concern. Of the thirty-seven examples of the type purchased during 1931, thirty were issued to the Cavalry Armoured Car Company for trials to determine their general suitability for normal service duties. (Fifteen of these were fitted with air cleaners.) Presumably, the model was found to be unsuitable as no further examples were ordered.

Matchless Model 36/G3 Clubman 347cc OHV Single-Cylinder – 1935 Evaluation Model

During 1935 Matchless was to supply the War Office with an example of its Model 36/G3 Clubman for evaluation and the one delivered (see p. 91) was subjected to the standard MEE 10,000-mile reliability test in the seven-make trials of that year.

Throughout the evaluation period, the model suffered minor problems (which were to be expected) and other, more notable faults, including soft hairpin valve springs (which Matchless offered to replace with stronger coil springs), collapsed rear wheel bearings, a badly worn gearbox (replaced at completion of 8,832 miles) and sprockets.

Official photograph of the 1935 Matchless G3 evaluation model, as used in the 1935 trials. (151/A2, The Tank Museum)

Many of the faults had arisen because the model was basically a standard commercial type, slightly modified for military testing but still ill-prepared for the extremely demanding MEE testing procedures. The minor modifications incorporated were different tyres, and the addition of a rear carrier, a low-level exhaust and, quite possibly, a lower bottom gear ratio.

It is worth noting that this example of the well-known Matchless Model G3 was considerably different from the later military Model G3 of the early war years. Among detail differences were the duplex cradle frame, the cylinder head with hairpin valve springs, a centre stand (rather than a rear stand), the foot brake pedal and the wheels.

Matchless G3 347cc OHV Single-Cylinder – 1936–39

Despite the problems noted about the G3 evaluation model of 1935, the War Office was evidently not deterred and subsequently ordered small quantities of the Model G3 under contract between 1936 and 1939 prior to the model undergoing redesign for the 1940 season.

Official photograph of the 1935-]36 Matchless G3 from contract C8239, which was the first production contract. (RLC Museum)

Official photograph of a 1938 Matchless G3, as bought to contract C2073. (REME Museum)

Those machines supplied before the war continued to have the duplex cradle frame and generally the same specification as the original test model of 1935, although certain annual changes to detail were incorporated as improvements were introduced, including a change to 14mm spark plugs, a new crankcase, the enclosure of the valve springs and changes to the fuel tank. Some models were also fitted with air cleaners.

A further MEE evaluation of the model during 1937 noted improved levels of reliability and wear over the original trial model of 1935.

Matchless G7 246cc SV Single-Cylinder – 1936

During late 1936 Matchless was to supply the War Office with a quantity of its Model G7 250cc SVs. These were all built to a standard 1937 civilian specification, with the type being destined for training purposes primarily with the Royal Corps of Signals.

Introduced into service without the usual MEE evaluation procedure, one example was eventually subjected to the standard 10,000-mile test at Farnborough. After 10,333 test miles, 801 of which were cross-country, the reliability of the model was described as only fair. Notable faults included considerable wear on the cylinder bore and the loss of grease from the wheel bearings. In summary, it was suggested that a more reliable and robust motorcycle should be found for training purposes, and no further Model G7 machines were purchased.

Official photograph of a 1936 Matchless G7. The left-side view of this motorcycle shows its registration to be C363877. (WO 194 45, The National Archives)

Novices on Matchless G7 learning to ride. (RLC Museum)

Matchless G80 Clubman 500cc OHV Single-Cylinder – 1940
Twelve examples of the 1940 civilian-specification model G80 were purchased by the War Office under contract during mid 1940 following the Dunkirk losses.

The machines supplied were standard civilian models, held at the factory and awaiting either completion or delivery to the commercial markets. When purchased by the authorities they were presumably finished in standard service colour schemes of the period.

Matchless G90 Super Clubman 500cc OHV Single-Cylinder – 1940
As with the twelve examples of Model G80 machines supplied during mid 1940, a solitary example of the Super Clubman version was available, held at the factory and ready except for the appropriate paintwork.

Matchless G5 Tourist 500cc SV Single-Cylinder – 1940
Along with the G80 models and the solitary G90 model, two examples of the company's G5 Tourist model were supplied from factory stock during mid 1940, again to 1940 specification.

Matchless G3 347cc OHV Single-Cylinder – 1940 Civilian Specification
A single civilian-specification G3 model was supplied from factory stock along with the G80, G90 and G5 models. The civilian-specification model was rather an oddity as, by then, the military model G3 machines were rolling off the production line in large numbers.

Matchless Experimental Lightweight 245cc OHV Single-Cylinder – 1940 Prototype (Contract C.6674)

Evaluated during the spring of 1940, this particular machine was loosely based around the company's existing civilian-specification model G2M.

The model had been developed in response to the War Office's requirement for a purpose-built lightweight military motorcycle. The reduction in weight had been achieved by using parts either manufactured lighter than standard or made from special lightweight alloys (in the case of castings). Other weight reductions were made, including the substitution of the standard heavy battery for lighting with a direct lighting system using an alternating generator for charging purposes.

After testing the model was considered good for a 250cc machine, although to keep it going across country it required considerable revving of the engine, which had the disadvantage of higher engine wear as well as an unwelcome increase in noise.

Testing was carried out against the Norton 350cc SV lightweight and the BSA 348cc OHV lightweight, where it was to perform better than the Norton (Matchless had claimed it would perform better than a 350cc SV) and comparable to the BSA, although it did not pull as well unless on full throttle. However, the testers were pleased with its fuel consumption.

Matchless Experimental Lightweight 245cc OHV Single-Cylinder – 1940 Pre-production Version (Contract C.8019)

This version was tested against the original model and the lightweight 350cc SV Royal Enfield over 5,000 miles, during which the performance of the engine deteriorated.

The conclusion on this model was that it should not be recommended for War Office use, as it considered that too much strain was placed on the 250cc engine, which needed more overhauls and adjustments than desirable, and that 340cc should be the minimum for War Office motorcycles.

Matchless Model 40 G3/L Experimental Lightweight 347cc OHV Single-Cylinder – 1940

During 1940 the War Office was clearly determined to reduce the weight of military motorcycles then in service, and several manufacturers, including Matchless, were developing and supplying prospective machines for evaluation. Matchless had taken note of the criticisms that its Model G3 was rather a heavy machine, particularly off-road, and thus set about pruning at least 56lb from the existing Model G3, the experiences gained from its experimental 250cc model proving useful in this venture.

Prototype Matchless G3L of 1940. (Mark Shemilt)

The resulting model was the machine destined to become the well-known Model G3/L, the 'L' supposedly standing for 'lightweight', which was generally applicable to the prototype model but rather less so to later production variants. In addition to the considerable weight saving, the model was fitted with the then revolutionary teledraulic front forks, which were based on pre-war forks of German design. They proved vastly superior to the previous girder fork design, still fitted to other motorcycles of the period, chiefly in terms of comfort and increased up and down travel when in use off-road.

At least two examples of the prototype lightweight Model G3/L are thought to have been built, but despite being a successful design War Office orders for quantities of the type did not appear straight away. The principal difficulty was the decision by the War Office to adopt one specific motorcycle for universal military service to replace the multitude of different types then in use.

Following considerable testing it was almost certain that Triumph's lightweight model 3TW would be chosen as the standardised War Office motorcycle, and had it not been for the German Air Force, this would probably have been the case. During November 1940 the city of Coventry was subjected to severe air raids, with the city centre virtually razed to the ground. Among the many buildings destroyed were the Priory Street works of the Triumph Motorcycle Company, and drawings, parts, plans and machines relating to the company's Model 3TW military lightweight twin were lost. Little could be salvaged from the rubble, and so the market was open once again for a lightweight machine to replace the unlucky 3TW. Matchless was able to offer its proven prototype Model G3/L to take up the position left empty by the elimination of the Triumph product.

Matchless G3WO 347cc OHV Single-Cylinder – 1940–42

Matchless had initiated several changes and improvements to its products for the 1940 season, which were introduced during late 1939; such changes affected the company's War Office specification Model G3, principally the fitting of the company's revised frame design incorporating a single front-down tube. Other changes included the fitting of a cylinder head from the similar AJS 350cc model, which used coil-type valve springs instead of the hairpin variety, a marginally redesigned cylinder barrel, incorporating the cutaway of some of the finning, and the fitting of a second toolbox above the existing one.

Some 18,500 examples of the Model G3WO were to be supplied to the military between late 1939 and early 1942 (before the type was withdrawn in favour of the new model G3/L) with minor detail differences between contracts. One of the changes was the phasing out of the tank-top instrument panel, which had been fitted to early examples before the issuing of contract number C.7183. However, 256 examples of the machines in contract number C.8078 still had the panel fitted, presumably to use up stocks of otherwise redundant components.

A 1941 G3 in the desert, as viewed from Edward Thorne's tent. (E. Thorne)

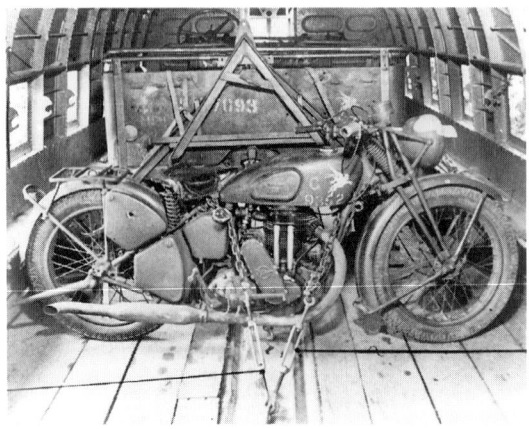

A Matchless G3 chained down behind a Jeep inside a Dakota. Note the bullet hole in the upper toolbox lid. (Airborne Assault Museum)

Official factory photograph of the Matchless G3WO. (KID 5392, IWM)

Interestingly enough, despite production of Model G3/L commencing during late 1941, the model G3WO continued to be built alongside the new machine, probably because War Office contracts for the type remained valid until early 1942. Certain Model G3WO machines produced in the last contract, during early 1942, were altered slightly to accept revised components from the new G3/L model, which included crankpins and brake shoes, probably because stocks of standard Model G3WO components had run out. Indeed, the last fifty Model G3WO machines produced became something of a hybrid, being fitted with, among other components, the engine and teledraulic front forks of the new Model G3/L.

Certain other detail differences between early and late production G3WO models included the fitting of a four-position headlight switch in place of the earlier three-position type, standard military specification speedometers superseding the earlier model, which had been fitted with a trip facility, and, on specifically fuel tank panel models, the substitution of the standard battery with a NiFe version.

Although officially replaced by the Model G3/L during 1942, the Model G3WO remained in War Office service until the end of hostilities, odd examples still being seen during the early 1950s, although the type was generally withdrawn from front-line duties by the end of 1943.

Unpopular when employed off-road because of its weight, the Model G3WO was, however, favoured for general road usage, principally because it possessed a good degree of performance and was not, in fact, too far removed from the pre-war civilian Clubman sporting model.

Matchless Model 41 G3/L 347cc OHV Single-Cylinder – 1941–45

The well-known Model G3/L motorcycle of the Second World War was the production model of the prototype lightweight Model G3, developed and tested during 1940. Once entered into military service it soon attained popularity among the majority of service users, principally because of the new teledraulic front forks. The G3/L, although mildly detuned compared with the earlier Model G3WO, was also still capable of decent performance both on- and off-road in comparison to other service models and thus was a machine much sought after by those issued with less sporting mounts.

Despite the prototype lightweight having been tested during 1940, the first production Model G3/L machines were not available until the latter half of 1941 and it was not until mid 1942 that the type appeared in any considerable numbers. The first Model G3/L machines delivered bore scant resemblance to the original prototype lightweight of 1940. This was mainly because of alterations made necessary by mass production, and also the incorporation of certain other components for service standardisation and use. Such changes increased the overall weight of the model over that of its prototype. Initially, ribbed front and rear mudguards, the large Matchless metal fuel tank emblems, and rubber handlebar grips and combination type control levers were fitted. Other points of note included the fitting of a revised lightened rear-frame section (only fitted to the first contract), only one fuel tap (which meant draining the tank before its removal) and the lack of a front stand, which rendered the front wheel difficult to remove. The universal pannier frames were also not fitted on the early G3/L machines as they had not yet been introduced into service.

Official photograph of a 1941 Matchless G3L. Note the ribbed front mudguard and lack of a front wheel stand. The picture was taken in Lincoln's Inn, London, and may show a pre-production version. (Airborne Assault Museum)

Matchless G3L from contract C14499, in use with RASC Coy 3rd Infantry Division. (John Tinley.)

Once entered into service, the Model G3/L was mildly developed as improvements were sought and changes were made to consecutive contracts issued for the type. Metal badges on the fuel tanks were replaced by transfers, rubber handlebar grips by canvas grips, and ribbed mudguards by plain ones. The engine-valve timing was improved and the teledraulic front fork yoke and handlebar lug altered to provide improved strengthening. Control levers were initially either of Bowden combination pattern or Amal single components, with the machine's crankcase often marked with an A or B to signify which type were fitted. (These were later substituted by 'standardised' universal components.) Pannier frames were fitted to virtually all machines produced from late 1942 onwards. Twin fuel taps and a front stand were also introduced about this time.

The wartime demands upon all manufacturers also affected Model G3/L production to a certain degree, for a short time the light-alloy engine-timing cover being produced from cast iron. During 1942 a shortage of electrical lighting components from Lucas led to some 5,000 Model G3/L machines being fitted with component parts of Miller manufacture, although the magneto was to remain of Lucas manufacture throughout. Although by and large the type remained fairly consistent throughout the remainder of the war, many other detail changes were made that affected the Model G3/L. The last

G3Ls packed into a Hamilcar glider. (Army Flying Museum)

examples produced had universal Vokes air filters factory fitted to the top of the fuel tank – a task that involved having to reintroduce the knee-grip fastening holes to mount the filter.

G3/Ls were retained by the services for use in the post-war period along with the BSA Model M20. The last examples of the type were disposed of during the 1960s when replaced by the BSA W-B40. Although held in high regard by those issued with one for riding, the Model G3/L was less popular with workshop personnel, largely because the sheer compactness of the model in the original design (to both increase ground clearance and reduce weight) led to time-consuming maintenance schedules, already hindered because almost all components were difficult to obtain. Virtually all engine maintenance required the fuel tank to be removed, and to simply take out the oil filter required the saddle to be taken off. Even worse, in order to remove the machine's dynamo, the entire primary chaincase and clutch had to be taken out, and the teledraulic front forks frequently caused overhaul difficulties to military personnel familiar only with girder forks.

Nonetheless, the Model G3/L attained a good reputation throughout the war and is well remembered.

Matchless OHV Single-Cylinder – 1944 (Rear-Sprung Prototype)

The Model G3/L, praised for its teledraulic front forks, still retained the conventional rigid rear frame and the possibility of some form of rear suspension system had been suggested on a number of occasions. During 1944 Matchless produced a prototype model to evaluate the suitability of this system and produced a specific machine that was loosely based on the existing Model G3/L, although generally constructed using several different parts from the Associated Motor Cycles (AMC) range. The machine had a Model G3/L front frame and similar teledraulic front forks with brake assembly. The engine fitted was of the pre-war AJS variety with the magneto mounted forward of the engine, necessitating the fitting of a different timing cover from that of the Model G3/L Matchless. A new rear frame was constructed and fitted with the new suspension arrangement, which was similar in appearance to a smaller version of the frontal teledraulic fork legs. Other details included the fitting of a centre stand and pillion footrests that actually rose and fell with the movement of the rear suspension.

MOTO-CHENILLE

Moto-Chenille Mercier 350cc OHV Single-Cylinder – 1939

This was very much an experimental motorcycle, and as such very unorthodox. It had a 4-wheel track-laying bogie in place of the front wheel and its engine and gearbox mounted on the handlebars.

When it was ridden, the testers considered it slow, noisy, unwieldy, very uncomfortable and requiring considerable skill even to ride it; consequently it was rejected.

It was of Swiss origin (although powered by a British 350cc OHV JAP) and was also tested by the French government. Pictures of this motorcycle sometimes show it with an armoured front, but it is thought the motorcycle tested by the British did not have this.

Demonstrated in mid 1939 by its designer, it proved to be useless at hill climbing and showered its rider with stones and mud. No road testing was conducted due to licensing restrictions and this may have been a blessing in disguise, as it was considered unsafe on the wet roads of the testing ground when it cornered at speed.

The military regarded it as having no value to it; its poor petrol economy of 24mpg and its weight of 375lb would certainly not have been acceptable.

NEW HUDSON

New Hudson Model 83e 350cc SV Single-Cylinder – 1929

A manufacturer from the 'veteran' motorcycling era, New Hudson supplied three of its models to the War Office for evaluation purposes, under contract, during mid 1929. These were assessed with the products of several other companies, who were hoping to secure government contracts. The three models from New Hudson were 350cc SV Model 83Es, which were supplied as standard except possibly for the finish, which was probably of service colour, and the use of non-bright components. It is not clear whether these models were fitted with the factory-specified 'long-lever' or the 'quadrant-type' gear change; both were listed as options in the company's 1929 sales brochure.

Evaluated during the 1929 trials, the New Hudson models were noted as being too heavy and were ultimately rejected as unsuitable for service use. Following this, New Hudson took no further part in the supply of motorcycles for War Office use. Only one example is believed to exist now, reputedly in Sweden.

Catalogue picture of a 1929 New Hudson Model 83E, similar to the version bought by the War Office. (New Hudson)

NEW IMPERIAL

Another motorcycle manufacturer from the 'veteran' era, New Imperial supplied one of its current models for War Office evaluation during the 1935 series of trials. Ordered and supplied under contract, the machine was a standard type New Imperial Model 40 OHV 346cc, possibly of 1936 specification.

In its advertisements New Imperial emphasised the Model 40's unit construction, praising the virtues of the helical gear wheels on the unit's primary drive as 'silent in operation, unbreakable and wear-proof'. This claim may well have been applicable to the average civilian user, but was found not to be the case with the War Office. After 7,000 miles of rigorous War Office testing, inspection of the engine revealed that it was noticeably worn. The evaluation report submitted considered the reconditioning of the unit to be of 'doubtful value' because an excessive amount of repair work was required. Needless to say, the War Office rejected the Model 40 as unsuitable for service use.

Four years later, during 1939, the New Imperial Company saw ownership pass into the hands of Triumph and only limited manufacture of the company's models continued, production ceasing altogether on 2 September 1939, the eve of Britain's entry into the Second World War. All the company's remaining tooling, machinery, completed machines and spares were then transferred to Triumph's factory in Coventry.

Following this, it was not expected that any further New Imperial motorcycles would be constructed, as most of the surviving remnants of the company had been placed in storage for the duration of the war. However, following the Dunkirk evacuation in May 1940 and the subsequent loss of huge amounts of equipment, Triumph, along with the majority of other motorcycle manufacturers, was inundated with large orders from the War Office for machines. In an attempt to meet the demand, Triumph offered the War Office a small quantity of New Imperial motorcycles, as well as recommencing production of its own models. Thirty-three New Imperial machines were therefore bought under contract and delivered to the War Office at Stirling, in Scotland. The exact details of these models, built by Triumph from parts held in stock, are unclear although it is known that all were of 496cc OHV unit construction, and most likely conformed to the specification of New Imperial's Model 76 or 76DL (de-luxe). Finish of the motorcycles would have been in the standard service colour of 1940, and it is not known whether the machines carried the New Imperial insignia or that of Triumph.

Following completion of this odd contract, no more New Imperial machines were constructed or supplied to the War Office, and the name disappeared.

New Imperial Model 40 350cc OHV Single-Cylinder – 1935

Supplied in civilian trim for the 1935 seven-make trial in the latter part of the year, this machine was rejected because of considerable wear on its engine and other components. Only 7,000 of the usual 10,000 miles were completed.

In some respects New Imperial was ahead of its time as its motorcycles were designed using 'unit construction', a trend not generally adopted by the British motorcycle industry until the early 1960s.

New Imperial Model 76 500cc OHV Single-Cylinder – 1940

These motorcycles were supplied when the company was under the ownership of Triumph, and were most likely built up from spare parts held at Triumph's factory in Coventry.

Whether the machines were the Model 76 or the 76DL (de-luxe) is not known, and it can also only be assumed that standard cradle frames were used rather than New Imperial's pre-war spring frame.

Official photograph of 1935 Model 40, as used in the 1935 trials. (138/E1, The Tank Museum)

Catalogue picture of a 1940 New Imperial Model 76 likely to have been offered to the War Office by Triumph (their owners) in 1940. (New Imperial Motorcycles)

NORMAN

A small manufacturer, Norman used proprietary engines of Villiers manufacture in its motorcycles. With small premises and limited production capability, only two models were produced by the company at the time, the 125cc 'Lightweight' and the 98cc 'Motobyk'.

For reasons that remain unclear, two contracts were issued to the company mid-war, around the same time that James and Royal Enfield were producing their 125cc models to War Office contract. However, it is unlikely that any of Norman's machines were used by the military services as this would have added to the existing problem of the authorities having too many models for which to cater adequately. Instead, these motorcycles were most probably issued to reserve occupation personnel, ARPs and other Civil Defence organisations.

Norman Lightweight 125cc Single-Cylinder 2-Stroke – 1943
This motorcycle used the Villiers 9D engine, as employed by James in its Model ML, although it is unclear whether it had an Amal carburettor, or a Villiers (as preferred by the military). Whether these machines were manufactured from a large stock of parts held by the company or production had to be resumed is not known.

Press advert of the Norman Lightweight 125cc. (Norman Motorcycles)

NORTON

Norton was one of the principal British motorcycle manufacturers for the armed services and other government organisations; production totals by the end of the war were second only to BSA. Further quantities were supplied for use by the Commonwealth services, largely the Canadians, with some of these machines occasionally being passed back to the British at later dates.

The first Norton motorcycles were supplied for military evaluation in 1932, these being a 16H, a Model 18 and a Model 19. Following these tests, another Model 16H 490cc SV was purchased for the seven-make trial in 1935 and subjected to evaluation by the MEE. It proved acceptable for military service providing that certain modifications were implemented. From late 1936 onwards, annual contracts were placed with the company for quantities of the model. Demand continued prior to and throughout the course of the Second World War, with the occasional contract calling for combinations. The machine was produced for ten years, the longest time the War Office ever kept to buying one model of motorcycle.

The 16H was used in numerous roles, and was perhaps the foremost British military motorcycle until early 1941, when models from other manufacturers began to appear in quantity. Many front-line units then swapped to these newer models, the Norton machines being relegated to second-line or training formations, although they continued in limited front-line use in all theatres until the war's end.

Following the end of the Second World War the Model 16H continued in use with the armed services, although in considerably reduced quantities. It remained in service in very limited numbers right up to the late 1950s.

Norton's other principal motorcycle supplied to the services was the Model No. 1 combination, commonly termed the Big 4, which employed a non-permanently engaged sidecar wheel drive. The model was originally designed to provide an all-terrain light vehicle for advance formation battlefield duties and general reconnaissance. Supplied up to the mid-war period, the unit was eventually rendered obsolete by the introduction of the American-produced Jeep, supplied to the War Department under Lend-Lease terms.

Other motorcycles supplied to the services included a number of experimental lightweight models, as well as other solo and combination prototypes for evaluation. The first of these experimental types, a lightened 16H, was supplied to the services as early as 1936, only a year after its introduction to the War Office. It was tested and then rejected on cost.

In 1937–38 Norton started development on its SWD prototype 16H for the War Office, which ultimately evolved into the well-known Big 4 outfit.

Some 350cc OHV motorcycles appeared in 1938, followed a year later by a special lightweight 350cc SV and two spring-frame motorcycles of 500cc (one SV, one OHV), all of which were well tested and subsequently rejected, as was a second attempt at a lightened 16H.

By 1940 the War Office needed a more powerful version of its Big 4 combination, so a 596cc OHV-powered outfit was supplied and tested; although its performance was better, it was not very reliable. After this failure Norton started working on a V-twin-powered outfit to achieve the new specification of a higher road speed of 55mph, which was felt necessary, but this project was killed off by the arrival of the Jeep from the USA.

In 1944 Norton also offered a new SV parallel twin in an attempt to win the contract eventually awarded to Triumph's TRW, after a long drawn-out test period.

Pre-war, Norton was often involved with development work with the authorities. Silencers and seats were two of the ideas explored, and the pannier bag racks fitted to all makes of Second World War motorcycles were, in fact, a Norton design.

Norton 16H 500cc SV Single-Cylinder – 1932

This motorcycle was loaned by Norton Motors for tests along with a Model 18 and a Model 19.

Of the three models tested, it obviously stuck in the minds of the War Office testers, as it was later selected as the model from Norton's range for the seven-make trial of 1935.

Results of the test are unknown.

Norton Model 18 500cc OHV single-cylinder – 1932

Like the 1932 16H and Model 19, this machine was on loan from Norton Motors for the same period of time. How it fared during testing is unknown, as the results no longer appear to survive.

Norton Model 19 596cc OHV single-cylinder – 1932

The Model 19 was supplied for testing along with a 16H and Model 18 in 1932, but only on an on-loan basis for the duration of testing. As with the Model 18, the test results no longer appear to survive.

Norton 16H 500cc SV Single-Cylinder – 1935

Delivered as a standard hand-change model, this machine was altered to foot change during testing, fitted with a different set of handlebars and given an 18-tooth engine sprocket as opposed to the previous 19-tooth version. The machine was delivered and tested in late 1935, so it is possible that the motorcycle was of 1936 specification.

After all the MEE tests of 1935, the 16H proved to be the best 500cc motorcycle and was therefore approved for service, even though it suffered some notable wear on the cylinder bore, a burnt exhaust, a broken headlamp bracket, a split rear mudguard and a broken petrol tank mounting bolt, to name but a few defects.

Official photograph of the 1935 Norton 16H as used in the 1935 trials. (RLC Museum)

Official photograph of the 1935–36 Norton 16Hs from the first major contract. Note the alterations to the trial model. (KID 5666, IWM)

Norton 16H 500cc SV Single-Cylinder – 1936–45

Following Norton's success in the 1935 tests, orders for 16Hs were issued every year until the end of the war, the occasional order being for combinations.

The first batch ordered was built with the requested modifications arising from the test model, the most obvious one being the installation of a foot-change gearbox replacing the original hand-change type. Some later 1936 motorcycles had an air cleaner fitted to the right of the rear wheel for use in dusty conditions overseas, and it also appears that none of these early 16Hs had speedometers fitted.

From 1937 onwards the air cleaner was not fitted until the Universal Vokes appeared, although it did not become a standard fitment until quite late in the war.

The next real visual change to the 16H came in 1938 when a crankcase shield was added. Two types are known to have been fitted, one devised by the MEE and the other by the India Office, which was the larger of the two.

1938–39 Norton 16H with twin outlet silencer. (RLC Museum)

A troop of Royal Corps of Signals riders with their 1940 Norton 16Hs. (Royal Signals Museum)

Corps of Military Police rider on his mid–late war Norton 16H. (RMP Museum)

More changes occurred in the early war years when pillion equipment and pannier bag racks were added. Other changes around this time included the repositioning of the speedometer, the removal of the number plates, the change to tubular footrests (rubbers removed) and canvas handlebar grips, and the installation of a new headlamp (the Lucas DU42).

It is worth noting that in 1940, just before the fitment of pannier bag racks and so on, Norton briefly fitted a pair of toolboxes, as a pair of 'saddle bags', over the rear wheel, and this was used on at least one contract.

Norton's 16H was supplied to all the services, as well as to the Canadian government. A proportion were fitted with sidecars, these coming from several manufacturers such as Swallow. Other notes of interest were the use of 1in-diameter handlebars (all the other manufacturers used ⅞in, with the exception of some Matchless and Triumph models), and interchangeable wheels.

Norton Model 16H (Lightened) 500cc SV Single-Cylinder – 1936

This was a test-only model taken to Farnborough in October 1936. It was a standard production 16H, made 28lb lighter by the use of light alloys.

Its performance was equal to that of the standard production model, but the MEE considered its additional cost was not justifiable.

Norton model 50 350cc OHV Single-Cylinder – 1938

Little is known about these models other than that in surviving documents for this contract the motorcycles are labelled as 'Gold Stars', a name more associated with BSA.

It can only be assumed that these must have been some form of competition model, bought for use by an Army team.

Norton 16H 500cc SV Single-Cylinder SWD Combination – 1938

Based around a trials competition outfit, this motorcycle was fitted with one of two possible systems for its SWD. It either had gears within the rear wheel and sidecar wheel or a Baughan Motor Cycles SWD system.

It is more likely that the Baughan system was used, as Dennis Mansell (Norton's works rider) had had this fitted to his 1935 works Norton by Baughans.

The Baughan system was simple yet very effective and relatively reliable. It consisted of a direct shaft drive from the rear wheel spindle through a simple dog clutch and two leather discs that acted as universal joints.

Trials carried out by the MEE showed that the SWD considerably improved cross-country performance, which was better than that of the 7hp Austin car.

Norton 16H 500cc SV Single-Cylinder – 1938

This was a civilian-specification motorcycle that was tested to see how good the engine improvements and modifications were and to determine whether they could be considered for the military 16H. (The most notable change was the use of fully enclosed valve springs.)

The MEE noted, that although the machine was 12lb heavier, its performance was comparable with that of the existing War Office machines and it considered it suitable for use. However, these 16H models were never to be bought as the War Office stuck to the 1937-specification engine to the end.

Norton Big 4 (Model No. 1) 633cc SV Single-Cylinder SWD Combination – 1938–42

Following the success of the 16H pilot model, a machine was developed with a 633cc engine to enhance its performance, an improved shaft drive (presumably by now Hardy-Spicer joints were used), and a sidecar suitable for carrying a Bren gun and ammunition.

Crew for the Big 4 was increased to three (there had been no pillion on the 16H pilot model) and further trials were carried out at the MEE and at Studland Bay. The machine's cross-country performance was now considered excellent and with various handles provided for lifting, it was possible for its crew to take the vehicle over very difficult country.

After this test, the remainder of the first contract was fulfilled with these motorcycles being issued to troops for trials.

Trials continued and the MEE noted that the defects in the design of the original pilot model, notably the SWD, had been overcome. Dunlop Sports-type tyres were also found to give better performance than the universal tyre and its performance was well maintained over the 10,000-mile trial. It was noted as suitable for War Office use, presumably late in 1938.

As with the 16H, the wheels of the Big 4 were interchangeable, but it used 18in rims and had 4.00–18 tyres (the 16H used 3.25–19).

Lend-Lease Jeeps from the USA eventually killed off the Big 4. Later they were released on to the civilian market, having had the SWD system cut off. This was done to prevent accidents; once the drive was engaged, the machine had no steering capability and it was feared that people would fail to disengage it once on tarmac.

A 1942 Norton Big 4 combination in use with the Free French. (REME Museum)

It has been noted that some Big 4s used by the RAF did not have the SWD system fitted and reasons for this can only be guessed at.

Surprising though it seems, the British airborne forces did use a few of these outfits, up to mid 1944 for glider-borne troops, but these were probably replaced by stripped down Jeeps as they became available.

In time the Big 4 was totally phased out and replaced by the Jeep. It ceased to be used as a front-line vehicle probably from about early 1943, somewhat sooner than its more complicated German equivalents, the Zundapp KS750 and the BMW R75. These lasted until 1944, when they were dropped on cost grounds and not because they had been proved inferior by a 4×4 car.

Norton Model 18 500cc OHV Single-Cylinder (With Spring Frame) – 1939

This was the first of the two spring-frame models offered for testing against an orthodox 16H in August 1939.

Testers noted that the spring frame gave increased comfort for the rider and reduced the level of strain, but they thought that the sprung rear wheel limited the ultimate performance of the motorcycle.

The test results concluded that it was impossible to differentiate between the orthodox 16H's frame and the spring-frame motorcycle because of the different engines and gear ratios used. It was therefore requested that a 16H-engined version be produced, for a better evaluation.

Norton 16H 500cc SV Single-Cylinder (With Spring Frame) – 1939

Following the testing of the first spring-frame model, this machine was submitted for testing at the MEE. It too had a sprung rear wheel and a plunger type front spring instead of the normal coil spring. It was 22lb heavier than an orthodox 16H.

Interestingly, when the motorcycle was tested in December 1939 the testers considered that it did not perform as well as an orthodox 16H across country, but it was far more comfortable for long-distance work on such terrain.

Also, the MEE considered that it gave a slightly inferior performance over loose surfaces as the rear wheel tended to ride over the top instead of digging into the hard sub-soil, with the rider unable to use his weight to get a grip. On roads, however, the comfort was increased and at very high speeds steering was improved. The MEE concluded that these advantages made up for the loss in performance, but the extra weight was a decided disadvantage.

Norton Experimental Lightweight 350cc SV Single-Cylinder – 1939

This first model was built to the War Office's specification for a new lightweight motorcycle with an engine of 350cc or greater, and a weight of 250lb or less.

Norton's 348cc SV single-cylinder offering just tipped the scales at 278lb and was the heaviest of the first batch of three lightweights tested in late 1939. The other two prototypes were Royal Enfield's 350cc SV (276lb) and Triumph's 350cc OHV parallel twin (263lb).

Tested over the usual 10,000 miles, the 348cc machine was found easier to handle than a standard 16H, but the motorcycle was not very reliable and its frame got badly damaged during the test.

For reasons unknown, at one stage of testing the motorcycle was sent to Universal Aircraft Ltd of Mitcham, Surrey.

Norton Experimental Lightweight 350cc SV Single-Cylinder – 1940

Following the 1939 version, two more similar motorcycles were supplied. This time the exotic materials used to build the first lightweight were dispensed with to make production cheaper, and consequently the overall weight went up slightly.

After rigorous testing the machine was still deemed unreliable and therefore not suitable for War Office use. It appears that the only two lightweights the authorities showed any interest in were BSA's WB30 and Triumph's 3TW, which were the best of the type. Both were OHVs, not the now out of favour SV singles, which testers were beginning to suggest were disposed of.

Norton Model 18 500cc OHV Single-Cylinder – 1940

Either seven or twelve of these 500cc OHV single-cylinder models were bought, at a time when the war was reaching its height and losses from Dunkirk had to be replaced. As the machines were bought immediately it is assumed that they were either built from stock at the factory or were already assembled and awaiting delivery to dealers.

Catalogue picture of a civilian 1939–40 Model 18. (Norton Motorcycles)

Norton Experimental Lightweight 500cc SV Single-Cylinder – 1940

This model was presumably offered in response to the criticisms of the 350cc lightweight's poor reliability, as it was fitted with a 16H engine, proven reliable after many years of service with the War Office.

With the 16H engine fitted, the lightweight weighed in at 304lb and gave a very satisfactory performance. It was deemed superior to both the standard 16H and the 350cc lightweight, but it still proved unreliable and was not approved by the War Office.

Norton Model 19 596cc OHV Single-Cylinder SWD Combination – 1940

This combination was produced in response to the need for a more powerful version of the Big 4.

Tested in mid 1940, it lost compression twice in 1,496 miles, the problem being caused by the exhaust valves overheating and not seating. Although the machine did perform better than the standard Big 4, its petrol consumption was worse.

Norton 1096cc SV V-Twin Combination – 1940–41

This SWD combination was built as a proposed replacement for the Big 4 in response to the War Office's request for a new model, which had to have a top speed of 55mph on the road. Power came from a JAP V-twin engine as Norton did not produce any engines larger than the 633cc of the Big 4.

Similar models were also being developed by Triumph and Sunbeam, until the arrival of the Jeep killed them all off.

Norton 500cc SV Parallel Twin – 1944 Prototype

Built as a result of the Standardisation Committee's search for a new standard motorcycle for War Office service, which had to be either a 500cc SV twin or a 350cc OHV twin, this model was tested against several other motorcycles

1944 Norton SV twin at some stage during its testing. Note the lack of pillion footrests, even though a dual seat is fitted. (MVE 27490/8, IWM)

from Douglas, Triumph, BSA and Royal Enfield. It was not chosen, the Triumph TRW coming out as the eventual winner. It is understood that this machine survives today.

OEC

OEC was a small company perhaps better described as a 'custom' manufacturer because of the wide range of options it offered in the choice of frames, engines and front forks in the construction of all its motorcycles.

Possibly OEC's first involvement with the War Office in the supply of motorcycles for the British armed forces was in the late 1920s, when the RAF ordered and took delivery of a number of 342cc Villiers 2-stroke powered motorcycles. Whether these were ordered over a number of years in several quantities under several contracts or as a one-off purchase is not known at the time of writing.

Also at about this time, in 1928, OEC became involved in the further development of the Army's 3-wheeled motorcycle concept, when it was asked to supply three machines, similar in design but different in weight.

The first, supplied in early 1928, was powered by a 490cc JAP engine, and was followed later in the year by two Blackburne-powered versions of 2¾hp and 3½hp. Testing of all three was carried out at Aldershot and later in Egypt and at Rawalpindi-Murree, India, although it had been discontinued in the UK certainly by late 1929 or 1930.

Interestingly, most of the documented testing in the UK seems to have been centred around the 3½hp version, whose duplex steering was proving unsatisfactory and was subsequently altered to pillar type. Although this provided better control, it was still difficult when compared to a 2-wheeled machine.

OEC literature called the 3-wheeler a 'Caterpillar Tractor' as the two small rear wheels could have a track fitted over them to turn the motorcycle into a half-track, thus improving its ability on loose surfaces or soft ground. (The track was usually carried on the rear mudguard when not in use.) These motorcycles could be converted to 2-wheelers by substituting the twin rear wheels for another single wheel, and also adapted to carry pillion passengers if required.

OEC's final involvement with the military was in 1929, when it supplied three 3½hp Blackburne-powered 2-wheeled solos for the seven-make trial of that year, during which the model was rejected, not even making the second round of testing.

OEC 342cc Single-Cylinder 2-Stroke – Late 1920s

This model was powered by a Villiers single-cylinder 2-stroke engine. Although it is known that the RAF was the only recipient of the machine, it has yet to be established just what quantities were delivered. Few other details on the model seem to exist. They were bought to replace the old Phelon & Moore (P&M) still in use at the time.

OEC 3-Wheeler 490cc SV Single-Cylinder – 1928

This 3-wheeler was delivered for trial in early 1928 along with two versions of slightly different design and also different engine capacities. Its first trial was finished by March 1928, and it was compared with the Army's earlier Triumph-based version.

A slightly surprising move by the War Office, considering the usual military secrecy, was to allow this motorcycle to be tested by the motorcycle press in mid March of the same year. Shortly afterwards magazines such as *Motor Cycling* and the *Motor Cycle* printed articles for friend or foe alike to read. Needless to say, this did not happen again until the war began, when results of Army motorcycle tests were again allowed to be published, presumably as an aid to recruitment, or even as a form of propaganda.

This version, unlike the other two, had a JAP SV engine, which leaned backwards in the frame, and an exhaust that ran down the left-hand side of the motorcycle. (On the 2¾hp and 3½hp versions, the exhaust ran down the right-hand side.)

The machine weighed a gigantic 453lb, approximately 100lb heavier than the 3½hp version, on which all test reports seem to centre. The extreme weight of the former machine may explain why testing on it was so short-lived, and why it was discarded so soon.

Official photograph of the 1928 OEC 490cc 3-wheeler, wearing a trade plate (later registered as MP8161) and yet to gain its pillion equipment. The battery and air cleaner were also revised later on, as were quite a few other items. (RLC Museum)

OEC 3-Wheeler 350cc SV Single-Cylinder – 1928

This version, weighing around 354lb and powered by a Blackburne SV engine, appears to have been the main test model, and testing continued at the MWEE until July 1929, with some trials also taking place in Egypt and India.

During testing the original duplex steering was altered to pillar type, as it was proving unsatisfactory for cross-country work. This change provided better control but, as with all the 3-wheelers, it was still not as easy to steer as a 2-wheeler and the rider was quickly exhausted. The MWEE's general conclusions were that the machine's cross-country performance was not sufficient to warrant the extra complications entailed, and that the extra weight over a 2-wheeled motorcycle (approximately 95lb) was not desirable.

OEC 3-Wheeler 250cc SV Single-Cylinder – 1928

This version is the one used in the OEC catalogue pictures. Although it was very similar to the 350cc version it had a number of lighter components on it, most notably the wheels and tyres, which reduced its weight to 310lb.

How it compared to the other two 3-wheelers has not been established at the time of writing.

The 1928 OEC 350cc 3-wheeler, being ridden in desert conditions. (RLC Museum)

Official photograph of a 1928 OEC 250cc 3-wheeler. It was this version that was shown in the OEC brochures of the time, where it was referred to as a tractor. (WO 194 [45]-5313, The National Archives)

Official photograph of a 1929 350cc model that was used in the 1929 trials. Note the large clearance between the rear wheel and mudguard. This was needed to allow fitment of the leather belt over the rear tyre to improve the machine's off-road abilities. When not in use it was stored on top of the rear mudguard. (KID 5589/HU63633, IWM)

OEC 2-Wheeler 350CC SV Single-Cylinder – 1929

Three of these machines were bought for the 1929 seven-make trial but after initial testing the model was not chosen for further trials.

Power was provided by a Blackburne SV engine, although not the same version as on the 3-wheeler, and it came equipped with a rear tyre belt for off-road use, as did all the 3-wheelers.

PANTHER

Under its previous name of Phelon & Moore (P&M), the company was well known for its association with the Royal Flying Corps during the First World War, and then the RAF from 1918 with its 3½hp machines.

From 1925 the name Panther started appearing on the RAF's new combinations, and later on its solo machines. With the arrival of these new machines, the old 3½hp P&Ms were slowly phased out, with the last leaving service around the late 1920s.

The Panther model was to stay in service until the mid 1930s, when it was replaced to some degree by BSA's War Office Twin. Although the arrival of this machine apparently caused the end of Panther's association with the RAF (and also with the War Office), it appears that some Model 100s were bought in about 1938–39.

Panther (Mark II to IV) Combinations and Solos, OHV Single-Cylinder – 1925 to 1930s

These OHV motorcycles were to replace 3½hp side valve P&Ms that were in use with the RAF. First appearing in 1925, they lasted until the 1930s, when newer models from other manufacturers began to replace them and effectively ended the bond between Panther and the RAF. The model that specifically caused this was BSA's War Office Twin, which was introduced in the early 1930s.

A few interesting features about these motorcycles were their interchangeable wheels, stands for all the wheels (including the sidecar) and massive butterfly nut-type oil-filler dipsticks, which could be removed without the use of a tool.

Panther Model 100 598cc OHV Single-Cylinder – 1938–39

Possibly 100 of these machines were ordered, although at the time of writing it is not known whether or not they were delivered.

Details of the model are scarce and only an official photograph in the Imperial War Museum's department of photographs confirms its existence as a War Office motorcycle.

One unusual feature was the separate dynamo and magneto set-up, which was quite different from the normal 1939 arrangement shown in catalogue brochures.

Official photograph of a 1938–39 Model 100, as investigated by the Ministry of Supply. (MH 11972, IWM)

ROYAL ENFIELD

The Enfield Cycle Company Limited, commonly known as Royal Enfield, of Redditch in the Midlands was a major supplier of motorcycles to the services during the Second World War, along with other products produced for the government. The War Department (Army) was by far the major user of Royal Enfield motorcycles, although both the Air Ministry (RAF) and Admiralty Department (Royal Navy), together with several elements of the Civil Defence services, also made use of certain quantities of machines.

This, however, was not the case up to the outbreak of the Second World War. During October 1935 the War Office purchased two Royal Enfield motorcycles as part of its evaluation programme. Those chosen were the Model C 350cc SV single-cylinder and the small-capacity Model B 250cc SV single-cylinder. Neither model coped with the rigorous War Office testing programme, both suffering considerable mechanical problems within the specified 10,000-mile assessment limit, and both were subsequently rejected by the War Office for their poor reliability and endurance in comparison to the other makes evaluated at the time.

It was not until April 1940 that Royal Enfield supplied any more motorcycles for War Office evaluation. Then two 350cc SV single-cylinder machines, manufactured from special lightweight steels and aluminium alloys in order to reduce the overall weight to the War Office's specified limit of 250lb or less, were delivered, tested and later rejected, on the grounds that they were neither reliable nor robust enough to withstand the rigours of military use.

Earlier, in May 1939, Royal Enfield had received a sizeable order from the Department of Air Defence of Great Britain (ADGB) (embracing several organisations) for the supply of 600 motorcycles, these being Model D 250cc SV machines, a type not previously evaluated by the military. The Department required these motorcycles for general message relaying between dispersed units and the low-performance Model D was considered both suitable and available at a time of increasing demand. Two months later, a further 900 Model D machines were ordered by the MoS for military use in the training programme of personnel as part of the build-up to war.

Following the outbreak of war, Royal Enfield received further orders for motorcycles, which were generally of the 1940 civilian model range finished, as appropriate, for the military. After the evacuation at Dunkirk and the loss of virtually all equipment, most major motorcycle manufacturers were inundated with huge orders from the War Office for machines, further contracts being placed well in advance of the completion of existing ones. Supply rather than suitability was paramount in the initial stages; once the situation had settled a little, the War Office specified the supply of one standard type of machine in order to avoid potential problems caused by having a wide range of different ones. The type that was specified from Royal Enfield was the 1940 specification Model C 350cc SV single-cylinder machine (much improved from the earlier 1935 offering), supplied and finished to War Office standard.

From 1942 onwards, the WD/C was superseded by the WD/CO, and production of the WD/C ceased in early 1942. During the course of the Second World War Royal Enfield also supplied the War Office with almost 8,000 lightweight 125cc 2-stroke WD/RE motorcycles. Again, this existing pre-war design was evaluated for potential service use and, with developments, ultimately adopted primarily for use by airborne formations and other assault troops in line with the instigation and rapid expansion of the British airborne arm after 1940.

In 1944, wartime production demands taking precedence, Royal Enfield (along with certain other manufacturers) did manage to undertake limited development work towards a new standardised model intended for military use as a replacement for many of the various types then in service. The particular machine it offered the War Office was a rather odd-looking 350cc SV twin-cylinder model, which was eventually rejected after due assessment.

Royal Enfield Model B 250cc SV Single-Cylinder – 1935

Only one civilian-specification model was supplied to the War Office for military evaluation alongside the 1935 series of trials. This model was evaluated for general road use only by the War Office but its poor reliability and endurance led to its rejection for service use. Problems encountered in its 10,000-mile test were a broken inlet valve, a bent exhaust valve, a broken magdyno, loosening of the tank-top instrument panel, a broken chain guard and a twisted frame, as well as other minor faults.

Official photograph of the 1935 Royal Enfield Model B, tested at the same time as the 1935 seven-make trials (but not as a part of them). (138/E5, The Tank Museum)

Royal Enfield Model C 346cc SV Single-Cylinder – 1935 Civilian Specification

As with the 250cc Model B, only one 346cc Model C was supplied to the War Office for evaluation in the 1935 trials; it too was a civilian-specification model. This model was evaluated for general service use, which included rigorous off-road testing as well as riding on normal roads. It was subsequently rejected for service use because of its poor robustness and reliability. Problems encountered in its 10,000-mile test were faulty timing gears, overheating, the piston crown breaking off (twice), stripped teeth on the magdyno driving gear, partial seizure, a blown head gasket (requiring a replacement to be fitted), a broken mudguard stay and a broken primary chain.

Official photograph of 1935 Royal Enfield Model C, as tested in the 1935 trials. (138/F1, The Tank Museum)

Royal Enfield Experimental Lightweight 350cc SV Single-Cylinder – 1940

Royal Enfield built two experimental lightweight 350cc SV machines for evaluation by the War Office in response to the requirement for a general-purpose motorcycle that could be produced for service use, of a capacity of 350cc or less and a maximum weight of 250lb or less. Royal Enfield was not alone in producing such a model and was competing against similar offerings from other major motorcycel manufacturers. Produced in the spring of 1940, the engine design of the machines was based around the 250cc SV Model D and, in common with their competitors, both were constructed of

1940 Royal Enfield Experimental 350cc Military Lightweight. (Royal Enfield Owners Club)

special steels and also of lightweight aluminium in order to keep the weight to a minimum.

Although the performance of both machines proved satisfactory, the Ministry of Supply held reservations about the model's robustness and reliability for service use. Consequently, none were ordered and the contracts went to BSA for its Model WB30 and to Triumph for its twin-cylinder Model 3TW.

The War Office serial numbers for these two motorcycles are not known, although they were both supplied under contract number C.6718 and were initially delivered to the War Office at Feltham, Middlesex. Incidentally, it is worth noting that the original lighting set was changed to the same type as that fitted on the Triumph 3TW.

Royal Enfield WD/D 248cc SV Single-Cylinder – 1939–40

The Royal Enfield 248cc SV Model D was an established pre-war design and was the first model in the Royal Enfield range of machines to be supplied in quantity to the War Office. The first large order for 600 Model D machines was placed by the Ministry of Supply in May 1939 during the preparations for war, for delivery to the Department of Air Defence, and were intended for light communications duties between the various locations of the many elements of this organisation. These machines were essentially civilian-specification models finished in the appropriate service colours. The machines supplied after the outbreak of war, generally in early 1940, were basically the same but lacked the valanced rear portion of the front mudguard.

Royal Enfield WD/D, as supplied in 1939 and 1940. (Royal Enfield Owners Club)

As time was at a premium, the model was considered suitable and ordered even though it had not been previously evaluated by the War Office. Further bulk orders followed for quantities of 900, 350 and 300 machines, along with several smaller orders.

In late 1939 and early 1940 small quantities of civilian Model D motorcycles were pressed into military service, overpainted in the appropriate colours. These were generally obtained from civilian stocks awaiting despatch at the factory or on sale in dealers' showrooms.

The Model D was employed mainly by the Army and its role was nearly always for training purposes or light communications duties. It was used to a considerable extent by female ATS (Auxiliary Territorial Service) personnel, for whom the Model D was both suitable and popular. Production of the Model D was halted during early 1941 and no further machines were made.

Royal Enfield G 346cc OHV Single-Cylinder – 1940

These motorcycles were accepted by the Royal Navy prior to their adoption by the War Office as Royal Enfield's main offering for the remainder of the war.

Pictures of these motorcycles (along with a rider from the Royal Navy) were used by Royal Enfield in advertisements to promote its products in the then current *Motor Cycle* and *Motor Cycling* magazines of 1941.

Perhaps surprisingly, there are many differences between the later WD/CO and this model, which is much more similar to the WD/L and the WD/J2.

Royal Enfield KX Combination 1140cc SV V-Twin – 1941

From the contract date it can only be assumed that these motorcycles were built up from pre-war stocks of parts still in the factory and that they were part of Royal Enfield's clear-out of old models, before the company switched over production entirely to WD/COs.

It is not known how the models were used, or whether they had passenger or box sidecars fitted.

Royal Enfield Model L 570cc SV Single-Cylinder – 1940

This motorcycle was loaned by the factory for testing in early 1940, when its suitability was compared with a standard WD 16H.

Although it was heavier than the 16H, testing showed that its petrol consumption was in fact better, and during its 1,000-mile test no mechanical failures occurred. It was considered to have stood up well to the test. Only two criticisms were noted, those being its ground clearance and the lack of a sump guard.

Interestingly, the test notes show this motorcycle as a 500cc, although the Model L was usually 570cc.

Royal Enfield WD/L 570cc SV Single-Cylinder – 1940–41

Not originally intended for use by the War Office, this model was readily available for production and delivery, and was supplied during a time of urgent demand. Two orders were placed in 1940, with the last delivery being completed in early 1941. No further machines were built or supplied after this date.

1940 Royal Enfield WD/L. (Royal Enfield Owners Club)

Although the WD/L was initially supplied to the War Department (Army), it is of note that subsequently many were transferred to the Admiralty Department (Royal Navy) for general shore-based duties, with a proportion going to the Air Ministry (RAF) as well. The WD/L continued in limited use with all three services until the end of the war, with the few survivors being sold off as war surplus almost immediately.

Royal Enfield KX 1140cc SV V-Twin Combination with SWD – 1941

Only one machine was produced in response to the brief need for a more powerful version of Norton's Big 4.

Powered by Royal Enfield's own SV V-twin, the model was short-lived, along with similar models from Sunbeam, BSA and Norton, because of the arrival of the Lend-Lease Jeep from America.

Royal Enfield WD/J2 499cc OHV Twin-Port Single-Cylinder – 1941

This machine was Royal Enfield's 499cc OHV model single-cylinder motorcycle fitted with a twin exhaust-port head, of which the Air Ministry ordered a small quantity during mid 1941 under a single contract, number C.10103.

The WD/J2 was similar in appearance and construction to the WD/G, with near-identical fittings including toolboxes and a large air cleaner box for the carburettor.

Interestingly, Royal Enfield publicity advertisements of the period always seem to show the WD/J2 on an airfield setting, complete with RAF rider.

Royal Enfield WD/J2 as used by the RAF. (Enfield Cycle Co.)

Royal Enfield WD/G 346cc OHV Single-Cylinder – 1940–41

Along with the WD/L, the WD/G was essentially a pre-war civilian version that was supplied to the War Office because it was readily available, along with tooling and parts, following the loss of equipment at Dunkirk.

The WD/G supplied was generally to a high-performance 'sporting' specification, the engine in some machines fitted with a cylinder head and barrel of aluminium, which gave a high compression ratio and consequent increase in top speed and overall performance.

Although the WD/G was seen to be the ideal replacement for the WD/C, two motorcycles from contract number C.9311 were tested for their suitability. The first did not live up to expectations and was considered to have a generally unsatisfactory performance, although it had handled well on the road. Modifications were suggested and carried out for the second motorcycle, consisting of wider gear ratios, a higher compression piston and a larger carburettor. Following 2,500 miles of testing in early 1941, the model was considered suitable for War Office use, but there was still concern over fuel consumption and it was also recommended that future motorcycles have their saddles raised by 1in and that a rear stand be specified as opposed to the centre stand currently fitted. The same testers also recommended that the current SV WD/Cs be fitted with OHV engines (this was noted on 28 May 1941).

1940 Royal Enfield WD/G. (Royal Enfield Owners Club)

It is quite probable that many of the WD/G machines remaining in use later in the war, after the introduction of the similar model WD/CO, lost much of their original identity during workshop overhauls and rebuild programmes. In such instances, replacement components fitted would most likely have been WD/CO fittings and, in the case of an engine overhaul, the original unit was replaced by a reconditioned standard WD/CO power plant.

Royal Enfield WD/RE 126cc Single-Cylinder 2-Stroke – 1942–45

The WD/RE was procured by the War Office primarily as a lightweight, expendable means of transport for use by the developing airborne elements of the armed services. The requirement was for a machine of adequate performance, reliable and robust enough for use off-road, of lightweight construction enabling it to be dropped by parachute or carried within aircraft or gliders, and capable of being manhandled by the rider over minor obstacles. The intended role of such a motorcycle was to provide an efficient means of relaying messages and signals with the minimum possible delay over relatively short distances between dispersed airborne and assault formations, particularly in situations where radio communications were difficult or non-existent.

Following the birth of the British airborne arm in early 1942, the War Office procured under contract twenty WD/RE motorcycles from Royal Enfield for evaluation. The company had the basic model readily available, having introduced it on to the civilian market during 1939 as a general utility, all-purpose lightweight. The models supplied for evaluation were essentially civilian model 1940 machines without modification, and had the pre-war frame design, a foot brake on the right, an Amal carburettor, a low-mounted toolbox and a single-box exhaust system.

The evaluation of the machines was generally successful, although modifications would be necessary before total acceptance by the War Office. These included installing a twin-box exhaust system to help suppress noise, replacing the Amal component with a Villiers carburettor (hence the 'V' prefix on the engine), repositioning the toolbox to below the saddle as the existing space had now been taken up by the carburettor and air cleaner assembly, installing a folding kick-start, folding footrests and folding handlebars to ensure compactness when packed, and modifying the frame, principally so that the saddle could be raised to a height of 29in. A revised, standardised Miller lighting system was incorporated into the design, a 35- instead of a 34-tooth rear wheel sprocket was fitted, a sealed vent was added to the filler cap to avoid fuel spillage when the machine was packed in its drop carrier and the foot brake was relocated to the left side of the motorcycle.

1942 Royal Enfield WD/RE as first supplied for evaluation. Note the many differences to the later production versions. (Royal Enfield Owners Club)

A much modified early WD/RE in first version of its proposed dropping cradle in late 1942. (Royal Enfield Owners Club)

Following the modifications, the first large contracts for the WD/RE were placed during early 1943, with deliveries commencing forthwith.

In early and mid 1942 two different protective cradles for the machine were developed by the AFEE to fulfil the War Office's requirement that the machine could be safely dropped by parachute into a landing zone along with troops.

All versions of the cradle had to withstand being dropped from the bomb racks of aircraft such as the Halifax, Dakota, Lancaster and Albemarle and be opened quickly on landing, with minimal damage to the motorcycle.

Subsequent testing of the first cradle showed it to be insufficiently rigid and protective. The second prototype was tested in September 1942, and proved infinitely better. This was then modified, incorporating heavier tubing and increased bracing, and, in December of the same year, handed over to Royal Enfield as a pattern for preparing the final version. These went into production at the Enfield Cycle Company, Calton Hill, Edinburgh, to be introduced in 1943.

It should be mentioned that not all WD/RE motorcycles were dropped into the battle area by parachute. In reality, only a small percentage would have arrived by this method along with the initial assault formation. A far greater

An early WD/RE in the 2nd version of its dropping cradle. Interestingly, the report from which this photograph comes describes the motorcycle as a DKW. (NB 3383-2, Crown Copyright, MoD Boscombe Down)

A production Royal Enfield WD/RE in either a pre-production or modified production cradle fitted with cast shoe-type wheel cradles. When tested, this design damaged the wheels more readily than the normal bar type wheel cradle. (NB 3383-6, Crown Copyright, MoD Boscombe Down)

A production Royal Enfield WD/RE in an Enfield-built production cradle. (NB 3383-5, Crown Copyright, MoD Boscombe Down)

A Royal Enfield WD/RE on No. 6 bomb rack of a Douglas Dakota. (NB 3383-4, Crown Copyright, MoD Boscombe Down)

percentage arrived in troop-carrying gliders whereby up to four machines, with riders, could land in one group, usually in one piece and in a specific area. When delivered by glider, the motorcycles were not carried within the protective frames, and were secured by harness straps that attached to the interior of the fuselage of the glider.

A percentage of WD/RE machines were also employed for use outside the airborne arm, principally by assault formations engaged in coastal landings during 1943 and 1944, when the machines were carried ashore from landing craft and used for communication duties on beachheads.

During the early post-war years, many surviving models were disposed of as war surplus, even though the type remained in limited service use until the end of the 1940s. Many were purchased by dealers and subsequently rebuilt as civilian models for sale to the public in the cheap utility class, and much sought after at the time.

Royal Enfield WD/C 346cc SV Single-Cylinder – 1940–42

The 346cc SV WD/C Royal Enfield became the company's main production model for the War Office for almost two years between 1940 and early 1942.

During the production period, the type was subject to numerous changes and improvements. There were specification changes for nearly every contract issued, although most of these modifications were to the cycle parts and fittings rather than mechanical components.

Early WD/Cs had bolt-together fork legs, aluminium brake plates, rubber-mounted handlebars (of which some had mounting points for the levers attached), a lock on the rectangular toolbox, number plates, a small rear carrier and a top-fed float chamber; they did not have filters on the timing-chest cover, pannier bag racks or pillion facilities.

As time went on changes had to be made to suit new requirements; the aluminium brake plates were replaced by steel ones (caused by shortage of aluminium and the needs of the aircraft industry), racks and pillion facilities were eventually added, a rigid fixing for the handlebars was introduced to prevent them rotating, and a filter added to the engine-timing cover to improve the life of the big-end. Other minor changes were made to the design of the forks, toolbox knobs and grass leg, among other things.

It should be mentioned that, contrary to popular belief, the WD/C was not identical to the later model OHV WD/CO (engines apart). It was virtually a completely different motorcycle, and very little was interchangeable between the two. (Engine crankcases, gearboxes and frames were totally different.)

Although production of the WD/C ceased during late 1941/early 1942 – deliveries to the War Office terminated in early 1942 – the model continued in service until the end of the war, chiefly with the Army and a number with

Official photograph of Royal Enfield's 1940 WD/C. (REME Museum)

the RAF. Most were used for light communications and convoy escort duty roles for most of their service, use of the type gradually diminishing during late 1944. When the war in Europe ended in May 1945, the WD/C Royal Enfield was among the first types of War Office machinery to be sold off to a transport-hungry public, with advertisements for the type 'Ex-WD Reconditioned As New' appearing in the motorcycle press as early as 1946.

Having been rebuilt from stocks of both new and reconditioned parts, these post-war 'new' Model C motorcycles were frequently fitted with an odd assortment of parts not specified for the type when originally constructed for the War Office. Examples of such include late-type WD/CO girder forks with side-mounted check springs and raised speedometer bracket. A further point is that many of the ex-military engines fitted into these post-war rebuilt WD/C machines are still marked as military units and usually carry the contract

Royal Enfield WD/C with bag racks shown on and off. (Royal Enfield Owners Club)

number on the cases. However, it will often be found that the engine number is a post-war restamp on top of the original number, carried out so that the engine number matches the frame into which the unit was fitted when rebuilt.

Royal Enfield WD/CO and WD/CO/B 346cc OHV Single-Cylinder – 1942–45

The Royal Enfield 346cc OHV WD/CO was introduced into War Office service in early 1942 as a direct replacement for the then current WD/C 346cc SV, which had been criticised throughout its service life for a general lack of overall performance.

During the four years of production the WD/CO, like the earlier WD/C, was subject to several noticeable changes and modifications. Some of these were the result of improvements while others were introduced because of the need to economise.

Early machines did not have the side-mounted check springs fitted to the forks as on all later models. Steering dampers were fitted, only to be removed in later years along with the footrest, handlebar grip, kick-start and gear-change rubbers, because of supply problems caused by the war in the Far East.

First contract WD/CO. Note that there are no check springs on the forks. (Airborne Assault Museum)

A Royal Enfield WD/CO/B, as supplied for one contract only. (Royal Enfield Owners Club)

Later models had canvas handlebar grips, only two toolboxes (the rectangular one was removed after the first contract), a new chain guard tail section, and a totally different frame. It is worth mentioning that there were in fact three styles of frames, of which the first two were similar, with different rear sections, but the third was vastly different.

One other major change, which was only temporary in 1942, was the installation of a Burman gearbox in place of the Albion type normally used for contract number C.13870. Machines so fitted were termed WD/CO/B.

Other changes to the WD/CO were minor, embracing horns, handlebar control levers and fittings, exhaust brackets, petrol pipes, chain guards and so on. Machines produced from late 1944 onwards were generally factory-fitted with tank-top-mounted universal type Vokes air filters; those produced from early 1945 onwards were almost certainly fitted with the late-war specification Lucas lighting equipment.

Between 1942 and 1945 the WD/CO served with elements of all three armed services, with a proportion also seeing service with certain Civil Defence units. Indeed, a large quantity were issued from Army stocks for the fire service from 1943 onwards. In comparison to the earlier WD/C, the WD/CO was employed in a wider range of uses, principally road communications and convoy escort duties. It did not see considerable usage in forward areas as perhaps originally intended, being generally rated below the Matchless G3/L and Ariel W/NG for performance and off-road suitability, chiefly because of the poor ground clearance of the frame. Furthermore, the crankcase bottom was exposed to a degree and not protected by either a shield or frame-member as on other makes – important considerations for off-road use.

As with the WD/C, WD/CO machines were sold off at the end of the war, the first quantities arriving on the civilian market during early 1946 having been either factory rebuilt or dealer reconditioned in the majority of cases. Again, mismatched components of various dates were frequently fitted and engines and frames restamped to match each other.

Royal Enfield 350cc SV Parallel Twin – 1944 Prototype
This was Royal Enfield's response to the military request for a new standardised motorcycle for post-war service.

Although it had many features that were favourable from a wear point of view (totally enclosed primary and secondary chaincases), it was not pursued as 350cc OHV twins or 500cc SV twins were considered to be the minimum requirement. The National Motor Museum at Beaulieu owns a surviving example.

RUDGE WHITWORTH

Rudge Whitworth supplied examples of its products for evaluation by the War Office during the mid 1930s. Government contracts were eagerly sought by all manufacturers as they provided a profitable bulk order, together with good publicity material – the government, it was generally assumed, only used the best of anything.

During the latter half of 1936 the War Office ordered under contract two motorcycles from Rudge Whitworth for evaluation purposes. These were delivered to the MEE at Farnborough, Hampshire. The two models supplied were to standard civilian specification, although the Army removed the linked front and rear brake arrangement in order to bring the model into line with other manufacturers' models being assessed at the same time. One of the models supplied was the 250cc OHV Rapid model, while the other was the well-known 500cc OHV Ulster model. After testing, however, both models were rejected.

Not to be defeated, and inspired to a degree by the partial success of its 250cc Rapid model in comparison to other manufacturers' products tested at the time, Rudge Whitworth concentrated on developing a model specifically for service use that incorporated the successes and recommendations from the War Office tests. The new model was loosely based on its 250cc Rapid, and was called the Service model. The company supplied an initial batch of twelve of these new models under contract during the latter half of 1938, all delivered to the War Office at Chilwell, Nottinghamshire.

According to War Office records, no further Rudge Whitworth machines were supplied following this delivery and information relating to the fate of the type is now almost non-existent.

It is known, however, that production of motorcycles at Rudge ceased on 18 December 1939, although Autocycles were still being made for some time into 1940. The fate of the twelve models delivered before the war is not entirely known, but one has been restored by a Rudge enthusiast.

A final note of interest is that in pre-war years, the Army display team (White Helmets) used a number of Rudge motorcycles in their displays, and it may well have been because of this that Rudges were originally tested by the MEE.

Rudge Rapid 247cc OHV Single-Cylinder – 1936

Initially loaned to Farnborough for testing in July 1936, this standard commercial model was to have some unspecified modifications carried out to it after its eventual purchase.

Official photograph of the modified 1936 Rudge Rapid test model. (WO 194 [45]-7897, The National Archives)

After the usual 10,000-mile test, of which nearly 2,500 miles were across country, the Rapid was only described as 'fair' in terms of reliability, even though its performance was generally good.

Its main problem was its gearbox, which persistently failed, and largely because of this it was not recommended as a suitable alternative to the standard War Office motorcycle.

Rudge Ulster 500cc OHV Single-Cylinder – 1936

Delivered to Farnborough at the same time as the 250cc Rapid, the Ulster was also initially on loan and purchased later following modifications.

Prior to the modifications to the gear-change position and brake pedal (which were deemed necessary to bring it in line with other service models) and the lowering of the first gear from 13.9 to 1 to 16 to 1, the machine's performance was described as promising, no doubt partly down to its 4-valve head.

Following all these modifications, the usual 10,000-mile reliability trial was conducted, of which 2,620 miles were across country. Afterwards the motorcycle was described as only 'fair' in terms of reliability, requiring a considerable number of replacement parts (mainly valve-gear components that suffered unacceptable wear). Needless to say, the Ulster was turned down.

Rudge Service 247cc OHV Single-Cylinder – 1938

Following the partial success of its Rapid, Rudge set about producing a purpose-made model for the War Office, loosely based on the earlier machine.

To overcome the main criticism of the Rapid (its gearbox), Rudge used its Ulster's gearbox, clutch (which then necessitated the use of a new chaincase), and rear wheel. Other notable changes included the use of a Lucas magdyno, a rear stand, uncoupled brakes, a right-side gear-change – left-side foot brake, and a prop-stand.

Twelve of these new Service models were purchased under contract and issued to units for extended trials in late 1938.

Finally, it is thought that Rudge was given the go-ahead to build another 200 Service models, which are reported to have been built, delivered, and later destroyed in an air raid. However, what is more likely is that Rudge, as a minor motorcycle manufacturer, was dropped when war broke out, as it could not supply the number of machines that would be needed, whereas larger manufacturers could. Also, the Hayes Middlesex factory, where the Service models were to be built, made radar and this was probably regarded as higher priority than a few motorcycles.

A 1938 Rudge Service, this left side view showing its serial number C3810116. (RLC Museum)

STEWART-EHRLICH

A prototype manufacturer, Stewart-Ehrlich offered the Ministry of Supply a proposed model, a 250cc split-single 2-stroke of unit construction, only for it to be turned down. Undeterred, it then offered a 350cc split-single 2-stroke, this now coupled to a Burman gearbox. This time the MEE did conduct a day's trial on the model on 15 October 1941. Although no further testing was conducted some development was continued, as this model later evolved into one of the post-war EMC motorcycles.

S.O.S.

A small manufacture that offered a prototype in 1940 and then an improved model in 1942. Both were powered by a 2-stroke engine and fared all right against the four strokes they were tested against. However, no contracts were awarded.

SUNBEAM

Sunbeam originally supplied equipment during the First World War, and produced ambulance-kitted combinations. Later the company tried several times to sell its models to the War Office, but it seems that each attempt was stopped because of a change of ownership.

In the late 1920s a Model 6 motorcycle was known to have been bought and it was about this time that the current owners, Marston, sold the name to ICI. (Whether Model 6s were also bought and supplied after the change of ownership is unknown.)

The next proposed Sunbeam was the 1936 Lion, which was specifically altered for the War Office during testing only to have its reliability trial stopped because of yet another change of ownership in 1937.

The final time a Sunbeam-badged military motorcycle appeared was during the war. This motorcycle was a Matchless-engined V-twin combination with SWD, which was specially developed as a proposed replacement model for the Norton Big 4. Once again there was a change of ownership, to BSA, but this time it was probably not the cause of the cancellation of the current motorcycle. The far more likely reason this time was the arrival of the Willys-Overland Jeep, after which development work on SWD models was stopped by all manufacturers.

Sunbeam Model 6 492cc SV Single-Cylinder – 1927

Details about this model are scarce and the only fact known to the authors is that the machine is now owned by a member of the Sunbeam Marston Register.

Whether the Model 6 was bought in limited quantities over a number of years or as a one-off in 1927 is not known.

Sunbeam Lion 500cc SV Single-Cylinder – 1936

This was a 500cc SV model (similar to the War Office's new Norton 16H) and had been specifically altered in the hope of meeting the requirements of the War Office.

Initially, this model was only loaned for testing at Farnborough, which started in October 1936. However, after its initial performance testing, which proved promising, it was bought. Certain modifications were carried out, most notably installing a lower first gear.

Following this, the MEE's obligatory reliability trial was commenced. This was never finished, however, as the company was bought out by AMC, which already had a successful military model of its own, the G3, and did not want a second. All testing stopped and the Lion was quietly forgotten.

Catalogue picture of a 1927 Sunbeam Model 6 492cc sv. (Sunbeam Motorcycles)

Official photograph of the 1936 Sunbeam Lion, seen at Farnborough in the winter of that year. (WO 194 [45], The National Archives)

Sunbeam Prototype 1000cc OHV V-Twin Combination (with SWD) – 1941

This was AMC's Sunbeam-badged offering to replace the Norton Big 4, but it was short-lived because of the arrival of the Willys-Overland ¼-ton 4×4 Jeep from America.

A 1941 Sunbeam combination with three soldiers. (John Tinley)

Essentially the model was a Matchless MX2 V-twin-powered combination, built to achieve the requested 55mph road speed (the Norton Big 4 was always regarded as slow) and fitted with heavy teledraulic forks and a 'transfer' box for forward or reverse gear selection.

Reputedly, an order for a batch was given but never fulfilled, and sadly the prototype no longer exists.

TRIUMPH

Triumph was a well-known name following the Armistice in 1918, its Model H machines having been employed in large quantities during the First World War, second only to the Douglas company in total numbers supplied. The Triumph models had earned a good reputation in service, which they retained in both public and military opinion throughout the years after the war. In the 1920s the Model H machines in War Office service were partially replaced by the company's Model P, and both types continued in service for the remainder of that decade.

Keen to retain government contracts, Triumph itself offered a replacement model for its Model P, the Model NL3. Although the NL3 was not one of the contenders in the seven-make trials of 1929, the War Office nonetheless conducted a comparison trial between it and the Douglas L29. Even though the War Office concluded that it was a considerable improvement over the Model P, the NL3 was not selected for further evaluation and the type was withdrawn.

During the late 1920s and the 1930s Triumph also supplied other models, the 494cc Model N and NP (although military records referred to both as the Model N) and the 549cc Model ND, but these were bought in only small batches. It is not known whether the MWEE tested either model.

A Triumph 1925 specification Model P was also used during the 1920s as the basis for an experimental 3-wheeler all-terrain machine. The sole example was constructed by the Royal Army Service Corps. Produced and evaluated in 1926, the model was found to require certain changes in order to improve performance, and the project was passed over to OEC for further development under War Office supervision.

The next seven-make trial was held by the War Office in 1935, and Triumph offered its Model 3/1 for assessment. Later that year, the company underwent considerable reorganisation and a change of name from Triumph Company Limited to Triumph Engineering Company Limited. Changes within the firm included the revision of all products and the Model 3/1 was dropped from the range. Its replacement was the Model 3S, a similar 350cc SV machine, which was supplied to the War Office for evaluation during 1936. The War Office consequently noted it as being suitable for use.

In 1939 the War Office requested Triumph, along with Norton and Royal Enfield, to supply a lightweight machine conforming to specific military requirements. Several prototype models were produced, the first incorporating special alloys to reduce its weight, although the final model dispensed with such features to offset high costs. These prototypes evolved into the military 3TW model, a 350cc OHV valve parallel twin-cylinder machine. The model so impressed the War Office that it decided to adopt the type as the standard military motorcycle for the duration of the war, the model replacing the multitude of others then in service. However, plans were cancelled overnight when the German Air Force blitzed Coventry, decimating the Triumph factory along with most of the city centre.

Despite the fact that it was virtually wiped out, Triumph did manage to continue with limited production in what remained standing of its Coventry works, and in temporary premises in Warwick. It concentrated primarily on military SV 3SW and some 5SW models. It was not until 1942 that Triumph was able to resume full-scale motorcycle production at its new premises at Meriden. The only model built from then on was the 350cc OHV 3HW. The proposed 3TW model was not resurrected, most probably because tooling for the model had been destroyed in the bombing.

During the latter half of the Second World War, Triumph developed another experimental model in response to War Office thinking. The model produced was a 500cc SV twin-cylinder machine termed the 5TW and fitted with telescopic front forks. Produced in 1942, the model was not fully assessed by the War Office until the end of the war, and formed the basis of the post-war military TRW model.

Triumph Model P 494cc SV Single-Cylinder – 1925–27

The Triumph Model P was purchased by the War Office as a partial replacement for the ageing Triumph Model H, which had seen active service during the First World War. The Model H was not completely withdrawn, however, the type continuing in use well into the 1920s alongside the Model P.

Triumph Model P in service overseas. (Authors' collection)

Triumph Model P combination in service with the RASC. (Authors' collection)

The total quantity of Model P machines supplied to the War Office is unclear, although it is known that the type was supplied in both solo and combination versions. Ultimately, the Model P was replaced by other motorcycles and the combination versions by light cars.

Triumph Experimental 3-Wheeled Motorcycle 494cc SV Single-Cylinder – 1926

This machine was the forerunner of the 3-wheeler machines later developed by OEC and was not actually constructed by Triumph itself. The machine was a civilian Model P, converted by the Royal Army Service Corps in the workshops of P Company.

The idea of a 3-wheeled machine evolved as a result of the success of the Army's new 6-wheeled lorries. The drive to the rear wheel was by chain with a linking belt between the rear wheels. For improved grip in certain off-road conditions a track could be fitted over the rear wheels, thus turning it into a half-track motorcycle.

Testing of the completed machine was conducted by Captain Bennet at Aldershot, the machine proving to be very good over soft ground and reasonably good over rough surfaces and tarmac. Although having many features in its favour, the machine did have certain problems, including both

Official photograph of the 1926 Triumph 3-wheeler. (RLC Museum)

weight and ground clearance. A further problem was a tendency for the rearmost wheel to lift clear off the ground when there was a surge of power.

An improved machine was suggested, although this version did not reach fruition, the entire project being passed on to the OEC company for further development.

Triumph Model N De-Luxe 494cc SV Single-Cylinder – 1927 and Triumph Model NP 494cc SV Single-Cylinder – 1928

Resembling the Model P machine at first glance, the Model N De-Luxe did have several differences. One of the main ones was a mechanically operated oil-pump in place of the Model P's hand-operated item, although the latter was in fact retained as an auxiliary item. Other differences included a heavier frame and different forks. The exact quantity of machines supplied to the War Office is not clear, nor has any evidence been found to indicate whether the type was ever evaluated by the MWEE prior to purchase.

Military records refer to both motorcycles as the Model N, which is correct in a way, but Triumph had to change the model name in 1928 to lessen confusion with its new N De-Luxe: it obviously could not have two motorcycles with the same name in its range.

1927 Triumph Model N in service with the Royal Green Jackets (170A12W_P_4972-2, Hampshire Archives/The Royal Green Jackets Museum)

Official photograph of a Triumph Model N combination, as in service in the 1920s. (WO 194 [45]-5316, The National Archives)

Triumph Model NL 494cc SV Single-Cylinder – 1928–29

This particular model was a saddle-tank version of the Model NP, still fitted with the 494cc SV single-cylinder engine and of de-luxe specification. The model name NL is an abbreviation of N De-Luxe (as it was called in 1928) and was kept for 1929. It shared many component parts with Triumph's Model NSD.

The Model NL was offered by Triumph in three optional guises. The base machine was the Model NL1, which was very utilitarian, without lighting or horn. The Model NL2 was fitted with a horn and Lucas acetylene lights, while the final optional version, the Model NL3, was fitted with a Lucas magdyno unit, electric lighting and a bulb-horn. The military authorities opted for the NL3 model, despite it being the most expensive.

Not a participant in the seven-make trial of 1929, the model was tested by the military in comparison with a 2¾hp. Douglas machine. The War Office, however, were impatient to receive a suitable new model for use and before all the trial results were collated they opted for the Douglas machines. The trials did not stop completely, however, the Model NL3 later being tested in

Official photograph of a Triumph Model NL3, as in service in the late 1920s. (WO 194 [45]-5549, The National Archives)

Egypt against the OEC 3-wheeled machine and the Levis company's '6-port' product. Ultimately, the War Office was to favour the Levis product, although the Model NL3 Triumph was noted as being the best machine produced by the company for military evaluation to date.

Triumph Model ND 549cc SV Single-Cylinder – 1933–34

Following the Model NL3, the next Triumph machine to see military usage was the Model ND. This machine had a 'sloper' engine configuration with a full sheet-metal enclosure over the crankcase and gearbox.

Only three small contracts for the supply of the model are known of and it has not been established whether the type was evaluated for suitability prior to purchase. It is probable that the machines supplied to the War Office were fitted with a small rear carrier along with conventional handlebars, as opposed to Triumph's alternative 'clean' type then on offer.

Stripped down Triumph Model NDs in use by the Signals display team between 1933 and 1937. (Royal Signals Museum)

Triumph 3/1 343cc SV Single-Cylinder – 1935

The Triumph Model 3/1 was one of the machines selected by the War Office for evaluation for suitability for military use in the seven-make trials of 1935. However, by the end of the year the model was withdrawn from testing, having been removed from the Triumph range after the company was reorganised.

At the start of the trials, the Model 3/1 was fitted with a hand-change gearbox that after 2,415 test miles, was converted to a foot change. Throughout the evaluation (between November 1935 and January 1936) the model suffered several problems, including persistent magdyno failures involving sheared armatures and stripped magneto driving wheels (on four occasions). Testing was halted by the time 4,530 miles had been completed.

Summarily, and despite the magdyno problems, the military assessed the performance of the machine as fair, with a good cross-country achievement.

Official photograph of a 1935 Triumph Model 3/1, as used in the 1935 trials. (138/E4, The Tank Museum)

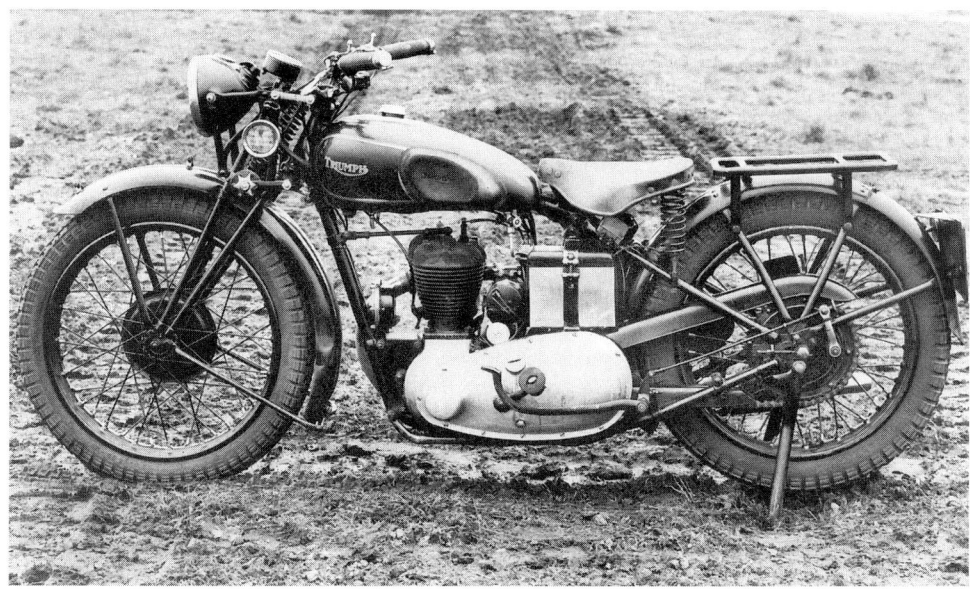

Official photograph of the 1936 Triumph Model 3S that was to replace the Model 3/1 in testing. (WO 194 [45], The National Archives)

Triumph 3S 343cc SV Single-Cylinder – 1936

The replacement model for the Model 3/1 following the reorganisation of the company, the 1936 Model 3S was offered to the War Office for military evaluation and delivered to the MEE at Farnborough in December of the same year, with testing continuing into 1937.

Similar in design to its predecessor, the Model 3S incorporated a new, strengthened frame and a new gearbox design. Other details of note include revised forks, wheels and fuel tank, among other items.

The War Office trials concluded that the type's performance was at least comparable to the earlier Model 3/1, despite suffering from excessive cylinder wear in the engine, which was partially remedied by the fitting of a new barrel and liner. Overall, the machine was noted as fair in both reliability and condition, and was summarily noted as being suitable for War Office use.

Triumph 3SW 343cc SV Single-Cylinder – 1938–41

Between 1938 and 1941 some 10,000 Model 3SWs were supplied to the War Office, although the final machines built may have been destroyed before completion or despatch from Triumph's Coventry premises during the bombing of the city in November 1940. Limited production of the 3SW continued in temporary premises at Warwick following the bombing and the move into new premises at Meriden during 1942 saw the 3SW withdrawn in favour of the similar OHV Model 3HW, which was produced for the remainder of the war.

The military model 3SW was based largely upon the civilian-specification 3SE model, a utilitarian version of the standard civilian 3S. However, there were a number of differences on the military version, including a low-compression engine, wide ratios in the gearbox, different handlebar controls, and a rear carrier and rigid-mounted handlebars. During its service, the 3SW underwent few changes. The most prominent alteration was the removal of the rear number plate during late 1940, which coincided with the fitting of the universal-pattern military tail/convoy light. Hooded blackout masks became a standard fitting from early 1941 onwards, and many of the later machines produced had an additional toolbox on the offside of the machine between the mudguard stays. Certain batches of machines also had some de-luxe items fitted such as 8in headlights and rod-operated brakes, presumably to use up stocks of parts.

The War Office was the main user of the Model 3SW, although limited numbers were also used by both the Admiralty Department and the Air Ministry. Judging from surviving photographs of the type in service, it appears to have been used frequently by women, although the type has also been noted in use for normal despatch duties in the Middle East during 1940.

Official photograph of a 1938 Triumph 3SW. (REME Museum)

Despite production of the Model 3SW ceasing during 1941, the type remained in service until the end of the Second World War, principally in training and second-line roles. Following the end of hostilities in 1945 the model was quickly disposed of, many of the survivors being rebuilt to civilian specification during the late 1940s.

Triumph 3TW Lightweight-Prototype 349cc OHV Parallel Twin – 1939 (Serial No. C.3937042)

The prototype Model 3TW was produced in response to the War Office's specification for a lightweight machine of 250lb or less, of 4-stroke engine design and having the performance of a 500cc SV machine. Triumph developed and offered its 350cc OHV parallel twin-cylinder Model 3TW for War Office evaluation and approval. It performed well enough to be proposed much later as the standard British military motorcycle for the duration of the war, the design to be produced by all other manufacturers.

In order to keep the weight of the machine within the limit specified by the military, liberal use was made of alloy steels and aluminium in the design, and direct lighting was fitted to further reduce the weight incurred by standard lighting systems, which incidentally did not work well enough until 30mph in top was reached. The 10,000-mile testing showed the engine performance to be exceptional, although at a cost of rather excessive wear to the engine components and a gearbox failure at 1,693 miles. It was thought, however, that such wear could be cured by modifying the design somewhat and suggestions were passed on to Triumph. The machine also had other peculiar design features including the gearbox being in unison with the engine (an idea possibly adopted following Triumph's purchase of the New Imperial Company?), a removable U-section for the top frame tube to which the fuel tank was attached and an alternator powering the direct lighting. Finally, the frame was welded together as opposed to the traditional brazing method. Tyres were 3.00–21 front and 3.25–19 rear.

Triumph 3TW Lightweight-Prototype 349cc OHV Parallel Twin – 1940 (Second Version)

Following the original Model 3TW, a second prototype example was supplied for evaluation during 1940. This model was essentially the same as the 1939 version but with a slightly less exotic specification listing for the materials used.

The original's alloy head and barrel were substituted for components made from cast iron, along with several other lightweight alloy components. The reason for the change was principally one of cost, but also because of the urgent demand for lightweight alloys from the aircraft industry, which took precedence over motorcycle manufacture. The substitution of iron and steel components increased the overall weight of the machine by some 12lb, although on testing, performance was still found to be satisfactory and largely unaffected by the increase. The engine wear problem was also largely resolved. Although this model and the original prototype had been considered to be rather 'sporty' in performance, the engine needed to be detuned to provide more bottom-end power, to enable the machine to be more suitable for novices to ride.

During testing (3,115 road miles and 2,519 cross-country) the gearbox fractured, so the Elektron casing was replaced by an aluminium version. Although other minor faults occurred elsewhere on the motorcycle, it was a considerable improvement over the first machine. However, more modifications were still requested for the next prototype, besides the detuning of the engine. These were a higher riding position and wider footrests, a lower front fork spring rate and dry plate Ferodo inserts for the clutch. During November 1940 the machine was also sent to Matchless to have teleforks fitted.

A second model (the third 3TW) was then modified (heavier flywheels, new camshaft with less dwell, modified carb slide) to give the required engine characteristics and a higher riding position with wider footrests. After testing

A rather battered Triumph 3TW prototype. (MVE 16384/2, IWM)

this motorcycle was considered superior to any other motorcycle submitted, although its fuel consumption needed improvement.

It is probable that, from this model on, the alternator was moved from its position on the engine-timing cover to outside the engine sprocket in an effort to overcome the criticism of poor low-speed lighting found on the first model.

Fifty of this model were then ordered in mid October, but this appears to have been amended shortly afterwards to two for verification with forty-eight to be delivered later on.

Triumph 3TW Pre-Production Version 349cc OHV Parallel Twin – 1940 Contract C.8020

This version of the 3TW model was the intended version for mass production and incorporated only minor modifications over the previous two contracts.

These two motorcycles were essentially the same as the third 3TW and were bought purely to verify the results of that motorcycle. Following these results, an order was placed for forty-eight (later amended to fifty) full production models for issue to various units.

Triumph Model 3TW Production Version 349cc OHV Parallel Twin – 1940 Contract c.8331

Once the pre-production version of the Model 3TW had received military approval, and various minor modifications had been completed, Triumph began to prepare for full-scale mass production of the 3TW model. Production of the first batch of fifty machines was under way at the Coventry factory when the premises were bombed in 1940. All machines were as good as destroyed along with plans, tooling for the model and spares. The company was able to salvage only a few examples of the 3TW from the ruins of the works, although, with production facilities destroyed, these were of little use. Following the bombing, the demand for other machines remained and Triumph concentrated its efforts on producing its 3SW and 5SW models from the limited facilities available for the time being.

Study of the production 3TW version indicates that the minor modifications to the pre-production and prototype models included the installation of a blackout shield to the headlight, the removal of the number plates, and the addition of a revised rear carrier, lightweight universal pannier frames, pillion-carrying facilities, and 3.25–19 tyres front and rear.

A sole surviving example of the Model 3TW from contract C.8331 can be seen at the National Motor Museum at Beaulieu; no other survivors of the type are known to exist today.

Triumph 5T (Speed Twin) 498cc OHV Parallel Twin – 1939

Only two examples of Triumph's renowned speed twin model are known to have been officially purchased by the War Office during December 1939, although it is known that further examples of the type were impressed into service from factory stocks at the same time, as were examples of the similar Tiger 100 machine.

With both machines being purchased late in 1939, it is likely that they were to 1940 specification complete with the larger 4-gallon fuel tank in place of the previous year's 3¼-gallon tank.

Considering the performance potential of the model, it was probably only employed in service by experienced motorcyclists. The ultimate fate of the two models officially supplied is not known. The impressed civilian versions are known to have served in instances up to 1941.

Triumph 5SW 493cc SV Single-Cylinder – 1940–41

Triumph's 5S model was introduced to its range just prior to the outbreak of the Second World War. However, the War Office did not consider the type for service because both Norton and BSA were supplying the 500cc machines required at the time.

Following the losses of equipment during the fall of France, the model was accepted for service and Triumph was able to supply some 1,500 models under two contracts placed.

The Model 5S was supplied to the same specification as the military Model 3SW and was thus termed the 5SW. It was identical to the Model 3SW in virtually all respects, the only difference being the increased engine capacity, which required the use of different pistons, flywheels, crankcases, cylinder head and barrel. At a time when machines were urgently required the 5SW was readily available and could be produced using Model 3SW components and stocks of 5S engine components, which were to hand in the works.

The 5SW model was quite popular with those to whom it was issued, principally because it was the size and weight of a 350cc machine but had the performance of a 500cc machine.

Triumph 3H 343cc OHV Single-Cylinder – 1940

According to the surviving records, only 140 examples of the OHV 3H model were officially supplied to the War Office in response to its requirement for machines following the losses inflicted during the fall of France.

The machines supplied were of 1940 civilian specification as the then official military Triumph product was still the Model 3SW. It is likely that the machines supplied were either readily available for delivery from the factory or able to be produced quickly from stocks of parts held at the works, these machines were therefore fitted with the civilian specification cylinder head rather than the later military specification 3HW component.

Triumph SWD Combination – 1940–41

Little is known about this model other than it was designed to have a road-speed capability of 55mph, and was killed off by the arrival of the Lend-Lease Jeep from America, as were similar offerings from Norton, Sunbeam and Royal Enfield. The machine concerned may possibly have been based on the SV Model 6S, or alternatively a 500cc twin.

Triumph 3HW 343cc OHV Single-Cylinder – 1942–45

By the time Triumph had moved into its new premises at Meriden during 1942, military thinking was favouring 500cc SV and 350cc OHV machines. Triumph therefore embarked on full-scale production of its 350cc OHV Model 3HW from April 1942 until the end of the war.

The military specification 3HW differed from the earlier civilian 3H model principally in the design of the cylinder barrel and head, an alteration established to simplify production methods. The Model 3HW shared virtually the same cycle components as the earlier 3SW and 5SW models; the early

Model 3HWs being very similar in appearance to the late 3SWs, having two toolboxes fitted, a small rear carrier with no pillion facility, full rubber fittings and the large 8in headlight. During 1943 the rubber fittings began to be withdrawn from new machines and the headlight was specified as the smaller 6in variety. Further, machines were now factory-fitted with pillion-carrying facilities, a large rear carrier and universal military pattern pannier frames.

As time progressed, the economies of war forced the aluminium alloy chaincase and oil-pump cover to be replaced with pressed steel items. By early 1945 machines coming off the production line were fitted as standard with universal pattern Vokes air filters on top of the fuel tank (frequently with a cutaway portion to the offside rear of the tank to accommodate the filter hose) and a revised lighting system incorporating a change-over switch atop the headlight, with the main lighting switch now located beneath the saddle.

With the end of hostilities, the 3HW models were rapidly disposed of by the military authorities, many being purchased by dealers for rebuilding and sale to the public, plus large numbers being supplied to Allied countries, such as Greece and India, as war aid. Triumph itself offered the military specification 3HW model for sale to the public, finished in civilian colours and constructed using stocks of parts available at the factory, although this had ceased by 1947 as stocks were exhausted. The Triumph Model 3HW was a popular machine during the war years, and this popularity continued after the end of the war. The type was held in high esteem by the grass-track, speedway and trials fraternity largely because of the flexible engine design and the compactness of the frame and associated components. Many machines were converted into specialist mounts, or were dismantled for parts to keep such machines running. Consequently, the Model 3HW Triumph is not commonly encountered today and surviving examples are few and far between.

Triumph 5TW 498cc SV Parallel Twin – 1942 and 1944

The Triumph Model 5TW was not simply an enlarged version of the earlier Model 3TW. Apart from having an SV rather than an OHV engine, there were many differences between the two machines.

The 5TW model was designed by Bert Hopwood following Edward Turner's move to BSA, and in certain quarters it has been suggested that the 5TW project was a political move to spite Turner. The machine was, however, quite different from the earlier 3TW model, particularly in basic engine design. It was also the first Triumph machine to be fitted with telescopic front forks.

Originally constructed for comparison testing against the company's own 3TW model, the model performed well and showed good prospects.

Official photograph of an early Triumph 3HW. (Airborne Assault Museum)

Official photograph of a Triumph 5TW side valve twin that has many 3TW features. This version may well be the resurrected 1944 version. (MVE 12850/2, IWM)

However, further development of the model had to be shelved from 1942 onwards in order to concentrate on model 3HW production, then heavily under way.

Resurrected again in 1944 following interest from the War Office, the project dragged on slowly, no doubt due to the imminent end of the war and the desire of the military to avoid suddenly having hundreds of unwanted machines. Interest in the project waned only to resurface yet again in the early post-war years when the model became the forerunner of the military TRW model.

VELOCETTE

Until just before the Second World War, Velocette had virtually nothing to do with the military and, as far as motorcycles were concerned, had not sought any involvement. Following the outbreak of war, however, two Velocette machines were purchased by the MoS for evaluation purposes by the MEE to assess their suitability for potential military service. The start of the war had prompted the requirement for large numbers of machines for the services and almost every potential product from the many motorcycle manufacturers of the time was considered.

The two Velocette models supplied for evaluation during October 1939 were the company's standard 1940 specification 350cc MAC and the larger 500cc MSS, both OHV types. Soon after, a military contract was placed for the supply of a militarised version of the MAC, although this was by the French government and not the British War Office. However, the contract was scarcely under way, let alone complete, when France fell to Germany in June 1940. Production was temporarily halted and the completed machines transferred to the British War Office, which eventually purchased under contract some 1,200 of the MAC models.

Following usage of this model by the services, Velocette produced an improved model called the MAF and managed to secure a War Office contract for the supply of 2,000 such examples. With the contract placed during 1941, production of the MAF commenced later that year with the first machines being delivered to the War Office during early 1942. Velocette, however, was still faced with the problem of a lack of bulk production facilities and was hampered to a considerable degree by the wartime demands of other production commitments that had increased as the war progressed. Production of the MAF was slow, delivery sporadic and never in great quantity. The result was that by September 1942 the contract for the MAF was terminated after the production of some 947 machines. At this stage of the war most of the other main motorcycle manufacturers were producing huge quantities of suitable service machines and the comparatively minor Velocette production was deemed unnecessary. Production thus ceased immediately for the remainder of the war, and the factory was put to use producing other war work.

The absence of surviving War Office Velocettes today has led to an abundance of stories surrounding the fate of the models. These include tales of sunken transport ships in either the Mediterranean destined for Africa, or in the English Channel destined for France, a rumour about quantities of the model going to Russia under Lend-Lease arrangements, and the notion that many of the military MAC and MAF models were returned to the factory after the war and rebuilt to civilian standard, having the original military frame and engine numbers removed and restamped.

Velocette MSS 500cc OHV Single-Cylinder – 1939
A sole example of the Velocette MSS was purchased by the Ministry of Supply for evaluation purposes by the War Office on 20 October 1939. The example supplied was a 1940 specification standard civilian model. Subsequent testing of the type revealed the machine to be rather powerful and a handful for anyone less than an experienced rider. This was probably why the MSS model was not accepted for military use.

It should be noted that the MSS was not simply an increased engine capacity 350cc MAC. Indeed, there were many differences between the two models including the gearbox, brakes, wheels, frame, petrol and oil tanks.

Velocette MAC 350cc OHV Single-Cylinder – 1939
Five days after the Ministry of Supply had purchased the MSS model for evaluation, a solitary Velocette Model MAC was purchased for similar testing by the MEE. This machine was again a 1940 specification standard civilian model and, on completion of the evaluation period, it was concluded that the MAC compared favourably with the 500cc SV BSA and Norton models already in service. It was relatively easy to control across country, and it was suggested that if certain modifications were carried out the type would be suitable for military service.

The testing of the MAC was observed by officials from both the British and French governments, and resulted in the latter placing an order for the type, which was never fulfilled.

It is of note that the MAC test model was, in fact, demonstrated to the respective governments by a BSA factory rider, as Velocette could not offer a skilled rider of its own, having no competition department within the company at the time.

Sergeant J.H. 'Crasher' White and Sergeant Freddie Frith, former racing and trials riders, then motorcycle instructors at an RASC driving and maintenance school at Keswick in the Lake District, October 1942. Both are on MAC(WD)s. (H24685, IWM)

Velocette MAC (WD) 350cc OHV single-cylinder – 1940

Ultimately delivered to the War Office, the militarised version of the civilian MAC was originally built for the French government. The model supplied was as originally tested by the War Office, but incorporating the various modifications suggested as a result of the previous testing. These modifications included a crankcase protective steel undershield fitted to the frame, a lower compression ratio engine, a lower bottom gear (16.8:1 as opposed to 14:1), a cylindrical fishtail silencer to increase ground clearance, a rear carrying rack in place of a pillion seat and footrests, a non-valanced front mudguard, an improved rear brake pedal, and dull chromium plate in place of normal bright chromium.

It is of note that the Velocette MAC (WD) model is sometimes referred to as the MDD, as this was the prefix stamped on to the frames and engines, although the majority of the surviving official references to the model refer to the type as the MAC (WD).

Velocette MAF 350cc OHV single-cylinder – 1941–42

The Velocette MAF was the result of development work carried out by the company on the MAC (WD) model then in service. Although this machine was generally well designed and adequately suited to use by the military in the majority of applications, the company felt that it could be improved upon and made considerably more suitable. Usage by the War Office had highlighted several areas that could be improved, and Velocette therefore took a standard MAC model, number MAC 6707, and progressively modified and tested it until it evolved into the form that became the MAF. The development work was carried out by Phil Irving (later famous for his Vincent connections) and the completed model was ridden during the period by the Velocette factory

Official photograph of a 1941/2 Velocette MAF. (KID 5355, IWM)

manager, Bob Burgess. Commencing in July 1941, the development of the MAC (WD) found favour with the War Office and a proposed second contract for MAC (WD)s was changed in favour of the improved MAF, an initial order for the supply of 2,000 being placed.

The modifications to MAC 6707 were as follows: a redesigned frame incorporating a large forging beneath the engine, which strengthened the frame and doubled as a protective shield for the crankcase; large rear carrier and standard military pannier frames plus a pillion seat and folding pillion footrests; one toolbox now fitted on the offside of the machine in a low position, rather than the previous pair fitted one either side in high-level positions; rubber bump-stops added to the front forks to avoid 'clashing' over rough ground; longer top links in the girder forks; the removal of the engine torque-stay; a re-profiled cam fitted to the engine; a different carburettor; an amended method for anchoring the rear brake plate (torque arm); a marginally smaller exhaust pipe diameter; improved routing of the exhaust system; a lower chain guard; a standard throttle control fitted in place of Velocette's own push-pull design; a clip fitted to the rear mudguard to hold up the hinged tail piece and facilitate the removal of the rear wheel; a pocket added to the interior of the singular toolbox lid to accommodate the rider's handbook and instruction manual, plus a length of Bowden cable fitted between the box itself and the hinged lid to stop the latter from falling fully open; a revised foot-change lever for the gearbox and linking mechanism which effectively reversed the gear-change operation to bring the type in line with other military motorcycles; a different gearbox end cover design; a revised rotating kick-start lever, which was an improvement on the existing swivelling variety; an even lower first-gear ratio of 18.17:1; a smaller diameter Miller headlight; the substitution of cast-steel for the alloy of the timing cover and the gearbox end-cover plate; and finally, the rear brake foot-control pedal adjustment method was revised.

These numerous modifications, however, had an adverse effect to a degree, as they raised the cost of the model considerably. By 1942 the MAF model was costing the Ministry of Supply at least £68 per machine, compared with, for example, the Matchless G3/L model, the Ariel W/NG, the Royal Enfield WD/CO and the Triumph 3HW, which all cost less than £60. Coupled with Velocette's limited bulk-production facilities, these figures were ultimately considered to be non-cost-effective and Velocette's facilities better directed at other forms of war production. The result was that by September 1942 the MAF model's contract was cancelled after the production of some 947 examples of the type. These continued in service along with existing MAC (WD)s, although many of the latter were subsequently transferred to various civil defence formations, including the National Fire Service, following the introduction of the MAF model. As with the MAC (WD), the MAF tended to be employed within the United Kingdom because of the comparatively small number in service.

8

Sidecars

During the war a number of contracts were issued for sidecars only (or sidecars and chassis). In the years after the First World War most manufacturers made their own sidecar bodies and chassis, and larger manufacturers continued to do so during the Second World War, although many, in fact, subcontracted to specialists (such as Swallow) for bodies.

Many different styles of sidecar bodies have been used over the years but not all have been for carrying passengers; during the war a number of box bodies were bought to fit BSA's M20, Norton's 16H and the Indian 741B.

At the outbreak of war quite a number of unapproved types were impressed into service from showrooms and factory finished goods areas. One notable model was the Matchless model X.

On the sidecar development front, besides the well-known SWD outfits from Norton (and the experimental versions from BSA, Triumph, Royal Enfield and Sunbeam), it is known that folding sidecars for carrying drop containers were experimented with, attached to Triumph 3HWs.

Matchless Model X combination fitted with anti-tank rifle in use with Royal Scottish Fusiliers. (H3983, IWM)

9

Miscellaneous Motorcycles

This chapter looks at machines from miscellaneous sources, which were pushed into service for one reason or another.

In desperate times many unapproved vehicles were drafted into service until the official versions could replace them, this being particularly the case after Dunkirk, when motorcycles were urgently needed. Thousands were put into service after being bought as 'local purchase' from showrooms, and more still taken from the finished goods areas of factories or even private owners, an operation known as 'impressing' equipment.

It is possible that some were donated as gifts for the war effort, with the owners not expecting them to be returned. This was certainly true of car owners, and it is reasonable to assume that motorcyclists were equally generous.

As the Second World War progressed, the local purchasing and impressing of vehicles slowed down as the large manufacturers got into their stride. By now damaged motorcycles were on the increase and the job of sorting them out fell to REME. They would often strip down the damaged motorcycles, restoring them to working order using parts from various machines. At big depots these rebuilt machines were reissued as such and carried new registration numbers beginning with the number C.1400000. This method of stripping down and reassembling continued after the war, hence very few War Office bikes have their original engines.

Any motorcycle that had seen a lot of military service (i.e. regularly damaged in use) would have had many rebuilds and consequently would have lost its original identity quite quickly. This is evident today from the number of mixed-up machines that can be found; that is machines that have engine and frame numbers from different contracts and/or parts that do not match their original contract.

It has also been known for home-made components or parts from another manufacturer's model to be fitted to machines. This happened especially when modifications had to be carried out in the field, and sometimes as a

A captured Zundapp KS750 combination, bearing its new British registration, C5321791. This motorcycle was picked up in the Middle East and has a variety of parts missing, and a makeshift rear light. (REME Museum)

NSU Kettenkrad captured in North Africa in 1942. (E12941, IWM)

A Matchless Model X in use with the Wehrmacht, probably a commandeered motorcycle. (John Tinley)

A Moto Guzzi Alce captured in North Africa in 1943 and brought back to the UK. (REME Museum)

preference; for example, Matchless teledraulic forks being fitted on BSA's M20 and Norton's 16H.

During the Desert War and thereafter many captured motorcycles were used, mainly of Italian or German origin. Towards the end of the war, these too were given their own series of registration numbers beginning with the number C.6000000.

10

The VAOS Spare Parts System

The origins of the Vocabulary of Army Ordnance Stores (VAOS) system date back to the 1860s and the basic principles of the system remained in use until after the Second World War (to around 1958), at which point the NATO system began to supersede VAOS.

In the beginning the stores lists were published and issued to the Army at intervals of between one and six months, simply to keep up with the latest changes in equipment. As time progressed and the Army became more mechanised, these stores lists became known as Proprietary Parts Lists.

With mechanisation of the Army, the Land Vehicle (LV) classification system was introduced by the VAOS. By the Second World War this was split into fifteen numbered LV sections covering all types of land vehicles, but the two of most interest to motorcycle enthusiasts searching for 'new old stock' spare parts are sections LV6 and LV7.

Key lists (Proprietary Parts Lists), and 'B' vehicle makers' parts lists were issued to all mechanised units in possession of the vehicles. All makers' spares were ordered from these lists.

When ordering parts, the VAOS MT section, designation (description of part), part number and quantity had to be entered on a form, with a separate sheet for each MT section. When ordering parts the vehicle contract number and catalogue reference number had to be referred to (the little brass or steel plate fitted to most Second World War motorcycles). The details on the plate would then be used to find the correct parts list, which would have the same numbers stamped in purple ink on the front cover and very often inside on the first page. Sadly, after a major REME rebuild this system fell apart – everything was mixed up from the strip-down, and when it came to putting things together again parts from different contract motorcycles and years were used to make a motorcycle again.

Matchless G3L Spares List for contracts C9506 and C9841. (Authors' collection)

PROPRIETARY PARTS LIST

for

MATCHLESS
Model 41-G3L, 350 c.c., O.H.V.

to

CONTRACTS C.9506, C.9841
Model 41-G3WO, 350 c.c., O.H.V.
CONTRACT C.8934

V.A.O.S.
SECTION LV7-MC

1944

Not to be published

(4201) Wt. T9788 G2146/3750 8/44 B & M Ltd. 7/8/7

Matchless G3 and G3L Propriety Parts List for contracts C9506, C9841 and C8934. (Authors' collection)

VAOS Section LV6

Described as 'the normal vocabularies of miscellaneous MT stores that are common to most vehicles and contain, in addition, lists of proprietary equipment', all the major mechanised units and RAOC establishments held these lists. The subsections were divided as follows:

LV6 CT   Handbooks

LV6 MT1   General MT stores: adaptors, belting, bin, blocks, cans, clips, Bowden cables, contract name plates, extinguishers, fibre washers, funnels, glasses for instruments, hooks, towing, jointing, keys, grease guns and lubricators/nipples, oilers/oil cans, pins, split cotters, circlips, plugs, petrol pipe nuts and nipples, scotches, saddles, taps, tins, tyre pumps, unions and washers. List of proprietary shock absorbers, speedometers, cables, pressure gauges, lubricating injectors and lubricators, lifting jacks, pumps/tyre inflator, saddles, twist grip, etc.

SM is Smiths, TT is Tecalemit, TE is Terry, LT is Lycett, EA is Ewarts, BN is Bowden, MS is Mansfield

LV6 MT2   Tools (except makers' special tools), tool chests, tool rolls, and list of contents.

LV6 MT3   Lamp holders and parts, ammeter and switch, bulbs, lamp glasses, mirrors, bells, list of lamps, horns and windscreen wipers.

LU is Lucas, MI is Miller

LV6 MT4   Electric cable (LT and HT), WD batteries, battery carrier for BSA M20, hydrometers, voltage regulators, dynamos, sparking plugs and electrical sundries (dipswitches, immobilisers, HT lead/ends, resistor for HT leads, rubber clips, flat clips). List of complete electrical equipment except lamps, horns and windscreen wipers.

LU is Lucas, MI is Miller, KL or KLG is KLG spark plugs, CHA is Champion, LO is Lodge

LV6 MT5   Bolts, machine screws, nuts, washers, rivets, etc.

LV6 MT6   Rubber hose, rubber mats, tyre repair kits/material, vulcanising material.

LV6 MT7 Bearings, loose balls and rollers.
TN is Timken, HN is Hoffman, SKF is SKF bearings

LV6 MT8 Mag-dynos, dynamos, distributors, ignition, coils, magnetos, etc.
LU is Lucas, MI is Miller, VS is Villiers

LV6 MT9 Machinery and parts.

LV6 MT10 Metals and metal tubing (locking wire).

LV6 MT11 Non-skid chains, transmission chains, chain links, and towing ropes.
RE is Reynolds

LV6 MT12 Carburettors, petrol filters, air cleaners, filters, autovacs.
AM is Amal, VS is Villiers

LV6 MT13 Coach materials and waterproof covers, shelters, pannier frames, pannier bags, pannier straps, towing attachments and body fitments.

LV6 MT14 Tyre covers (tyres), tubes and valves, WD standard and proprietary wheels, wheel nuts and studs, wheel rim security bolts, wheel flanges, spokes and nipples.

LV6 MT15 Special miscellaneous stores and proprietary equipment parts for 'A' vehicles only (armoured cars and tanks).

VAOS SECTION LV7

LV7 was the section covering non-standard British 'B' vehicles, which covered 'soft-skin' vehicles such as lorries, cars and motorcycles and major component suppliers.

The following is a list of the main motorcycle manufacturers' identifying codes. These were applied to all supplied spare parts:

AI	=	Ariel
BC	=	BSA
BGB	=	Burman gearboxes

Original packing boxes and spares, mainly Matchless. (Authors' collection)

EM	=	Excelsior
JM	=	James
MC	=	Matchless
NC	=	Norton
RE	=	Royal Enfield
TC	=	Triumph
VC	=	Velocette

11

Colour Schemes

With the exception of certain test models, motorcycles procured by the War Office during the years before the outbreak of war in September 1939 were generally finished in the standard colour scheme of the majority of other service vehicles of that period. This comprised an overall colour of bronze green (a somewhat deep shade of green), with quite a glossy finish. Normally, engine and gearbox casings were left in unpolished bare metal and ancillary components, such as control levers, exhaust systems, nuts, bolts and studs, were in such finish as supplied by the respective manufacturer, usually dull chromium plate, nickel plate, cadmium (dull) plate, enamel or 'coslettised' – a dull black. Certain machines, principally those for evaluation purposes, were supplied to the War Office in standard civilian colours.

The paint used on War Office machines was manufactured and supplied by external sources and complied with War Office guidelines, although in practice there existed a wide variation of the one specific colour and the shade could vary considerably.

Before the war, the peacetime parade-ground finish of vehicles was unsuitable for camouflage and concealment purposes. Manufacturers therefore began to apply paint that incorporated a matt, non-reflective finish. Officially, this paint was a light khaki-green colour. In reality, due to wartime demands, the colour could vary from a distinct brown shade through to dark green. The paint was supplied to individual units for repainting pre-war machines already in use, and was applied either by brush or by spraying; the latter particularly if the quantity of machines to be finished was considerable. Impressed civilian models, machines of 1940 specification waiting at factories and those in showrooms were grouped together and finished in the wartime service colour. The application of paint was often quite liberal, resulting in the saddle, engine and tyres being painted along with the rest of the machine.

Two-colour camouflage schemes were both officially and unofficially applied to many War Office vehicles during the course of the war, notably between 1940 and 1943. The scheme usually consisted of a light khaki-brown base colour overpainted with random areas of dark brown. Motorcycles were normally exempted from this practice because of their considerably smaller surface area. Examples bearing this two-colour scheme have been noted, notably motorcycle combinations such as the Norton Big 4, which was the size of a small vehicle.

In 1942–43 some contracts for machines from manufacturers were finished in an earth-brown colour, a milk-chocolate brown shade, because of shortages in the components necessary to manufacture green-shade paint. However, existing stocks of khaki-green paint had to be used up before the new colour was adopted. In 1944, before the D-Day landings in June, motorcycles arriving from the manufacturers were finished in matt, non-reflective olive drab. This was a medium-depth colour, of a shade midway between brown and green, although there were many variations of the official specification.

Those machines still bearing earlier finishes retained them until repainting was necessary, typically completed following a major overhaul or rebuild at base workshops. The olive-drab shade in reality was little different from the earlier khaki-green.

After the war, most War Office machines retained their wartime finishes until repainting was necessary or until the instigation of peacetime directives, which demanded a reversion to semi-gloss bronze or Brunswick-green colours, though of a lighter shade than previously.

AIR MINISTRY (ROYAL AIR FORCE) COLOUR SCHEMES

Before 1939 motorcycles employed by the Air Ministry were finished either in a gloss dark blue-grey or the bronze-green colour of the War Office.

The outbreak of war and the consequent reversion to camouflage colours affected the RAF perhaps to a greater extent than the Army, as the airfields where many vehicles were employed were considered prime targets for air attacks. Pre-war finished machines were hurriedly repainted with any suitable camouflage colour available. This frequently involved using paint intended for aircraft, usually matt green or matt earth-brown, or dark grey or dark brown paint intended for hangar camouflage. Other paint shades employed were similar, if not identical, to those employed by the War Office.

Motorcycles supplied direct to the Air Ministry were finished by the manufacturers in exactly the same colour schemes as those supplied to the War Office, this trend remaining for the duration of the war.

During early 1946 certain RAF units repainted motorcycles and other vehicles in a gloss blue-grey colour, either utilising pre-war stocks of paint or locally mixed colours, which led to a wide variation in shade. Other machines retained wartime camouflage colours or were repainted in the post-war War Office bronze-green colour, until such time as glossy blue-grey finishes were officially reintroduced.

ADMIRALTY DEPARTMENT (ROYAL NAVY) COLOUR SCHEMES

Until 1939 motorcycles employed by the Admiralty Department were finished in several different colour schemes. Whether these were applied by the manufacturer or completed by individual establishments is unclear. The colours noted, all of a gloss finish, were dark navy blue, varying from a medium shade through to near-black, dark grey and light grey. The latter two colours may well have been the same paint used for warships, applied at the factory or locally. The pre-war War Office colour of bronze-green (most probably Royal Marine motorcycles) has also been noted. In accordance with the other services, machines were kept in a presentable condition.

Once war had broken out, machines were repainted in available camouflage colours, although perhaps to a lesser extent than the other services. A paint occasionally used on naval motorcycles was a dockyard or battleship camouflage-grey colour, although it did not have a true matt finish.

As no special colour was supplied for machines destined for the Navy, motorcycles supplied to the Admiralty Department were finished in the standard camouflage colour of the period, which was whatever the manufacturers had to use.

After the cessation of hostilities, naval motorcycles, along with those from the other services, continued to carry their wartime colours until a repaint was necessary. When this happened, the colour was usually changed back to the War Office bronze-green colour, although sometimes pre-war colours were used.

OVERSEAS COLOUR SCHEMES FOR SERVICE MOTORCYCLES

Contrary to popular belief today, it was rare to find a motorcycle manufacturer finishing a machine in a colour scheme for service use outside the European theatre of war. Virtually all motorcycles were either collected from the manufacturer by the service concerned, or delivered to a specific ordnance depot or other such location of that service. Following delivery, the service then allocated specific machines for issue to units where and when required.

BSA M20 and Ariel W/NG in the distinctive colour scheme and pattern used only in Malta during the Second World War. (National War Museum Association, Malta, via Clive Micallef)

Norton 16H in Malta with a motorcycle-loving dog. (National War Museum Association, Malta, via Clive Micallef)

Very occasionally, a batch of motorcycles destined for overseas service, for example North Africa, would be repainted by the distribution depot in the appropriate desert camouflage colour, although urgency of delivery normally prevented this.

Refinishing was occasionally carried out by the unit receiving the machines on arrival overseas, although this time-consuming practice was not as commonly followed as is often thought today. The large proportion of the motorcycles sent to the Middle and Far Eastern theatres of war served there in their standard European colour schemes. In the case of a motorcycle, this was considered acceptable because of its small surface area. In North Africa, the European camouflage colour of matt khaki-green soon faded under constant exposure to sunlight and desert elements. Likewise, in the Far East the European green colour was equally effective in the tropical environment. Those machines repainted overseas, particularly in the Middle East, were usually painted a camouflage colour that matched the local terrain. In Malta, for example, all motorcycles (including solos) were repainted with the island's distinctive colour scheme, which incorporated a crazy-paving pattern (see photograph on p. 175). Paint was often mixed locally as a result of supply difficulties and was liberally applied to the machine's main surfaces, usually rather crudely. Dust and sand were frequently thrown on to the paint while it was still wet to further dull the finish.

Appendix 1

Contract Notes

The information contained in the production tables has come from many sources, namely original manufacturers' drivers' handbooks and parts lists, a B-vehicle census document dated November 1944, manufacturers' ledgers, Ministry of Supply ledgers and vehicle test reports.

Dates in these documents very often conflict, and in the case of delivery dates it is sometimes not clear whether the date given is a commencement date, during or completed contract date. Some dates, although known, have not been filled in, as it could not be firmly established to what exactly they were referring.

Inevitably there are gaps in the tables and the authors would be most grateful to hear from anyone with additional information so that any reprints can be updated. Likewise, the authors would be pleased to hear about any photographs that might exist of the many models not illustrated.

Key
CD	=	Contract date
COD	=	Central Ordnance Depot (Army)
CP	=	Completed contract
DL	=	Delivered
DM	=	Demand
EX CAN	=	Ex-Canadian Commonwealth Forces
MAP	=	Ministry of Aircraft Production
M/C	=	Motorcycle
MOWT	=	Ministry of Works Transport
MU	=	Maintenance Unit
NC	=	Not confirmed
NK	=	Not known
PL	=	Parts list
ROD	=	Regional Ordnance Depot (Army)
SAS	=	Special Air Service (Army)
VRD	=	Vehicle Receiving Depot (Army)

Appendix 2

Production Tables

AJS

Maker's Type	Military Class	WD Serial No. Allocation	Contract Number	CAT. REF.	Frame Number	Engine Number	Qty Prod'd	Dates	Price(s)	Delivery Destination & Notes
M5	M/C solo 350cc SV	20533, ?, ?					?	Late 1920s		India Office
M6	M/C solo 350cc OHV	20533, ?, ?	C.1933		M106173, ?, ?	M6/106173, ?, ?	3	04/05/29 DM 18/06/29 CD 02/08/29 DL	£46.6s	Civilian reg. MG 9001
M6	M/C solo 350cc OHV		C.3512				6	09/02/31 DM 06/03/31 CD	£47.15s	Feltham
M6	M/C solo 350cc OHV	22304, 22316	C.4259	1			2	1931	£51.19s 40/8 £55.2s 1d 8SS £47.4s 6d 40/9	
40/8, 8SS, 40/9	M/C solo 350cc SV or OHV	419344-7 419760	C.7373	2				26/05/40	40/8-1 8SS-2 40/9-2	Stirling or Catterick
40/26	M/C solo 350cc OHV	419751	C.7353	3			1	26/05/40	£44.17s 2d	Stirling or Catterick

ARIEL

Maker's Type	Military Class	WD Serial No. Allocation	Contract Number	CAT. REF.	Frame Number	Engine Number	Qty Prod'd	Dates	Price(s)	Delivery Destination & Notes
VA3	M/C solo 557cc SV	35797	C7641		Y10075	KA2590	1	09/09/35 DL		Westminster, civilian reg. CMM750
Square 4	M/C solo 600cc OHC				P120	EC102	1	02/10/36 DL	On Loan	Returned to Ariel 02/10/36 (same day!)

Maker's Type	Military Class	WD Serial No. Allocation	Contract Number	CAT. REF.	Frame Number	Engine Number	Qty Prod'd	Dates	Price(s)	Delivery Destination & Notes
Square 4	M/C solo 1000cc OHV				P109	DB107	1	02/10/36 DL	On Loan	Returned to Ariel 02/10/36 (same day!)
W/VA	M/C solo 500cc SV	4111501-4111600	C5111	1	10001-19, 10022-48, 10050-100	CH 147, 160, 454, 724, 994, 502-8, 519-28, 603-12, 623-31, 643-82, 684-99	97*	27/09/39 DM 06/01/40 CD 11/39 DL 1939 PL		Feltham 30, Chilwell 70 *3 frames not allocated
W/VA	M/C solo 500cc SV	RAF			10634, 10940, 10895, 10981, 11050, 10773, 11183, 10909, 10740, 11126, 11099, 10771, 10912, 10646	CH 1102, 1103, 1131, 1132, 1133, 1134, 1192, 1193, 1195, 1196, 1197, 1198, 1199, 1200	14	04/40		Chilwell, Abingdon, ?, Glasgow, Fareham, ?, Middlesex, Shetlands, Liverpool, Sheffield, S?, Manchester, ?, Plymouth
W/VA	M/C solo 500cc SV	MoA			9639, 9777, 10195, 10217, 10639, 10709, 10739, 10766, 10772, 10942, 11006, 11008, 11016, 11018, 11025, 11026, 11028, 11049, 11102, 11106, 11107, 11110, 11112, 11119, 11121, 11131, 13284, 13376, 13381, 13387, 13388, 13397, 13401, 13405, 13407, 13410, 13413, 13414, 13422, 13425, 13442, 13444, 18874	CH 1468, 1469, 1637-45, 1647-61, 1663, 1665-7, 1672, 1674, 1676, 1678, 1680, 1684, 1696, 1702, 1713-17	43	August to October 1940		

Maker's Type	Military Class	WD Serial No. Allocation	Contract Number	CAT. REF.	Frame Number	Engine Number	Qty Prod'd	Dates	Price(s)	Delivery Destination & Notes
?	M/C comb.	MAP	B7402				64	21/03/40 CD Delivery between 9/08/40 and November 1942	21 at £56.17s 6d 11 at £64.7s 6d 32 at £67.17s 6d	50 per cent commercial box sidecars 50 per cent passenger-carrying sidecars. Contract possibly amended to 23 solo 500ccs, 63 solo 350ccs, 23 500cc combinations and 52 500cc combinations standard
?	M/C comb. 500cc		C8882				1	05/10/40 DM 18/03/41 CD 27/09/40 DL	£73.3s	Dds 1775
VG	M/C solo 500cc		C9258		10319, 10914, 19449	CH 1591, 1593, 1594	3	16/12/40		Dds 1852. MoS, Kent
VB	M/C solo 598cc SV				10795, 13292	1475, 1457	2	08/40 DL		MoS and M/C section D, Newcastle
VH	M/C solo 500cc OHV	4191554-558, 561, 563, 565, 566, 568, 569, 571, 573-578, 581, 583, 629, 631, 633, 634, 636-638, 660, 661, 663, 664, 670, 672, 673, 676-678, 681, 683, 684, 703,	C7372	2	733, 9316, 9322, 9345-7, 9352, 9356, 9359, 9842, 9847, 9851, 9852, 9871, 9881, 9891-2, 9903, 9906, 9910-1, 9915, 9988, 10605, 10815, 10827, 10834, 10836, 10873, 10885, 10889, 10916, 10927, 10933, 10945, 10964, 10967,	CH 515, 1240, 1248, 1250, 1485-94, 1497-1507, 1526-1545.	45	28/05/40 DM 17/04/40 CD	£57	Catterick

Maker's Type	Military Class	WD Serial No. Allocation	Contract Number	CAT. REF.	Frame Number	Engine Number	Qty Prod'd	Dates	Price(s)	Delivery Destination & Notes
		713, 715-717, 721, 722, 724, 726, 730, 733, 734, 737-739, 741, 858, 861, 863, 865, 884, 885, 887, 888, 890, 894, 898, 900-903, 908, 910-912, 915, 919, 924, 926, 929, 940, 941, 945, 946, 948, 950, 957			10983, 10991, 11057, 11067, 11132, 11147, 11160, 11182					
VG	M/C solo 500 OHV	4191559, 567, 635, 655, 659, 665-668, 671, 674, 675, 682, 685-688, 690, 691-702, 704, 705, 708, 720, 723, 725, 731, 735, 736, 740, 886, 892, 899, 904, 905, 907, 909, 913, 916-918, 927, 928, 931-936, 939, 947, 953, 954	C7372	5	9323, 9341, 9344, 9351, 9360, 9819, 9875, 9908, 9912-4, 9973, 10317, 10714, 10829, 10892, 11010, 11021, 11023, 11041, 11043, 11045, 11054-5, 11058-9, 11063, 11068, 11090, 11100, 11117, 13429, 19447	CH 1252, 1256, 1430, 1432, 1433, 1436-9, 1508-10, 1512-21, 1546-50, 1552, 1554-5, 1591, 1593-4, 1596	34	26/05/40 June and September 1940 and January 1941		Catterick Deliveries in April
VA test model	M/C solo 500cc SV				XG 9567	CH 107	1	02/11/39 DL		Returned to Ariel on 02/12/39
VA lightened	M/C solo 500cc SV				XG 10208	CH 683	1	17/11/39 DL		Returned to Ariel on 21/12/39

Maker's Type	Military Class	WD Serial No. Allocation	Contract Number	CAT. REF.	Frame Number	Engine Number	Qty Prod'd	Dates	Price(s)	Delivery Destination & Notes
NG & NH	M/C solo 350cc OHV		CIST Batch		8141-9223	BE1467-1687	29 NG 157 NH	2/09/39 to 6/10/39 DL		
NG & NH	M/C solo 350cc OHV		CIST Batch		9211-9773	BH101-288	71 NG 109 NH	5/10/39 to 22/10/39 DL		
NH	M/C solo 350cc OHV	4191570, 572, 580, 582, 628, 630, 632, 679, 689, 707, 709, 711, 714, 718, 732, 855-857, 859, 860, 862, 864, 891, 893, 895-897, 906, 930, 937, 938, 943, 944, 949, 951, 952, 955, 956	C7372	3	9838-11178	421-687	38*	26/05/40	£55.19s	*29 in ledgers. 3 with spring frames (frames BX713, 729 & 762)
NG	M/C solo 350cc OHV	4191560, 562, 564, 579, 654, 656-658, 662, 669, 680-706, 710, 712, 719, 727-729, 742, 889, 914, 920-923, 925, 942	C7372	6	See Cat Ref 3	See Cat Ref 3	27*	26/05/40	£15.15s	*28 in ledgers
?	M/C solo 350cc	1038301	NK				1	1941?		
W/NG proto	M/C solo 350cc OHV		Unknown		XG12179	BH 1700	1	18/07/40 DL		
W/NG	M/C solo 350cc OHV	4311978-4314677	C8302	4	XG11186-13285, 13554-14153	BH 600-3299	2,700	08/08/40 DM 10/12/40 CD 18/07/40 DL	c. £55	Chilwell, with 153 to French government

Maker's Type	Military Class	WD Serial No. Allocation	Contract Number	CAT. REF.	Frame Number	Engine Number	Qty Prod'd	Dates	Price(s)	Delivery Destination & Notes
W/NG	M/C solo 350cc OHV	4381388-4381737	C8574	7	XG14154-14503	BH 3300-3649	350	27/08/40 DM 01/11/40 CD 01/11/40 PL	£55.18s 1d	Chilwell
W/NG	M/C solo 350cc OHV	4459718-4461717	C8722	8	XG14759-17000 with gaps	BH 4131-6149 with gaps	2,000	18/09/40 DM 07/12/40 CD Early 1941 DL December 1940 PL	£54.10s 6d	Chilwell. C4460559 had cast-iron gearbox casing (XG 15626/BH 5024). C4460175 had engine BH 4423 enlarged to 500cc
W/NG + Ariel-Matchless + Ariel-BSA	M/C solo 350cc OHV	4553325, 4553326, 1034001-1037500	C9387	11	XG15685, 15690, XG17001-20999	BH 6150-9999	3,500* 1 1	07/03/41 DM 28/01/42 CD Mid 1941 DL May 1941 PL	£54.10s	2 to Tewkesbury rest to Chilwell. Some to RAF. C4553325/XG15685 had Matchless engine fitted on 29/05/41. C4553326/XG15690 had BSA WB30 engine/523 fitted on 20/02/41. Bag racks and pillion parts added to contract. Quantity added to on 30/3/43. Contract includes spare frames/engines. **total built 3,473

Maker's Type	Military Class	WD Serial No. Allocation	Contract Number	CAT. REF.	Frame Number	Engine Number	Qty Prod'd	Dates	Price(s)	Delivery Destination & Notes
W/NG	M/C solo 350cc OHV	4589426-4590925 (RAOC) 1038302-1039801 (RASC)	C10477	9	XG20501-23500	BH10777-13776	3,000	26/04/41 DM 24/01/42 CD By February 1942 DL	£57.15s	Chilwell 1,500 and Ashchurch 1,500. Some to RAF & RN. 600/month. Bag racks and pillion parts added to contract
W/NG	M/C solo 350cc OHV	4692899-4696398	C11103	10	XG23751-27250	BH15001-18500	3,500	05/07/41 DM 27/03/42 CD By August 1942 DL April 1942 PL	£57.15s	Chilwell. Fitted with bag racks. 650/month after C10477
W/NG	M/C solo 350cc OHV	4850001-4852000	C12450	13	XG29751-31750	BH19001-21000	2,000	12/11/41 DM 24/01/42 CD By August 1942 DL	£57.15s*	Tewkesbury at 650/month. Bag racks and pillion parts added to contract. *Price increased to £62 with added parts
W/NG	M/C solo 350cc OHV	4812104-4815603	C13871	12	XG31751-35250	BH21501-25000	3,500	14/03/42 DM Nov 42 PL By April 1943 DL 16/01/43 CD	£63.11s 10d	
W/NG	M/C solo 350cc OHV	RN	S308		XG35251-35300	BH14946-14995	50	02/07/42 DM 08/09/42 CD		Portsmouth 15, Clyde 11, 8 each to Mersey, Rosyth, Chiswick
W/NG	M/C solo 350cc OHV	5167181-5170430	S1049	14	XG37281-40530	BH27501-30750	3,250 (+162?)	30/09/42 DM 02/04/43 to 15/11/43 DL May 1943 PL 05/02/44 CD		Chilwell

Maker's Type	Military Class	WD Serial No. Allocation	Contract Number	CAT. REF.	Frame Number	Engine Number	Qty Prod'd	Dates	Price(s)	Delivery Destination & Notes
W/NG	M/C solo 350cc OHV	5360771-5363020	S2601	15	XG42001-44250	BH32001-34250	2,250	03/03/43 DM September 1943 to February 1944 DL March 1943 PL 30/07/43 CD		Chilwell. Original quantity was set for 4,500 but reduced to 2,250
W/NG	M/C solo 350cc OHV	5490401-5494400	S4554	16	XG47251-51250	BH35001-39000	4,000	20/09/43 DM 31/12/43 to 07/09/44 DL	£62.13s 6d	
W/NG	M/C solo 350cc OHV	5363021-5366020	S5514	17	XG44251-47250	BH42001-45000	3,000	06/01/44 DM September 1944 on for DL November 1944 PL	£62.13s 6d	Possibly 2,957 delivered
W/NG	M/C solo 350cc OHV	6193966-6197465	S6287	18	XG51856-55355	BH45701-49200	3,500*	31/03/44 DM Mid 1945 DL Mar 1945 PL 17/02/45 CD	£65	See Cont. S6197. No tyres fitted. *Reduced to 2,000 in May 1945
W/NG	M/C solo 350cc OHV	RN	S6197		XG57221-57520	BH47801-48100	300	12/06/45 to 21/08/45 DL	£60	See Contract S6287
W/NG	M/C solo 350cc OHV	RN	S1494		XG35441-35480	BH18924-18963	40	20/11/42 CD		
W/NG	M/C solo 350cc OHV		C/S12928				100	26/12/41 DM 28/01/42 CD January 42 to mid 1942 DL	£57.15s	As per C12450. Del. at 25/month. Oil pressure reg. and breather pipe from timing cover eliminated within this contract
W/NG	M/C solo 350cc OHV	RAF	C/S11464		XG27501-28240	BH9561-10788	750	12/08/41 DM 17/01/42 CD	£56.12s 6d	

Maker's Type	Military Class	WD Serial No. Allocation	Contract Number	CAT. REF.	Frame Number	Engine Number	Qty Prod'd	Dates	Price(s)	Delivery Destination & Notes
W/NG	M/C solo 350cc OHV	RAF	C/S12427		XG28750-29050	BH13020-13885	300	10/11/41 DM 20/01/42 CD 31/01/42 CP	£57.15s	As per C/S 11464 Del. at 75/week from January 1942
W/NG	M/C solo 350cc OHV		S788				105?	02/02/42 09/10/42 CD	Total cost £6,383.4s 9d	
W/NG	M/C solo 350cc OHV	RAF	C/S14218		XG35481-37280	BH25201-27000	1,800	09/04/42 DM 26/01/43 CD 15/01/43 to 23/12/43 DL	£61	
W/NG	M/C solo 350cc OHV	RN 17290-17339	S2037		XG41281-41330	BH21101-21150	50	21/01/43 13/04/43 to 16/07/43 DL	£60	Frame and engine nos for contract derived from factory records
W/NG	M/C solo 350cc OHV	RN 20265-20364	S3174		XG41831-41930	BH21151-21250	100	05/05/43	£6,162.4s 5d	Frame and engine nos for contract derived from factory records
W/NG	M/C solo 350cc OHV	RN 26032-26281	S4670		XG51251-51500	N/BH40001-40250	250	09/10/43 09/02/44 CD Jan 44 to Apr 44 DL	£61	
W/NG	M/C solo 350cc OHV		S6151		XG51501-51505	BH30751-30755	5	25/03/44, 19/04/44 CD	£62	
W/NG	M/C solo 350cc OHV	RN 35151-35500	S6520		XG51506-51855	NBH40251-40600	350	16/06/44 CD	£61	
W/NG	M/C solo 350cc OHV	RN 46014-46163, 49312-49411	S8049		XG56928-57015, 57017-57177	NBH40601-40699, 45101-45250	249	31/01/45 CD 12/01/45 to14/05/45 DL	£64.12s	Contract may have been for 250 not 249

Maker's Type	Military Class	WD Serial No. Allocation	Contract Number	CAT. REF.	Frame Number	Engine Number	Qty Prod'd	Dates	Price(s)	Delivery Destination & Notes
W/NG	M/C solo 350cc OHV	RAF	S7011		XG55356-56477	BH40701-41822	1,572*	15/02/45 CD 25/07/44 to 11/05/45 DL		*Reduced to 1,122 in June 1945
W/NG	M/C solo 350cc OHV	RN 54096-54138	S8574		XG57178-57220	NBH45251-45293	43	27/01/45 14/02/45 DL	£64.13s 6d	
W/NG	M/C solo 350cc OHV	RN 58403-58702	S9167		XG57221-57520	NBH47801-48100	300	07/04/45	£64.13s 6d	Preserved against rust and tropicalised
W/NG	M/C solo 350cc OHV	French (See contract C8302)			XG11186-11213, 11217-11230, 11232-11240, 11245, 11248, 11250-11252, 11255, 11257, 11258, 11260, 11264-11265, 11267-11270, 11272, 11276, 11278-11284, 11286-11291, 11293-11295, 11300-11301, 11304, 11306-11308, 11310-11311, 11313, 11315, 11317-11319, 11321-11323, 11327, 11329-11331, 11333-11335, 11337, 11339-11342, 11345, 11347-11349, 11352, 11354, 11356, 11358-11359, 11361-11362, 11365, 11368, 11371, 11377-11379, 11381, 11385-11389, 11391, 11396, 11397, 11402, 11406, 11407, 11412, 11416, 11421, 11424, 11426, 11431, 11435, 11438, 11446, 11451, 11464, 11470, 11500		153			

Maker's Type	Military Class	WD Serial No. Allocation	Contract Number	CAT. REF.	Frame Number	Engine Number	Qty Prod'd	Dates	Price(s)	Delivery Destination & Notes
W/NG	M/C solo 350cc OHV	RAF	?		XG27501-28083, 28085, 28086, 28088-28091, 28093-28095, 28099, 28100, 28102, 28104, 28105, 28107, 28108, 20127, 20129, 20135, 20168, 20181, 20184, 20190, 20192, 20194-20197, 20199, 20200, 20202-20206, 20208-20210, 21212, 21213, 21215, 21216	BH9635, 9637-9644, 9648, 9650-9652, 9655-9657, 9662-9667, 9674, 9677, 9678, 9683, 9684, 9758, 9849, 9896, 9900-9902, 9904-9912, 9914-9916, 9919, 9922-9928, 9930-9944, 9946, 9947, 9952-9956, 9959-9984, 9986-9991, 9993-10004, 10006-10015, 10017-10025, 10028-10032, 10035, 10036, 10039-10042, 10044-10050, 10052-10055, 10057-10060, 10062-10075, 10078, 10080, 10081, 10084-10086, 10088-10098, 10100, 10102-10109, 10111-10116, 10118, 10120, 10121, 10123-10129, 10132-10137, 10139-10146, 10149-10156, 10158-10173, 10175-10181, 10184-10188, 10190-10194, 10196-10199, 10201, 10203-10210, 10213-10221, 10223-10231, 10235-10243, 10246-10254, 10256-10265, 10268-10276, 10278-10285, 10287, 10290-10298, 10301-10310, 10312-10320, 10323-10331, 10334-10340, 10342-10353, 10356-10364,	625	August 1941 DL		Could be contract C/S11464

Maker's Type	Military Class	WD Serial No. Allocation	Contract Number	CAT. REF.	Frame Number	Engine Number	Qty Prod'd	Dates	Price(s)	Delivery Destination & Notes
						10367-10377, 10379-10385, 10388-10396, 10398, 10400-10408, 10411-10418, 10422-10425, 10427-10430, 10433-10441, 10444-10452, 10455-10462, 10466-10474, 10477-10485, 10488-10496, 10499-10518, 10521-10530, 10533-10540, 10543-10551, 10554-10562, 10565-10573, 10576-10584, 10587-10594, 10597-10607, 10610-10618				
W/NG	M/C solo 350cc OHV	RAF	?		XG28110, 28111, 28113-28115, 28118, 28120, 28124, 28125, 28128-28131, 28135-28140, 28142-28146, 28148-28180, 28182-28183, 28185-28188, 28190-28203, 28206-28207, 28209-28212, 28214-28216, 28218-28219, 28221-28223, 28225, 28227-28230, 28233, 28235-28237, 28240, 28243, 28265, 28321-28322	BH10685-10705, 10709-10733, 10736, 10739, 10741-10748, 10752-10760, 10763-10771, 10774-10782, 10785-10788	107 frames 87 engines	September 1941 DL		Some frames with no engines allocated

Maker's Type	Military Class	WD Serial No. Allocation	Contract Number	CAT. REF.	Frame Number	Engine Number	Qty Prod'd	Dates	Price(s)	Delivery Destination & Notes
W/NG	M/C solo 350cc OHV	RN	?		XG29059, 29075-29077, 29079-29088, 29090-29102	BH14220-14246	27	20/02/42 February 1942 DL		
W/NG	M/C solo 350cc OHV	RN	?		XG29103-29105, 29107-29112, 29114-29119, 29121-29125, 29127-29230	BH14666, 14670, 14686-14692, 14695, 14697, 14699	24	March/April 1942 DL		
W/NG	M/C solo 350cc OHV	RN	?		XG35079, 35301-35353, 35355, 35358-35360, 35362, 35363, 35366, 35368, 35369, 35371-35375, 35378, 35380-35383, 35390, 35399	BH18824-18882, 18885, 18886	75	27/08/42 to 19/09/42 DL		Could be contract S788

AVELING BARFORD

Maker's Type	Military Class	WD Serial No. Allocation	Contract Number	CAT. REF.	Frame Number	Engine Number	Qty Prod'd	Dates	Price(s)	Delivery Destination & Notews
Exptl. LW	M/C solo 125cc	3921638	V.7235			AAA 8335	1	24/11/38 DL	£250	Farnborough 2-stroke

BMW

Maker's Type	Military Class	WD Serial No. Allocation	Contract Number	CAT. REF.	Frame Number	Engine Number	Qty Prod'd	Dates	Price(s)	Delivery Destination & Notes
		4339541, 4339542	57/Vehs/7487	M/C solo			2	1940?		

BSA

Maker's Type	Military Class	WD Serial No. Allocation	Contract Number	CAT. REF.	Frame Number	Engine Number	Qty Prod'd	Dates	Price(s)	Delivery Destination & Notes
S 29 De-Luxe	M/C solo 500cc SV	20530–20532	C1933		XH 213, XH ?, XH 221	XS 311, XS ?, XS 312.	3	04/05/29 DM 18/06/29 CD 02/09/29 DL	£42.0s	Farnborough. Civilian registration of one was MT6498
WO Prototype Twin (A14)	M/C solo 500cc OHV V-twin				EX 146	Not stated	1	02/05/32 DL		BSA property, only on loan
WO Twin A14	M/C solo 500cc OHV V-twin	33206–33271, 33277–33416	C4845	1	A14.101–197, 199–223, 225–226, 228–285, A14.288–290, 293, 295–314, 316–317	A14	208*	17/10/32 CD		*Not enough serial numbers. Civilian registration of one was MV5768I
WO Twin B15	M/C solo 500cc OHV V-twin	33579–33654	C5678	2			76	31/08/33		
?	M/C solo		DDS.1317	3			?			
WO Twin B15	M/C solo 500cc OHV V-twin	34055–34232, 34250–34279	C6264	4			208	18/04/34 26/04/34 CD		
WO Twin B15	M/C solo 500cc OHV V-twin	RAF	311916/34 C1(d)		B15–233 to B15–270	B15–185 to B15–222	38			Frame type 'A'

Maker's Type	Military Class	WD Serial No. Allocation	Contract Number	CAT. REF.	Frame Number	Engine Number	Qty Prod'd	Dates	Price(s)	Delivery Destination & Notes
WO Twin E15	M/C solo 500cc OHV V-twin	34561-34660	C6264	5	E15-114, 134, ?, ?	E15-119, 101, ?, ?	100	18/04/34		Civilian registration of one was BMM 431
WO Twin E15	M/C solo 500cc OHV V-twin	34963-34999, 341000-341089	C7090	6	E15-251, 299, 272, 229	E15-251, 299, 272, 229	127	14/01/35 CD 05/04/35 DL		C341013 was control M/C in seven-make trial (E15/251). BMM 642. Pillion seating fitted
WO Twin E15	M/C solo 500cc OHV V-twin	35586-35765, 35803-35828, 351837-351932, 352140-352187	C7487	7			350	05/06/35		
WO Twin E15	M/C solo 500cc OHV V-twin		7876				96	18/10/35 DM		As contract C7487
WO Twin E15	M/C solo 500cc OHV V-twin		8518				48	26/11/35 DM		As contract C7487
WO Twin E15	M/C solo 500cc OHV V-twin	RAF	412315/35 C2(b)		E15-521 to E15-559	E15-521 to E15-559	39			Frame type 'B'
WO Twin E15	M/C solo 500cc OHV V-twin	RAF	41235/35 C10(b)		E15-586 to E15-604	E15-586 to E15-604	19			Frame type 'B'
WO Twin E15	M/C solo 500cc OHV V-twin	RAF	559903/36 C10(b)		H15-101 to H15-130	H15-106 to H15-135	30			Frame type 'C'
WO Twin E15	M/C solo 500cc OHV V-twin	RAF	632331/37 C12		H15-150 to H15-319	H15-150 to H15-319	170			Frame type 'D'

Maker's Type	Military Class	WD Serial No. Allocation	Contract Number	CAT. REF.	Frame Number	Engine Number	Qty Prod'd	Dates	Price(s)	Delivery Destination & Notes
WO Twin lightened	M/C solo 500cc OHV	33969	Dds/1317		B15-J15X	B15-113	1	11/04/34 DL		Civilian registration was AMP 366
W.35-6	M/C solo 500cc SV	35796	C7641	8	D6-224 and E6-877	D6-684 and E6-966	1	29/05/35 DL		Dunstable. Civilian registration was CMM 798
M20 prototype	M/C solo 500cc SV	363543	C9131	9	EX 197	EX 197	1	31/07/36 DM 28/08/36 CD 02/06/36 DL	£42.5s	Farnborough. Civilian registration was EMV 196
M20 prototype	M/C solo 500cc SV	371l350-371l352	C991	12	EX 232, EX 233, EX 234	EX 232, EX 233, EX 234	3	13/11/37 DM 15/12/37 CD 19/10/37 DL	£47	Farnborough. Civilian registration were HMP 803, HMP 804 and HMP 805
M20	M/C solo 500cc SV	389144-389441 391733-391832	A9764	14	KM20-301 to 598	KM20-301 to 598	298	19/07/38 DM 10/10/38 CD 06/12/38 DL	£42	398 serial numbers
M20	M/C solo 500cc SV	398052-398434	C3139	16	KM20	KM20	383	24/02/39 CD	£42.5s 9d	
M20 De-Luxe	M/C solo 500cc SV	398435-398733, 3914359-3915660	C3655	18	KM20-3001 to KM20-4602	KM20-2001 to KM20-3602	1,602	24/07/39 DM 15/08/39 CD		
M20	M/C solo 500cc SV		?		KM20-4603 to 4662, 4676, 4678, 4692, 4695, 4700, 4705, 4709, 4938, 4941, 4958, 4976, 4985, 4986, 4987, 4998, 5000, 5005, 5008-5010, 5012,	KM20-156, 162, 187, 188, 195, 711, 980, 1022, 1024, 1818, 1819, 1824, 1846, 1889, 1891, 1897, 1900, 1902, 1909, 1911-14, 1917, 1921-29, 1931-3, 1935, 1936, 1939, 1941-49, 1950-57, 1959-1961,	117	September 1939 DL		

Maker's Type	Military Class	WD Serial No. Allocation	Contract Number	CAT. REF.	Frame Number	Engine Number	Qty Prod'd	Dates	Price(s)	Delivery Destination & Notes
M20	M/C solo 500cc SV				5018-5022, 5024, 5025-5027, 5030-5032, 5672-5674, 5677, 5679, 5680, 5682-5684, 5687, 5693, 5694, 5698, 5699, 5701, 5703, 5708, 5710, 5711, 5720, 5730-5732, 5734	1963, 1965, 1967-70, 1972-75, 4676, 4692, 4695, 4700, 4705, 4709, 4958, 4986, 4987, 5003, 5005, 5008, 5009, 5010, 5012, 5018-5022, 5024, 5025, 5030-5032, 5672-5674, 5677, 5679, 5680, 5682, 5683, 5684, 5687, 5693, 5694, 5698, 5699, 5701, 5703, 5707, 5708, 5710, 5711, 5720, 5730-5732, 5734				
M20	M/C solo 500cc SV		?		KM20-5712, 5728, 5729	KM20-121, 120, 122	3	November 1939 DL		
?	M/C solo 500cc SV				EX 315	WM20-499	1	27/12/40 DL		Lightened M20?
M20	M/C solo 500cc SV		?		WM20-111 to 122, 124, 125A, 125B, 126-32, 134-84, 186-94, 195A, 195B, 196-99, 201-19, 220A, 220B, 221-52, 420, 501-06, 508, 511, 513-15, 517, 520-23, 527, 528, 530, 534, 535, 541, 542, 544, 545, 550, 556, 559, 562, 570, 572, 573, 575-78, 580, 585, 587-592, 596, 733, 1501-60, 1562-66, 1568-64, 1574-29, 1631-53, 1655-64, 1666-71, 1673-75, 1677-80, 1682, 1684-1714	WM20-244 to 249, 251, 252, 420, 501-06, 508, 511, 513-15, 517, 520-23, 527, 528, 530, 534, 535, 541, 542, 544, 545, 550, 556, 559, 562, 570, 572, 573, 575-78, 580, 585, 587-92, 596, 841, 868, 1501-60, 1562-66, 1568-72, 1574-1629, 1631-53, 1655-64, 1666-75, 1677-80, 1682, 1684-1714, 1716-18, 1720, 1722-60, 1762-69, 1771, 1773-1805, 1807-14, 1816-17, 1822, 1825, 1826, 1828-32, 1835-40, 1842-43, 1845, 1847, 1848, 1850-56, 1858-67, 1869, 1872,	474	September 1939 DL		

Maker's Type	Military Class	WD Serial No. Allocation	Contract Number	CAT. REF.	Frame Number	Engine Number	Qty Prod'd	Dates	Price(s)	Delivery Destination & Notes
M20	M/C solo 500cc SV	4191743-4191748, 4191761-4191801	C7370	26	1716-18, 1720, 1722-60, 1762-69, 1771, 1773-82, 1784-92, 1794, 1795, 1797-1800, 4501, 4619, 4689, 4846, 4899	1873-88, 1890, 1892-96, 1898-1899, 1901, 1904-08, 1910, 1913, 1915, 1916, 1918-20, 1930, 1932, 1934, 1940, 1944, 1955, 1963, 1964, 1966, 4501, 4619, 5689. Repeated nos 1776, 1778, 1779, 1781, 1782, 1784-92, 1794, 1795, 1797-1800, 1813, 1814, 1837, 1840, 1851, 1866, 1869, 1871, 1876, and 1791 yet again!	147	28/08/40 DM 14/09/40 CD	£49.9s 9d	Colchester or Catterick. *Only 47 serial numbers. 145 were demanded
M20	M/C solo 500cc SV		?		WM20-256	WM20-256	1	03/11/39 DL		
M20	M/C solo 500cc SV		?		WM20-4251	WM20-533	1	31/03/41 DL		
M20	M/C solo 500cc SV		?		WM20-255, 239, 2232, 2241, 2264, 2275, 2276, 2280, 2283, 2284, 2289, 2296, 2297, 2299, 2300, 2309, 2312, 2371, 2372, 2373, 2378, 2380, 2795, 2863, 2864, 2868, 2873, 2875, 2876, 2879, 2881, 2887, 2889, 2892, 2898, 2900, 2902, 2908,	WM20-255, 348-359, 361, 362, 364, 366-68, 370, 371, 374-76, 378-81, 384, 385, 387, 388, 390, 391, 394-97, 2232, 2241, 2267, 2275, 2276, 2280, 2283, 2284, 2289, 2296, 2297, 2299, 2300, 2309, 2312, 2371, 2372, 2373, 2378, 2380, 2795, 3904	60	29-30/05/40 01/06/40		

Maker's Type	Military Class	WD Serial No. Allocation	Contract Number	CAT. REF.	Frame Number	Engine Number	Qty Prod'd	Dates	Price(s)	Delivery Destination & Notes
M20	M/C solo 500cc SV				2909, 2911, 2914-17, 2981, 2982, 2987, 2988, 2990, 2993, 2995, 3000, 3074, 3904, 3978, 3982, 3984, 3995, 4001, 4002					
M20	M/C solo 500cc SV		8152/9064		WM20-3101 to 3557	WM20-3101 to 3557	457	20/02/40		To the India Office
M20	M/C solo 500cc SV		?		WM20-4240, 4243-51	WM20-502 to 505, 508-13	10	09/03/41 DL		
M20	M/C solo 500cc SV		?		WM20-4216	WM20-42116	1	20/03/41 DL		
M20	M/C solo 500cc SV		?		WM20-4222	WM20-42121	1	20/03/40 DL		
M20	M/C solo 500cc SV		?		WM20-4253	WM20-630	1	06/02/41 DL		
M20	M/C solo 500cc SV	RN	?		WM20-4050 to 4061	WM20-4050 to 4061	11	26/05/40 DL		Bath
M20	M/C solo 500cc SV	RN	?		WM20-4161, 4163-4165, 4167, 4173	WM20-473 to 476, 479, 483	6	20/09/40 and 14/10/40 DL		Bath
M20	M/C solo 500cc SV	3928419-3931195, 3934710-3935709, 4105401-4107400, 4123773-4125995, 4137042-4137141	C5110	20	WM20-5001 to 7099, WM20-7201 to ?	WM20-5001 to 7099, WM20-7201 to ?	8,100?	27/09/39 DM 04/02/40 CD 21/08/40 CP		Chilwell at 600 per week from 16/09/39 De-Luxe models

Maker's Type	Military Class	WD Serial No. Allocation	Contract Number	CAT. REF.	Frame Number	Engine Number	Qty Prod'd	Dates	Price(s)	Delivery Destination & Notes
M20	M/C solo 500cc SV	4140434-4144433	C5610	21	WM20-14001 to 18000	WM20-14001 to 18000	4,000	21/11/39 DM 19/01/40 CD 04/06/40 CP	£44.4s 6d	Chilwell at 450/500 per week from 10/02/40
M20	M/C solo 500cc SV	4170215-4173214	C6126	22	WM20-18001 to 21000	WM20-18001 to 21000	3,000	25/01/40 DM 14/06/40 CD	£48.5s	Chilwell at 1,500 per month after C5610
M20	M/C solo 500cc SV	4196513-4199999, 4300000-4300512	C6654	23	WM20-21001 to 25000	WM20-21001 to 25000	4,000	21/03/40 DM 17/07/40 CD 04/08/40 CP 1940 PL	£49.10s	Chilwell after C6126
M20	M/C solo 500cc SV	4341593-4358592	C7287	24	WM20-25001 to 42000	WM20-25001 to 42000	17,000	25/05/40 DM 30/11/40 CD 28/08/41 CP	£49.15s	Chilwell at 2,000 per month after C6654. 1,375 sent to Australia
M20	M/C solo 500cc SV	RAF	C9893				115	17/02/41 DM 29/08/41 CD	£49.12s	Hartlebury at 40 per week
M20	M/C solo 500cc SV	RAF	C9892		WM20-42116 to 42121, 42201-44106	WM20-42116 to 42121, 42201-44106	1,912	17/02/41 DM 03/01/42 CD	£51.9s 6d	Hartlebury. Fitted with sidecar lugs
M20	M/C solo 500cc SV		C10021				2	04/03/41 DM 02/05/41 CD	c. £50	
M20	M/C solo 500cc SV		C10119				100	18/03/41 DM 20/10/41 CD	£57.11s 6d	Similar to C9310
M20	M/C solo 500cc SV		C11440				10	09/08/41 DM 02/12/41 CD	£56.5s	Crated for colonies
M20	M/C solo 500cc SV	4553722-4562721	C9310	30	WM20-44213 to 53212	WM20-44213 to 53212	9,000	03/12/40 DM 30/12/40 CD 21/01/42 DL	£56.5s	Chilwell. Bag racks fitted. 1,175 sent to Australia
M20	M/C comb. 500cc SV	RAF	C10655		WM20-53213 to 53412	WM20-53213 to 53412	200	10/05/41 DM 30/12/43 ?/01/44 DL	£85.19s 7d	No panniers

Maker's Type	Military Class	WD Serial No. Allocation	Contract Number	CAT. REF.	Frame Number	Engine Number	Qty Prod'd	Dates	Price(s)	Delivery Destination & Notes
M20	M/C solo 500cc SV	4635001-4640000, 4662156-4667155	C11101	31	WM20-53413 to 61412, 61448 to 63447	WM20-53413 to 61412, 61448 to 63447	10,000	05/07/41 DM ?/?/42 DL	£64.12s	Order originally for 350cc OHV
M20	M/C comb. 500cc SV		C12586				35	24/11/41 DM, 06/01/44	£85.19s 7d	
M20	M/C solo 500cc SV	4699545-4707544	C12424	32	WM20-63448 to 71447	WM20-63448 to 71447	8,000	10/11/41 DM	£64.12s	Order originally for 350cc OHV
M20	M/C solo 500cc SV		C13048				1	06/01/42 DM 24/01/42 CD	£61.3s 6d	
M20	M/C solo 500cc SV		C13213				2	21/01/42 DM 18/02/42	£63	
M20	M/C solo 500cc SV	4752401-4757400, 4860801-4865800	C13290	33	WM20-71818 to 81817	WM20-71818 to 81817	10,000	26/01/42 DM	£64.12s	
M20	M/C comb. 500cc SV		C13322				50	29/01/42 DM 16/02/44	£96.4s	
M20	M/C solo 500cc SV		C13441				2	06/02/42 DM 24/02/42 CD	£63.0s	
M20	M/C comb. 500cc SV		C13873				35	14/03/42 DM 31/12/43	£87.3s 7d	
M20	M/C comb. 500cc SV		C13909				25	18/03/42 DM 30/12/43	£87.3s 7d	
M20	M/C comb. 500cc SV	RAF	C14052		WM20-71509 to 71817	WM20-71509 to 71817	309	31/12/43, 01/44 DL	£86.17s 7d	To India? No panniers
M20	M/C solo 500cc SV		C14330				2	26/05/42 CD	£58.10s	No pillion equipment

Maker's Type	Military Class	WD Serial No. Allocation	Contract Number	CAT. REF.	Frame Number	Engine Number	Qty Prod'd	Dates	Price(s)	Delivery Destination & Notes
M20	M/C solo 500cc SV		S38				2	05/06/42 DM 24/09/42	£63	
M20	M/C solo 500cc SV		S364				4	10/07/42 DM	£63	
M20	M/C comb. 500cc SV		S649				1?	02/10/42	£93.12s	
M20	M/C solo 500cc SV	5115218-5130217	S1048	34	WM20-81818 to 96817	WM20-81818 to 96817	15,000	24/09/42 DM? 03/11/43	£62.15s	
M20	M/C solo 500cc SV	5207518-5215517	S2603	35	WM20-96818 to 104817	WM20-96818 to 104817	8,000	03/03/43, 01/07/44	£63.10s 6d	
M20	M/C solo 500cc SV	5545518-5557517	S5209	36	WM20-104818 to 116817	WM20-104818 to 116817	12,000	02/12/43, 28/07/45	£64.10s	
M20	M/C solo 500cc SV		S5773				5	26/05/44	£63.10s 6d	
M20	M/C solo 500cc SV		S6003				1	31/05/44	£63.10s 6d	
M20	M/C solo 500cc SV		S6050				1	31/05/44	£63.10s 6d	
M20	M/C solo 500cc SV		S6061				5	31/05/44	£63.10s 6d	
M20	M/C comb. 500cc SV		S6506				1	16/06/44	£63.10s	
M20	M/C comb. 500cc SV		S6507				4	16/06/44	£63.10s 6d	
M20	M/C solo 500cc SV	5885918-5895917	S7218	37	WM20-116818-126817	WM20-116818-126817	10,000*	10/08/44, 19/01/46	£69.2s 3d	*Reduced to 5,870
M20	M/C solo 500cc SV		S9330				14	12/12/45	£69.2s 3d	

Maker's Type	Military Class	WD Serial No. Allocation	Contract Number	CAT. REF.	Frame Number	Engine Number	Qty Prod'd	Dates	Price(s)	Delivery Destination & Notes
M20	M/C solo 500cc SV		S10277				3	05/08/47	£79.14s	
B20	M/C solo 250cc SV	377600–377629	C174	10	HB20-4086, 4088-4090, 4092, 4093, 4098-4100	HB20-2009 to 2017	30*	04/05/37 DM 15/06/37 CD 20/07/37 CP 07/07/37 delivery	c. £30	Chilwell at 20 per week. *Only 9 machines listed in BSA ledgers.
B20	M/C solo 250cc SV	383859–383982	C912	11	JB20-3101 to 3224	JB20-901 to 1024	124	14/10/37 DM 06/12/37 CD 05/02/38 CP	£31	Chilwell at 20 per week
C10	M/C solo 250cc SV	399327–399926	C3739	17	KC10-3015 to 3600	1415-2000	585*	03/05/39 DM 10/06/39 CD	£29.5s	Chilwell at 125 per week. De-Luxe model. *600 serials issued
C10	M/C solo 250cc SV	3922946–3924295	C4452	19	WC10-101 to 1451	WC10-101 to 1451	1,350	15/08/39 1940 DL		Chilwell
C10	M/C solo 250cc SV	RN	?		WC10-3804 to 3807	WC10-3804 to 3807	4	02/04/40 DL		Deptford
?	M/C solo 250cc		C11135				3		£34.7s 6d	Bromsgrove. Civilian model
C11	M/C solo 250cc OHV	India Office	Y8142/9064		WC11-4001 to 4531	WC11-4001 to 4531	530	09/07/41 DM 26/08/41 CD 20/02/40		India
C12	M/C solo 350cc SV	RN			C12-3848 to 3852, 3854-3864, 3615, 3862, 3625, 3849, 3634, 3860, 3863, 3616, 3851, 3631, 3667, 3858, 3618, 3628, 3647, 3661, 3637, 3852, 3657, 3620, 3655, 3621, 3861, 3658, 3626, 3856, 3854, 3848, 3857, 3642, 3850, 3859, 3627, 3855	C12-401 to 413, 416 to 436, 439	35	September 1940 DL		Bath

Maker's Type	Military Class	WD Serial No. Allocation	Contract Number	CAT. REF.	Frame Number	Engine Number	Qty Prod'd	Dates	Price(s)	Delivery Destination & Notes
WB30 prototype	M/C solo 350cc OHV	4369675	C6623		EX 290	EX 291	1	30/03/40 DM 12/06/40 CD 25/01/40 DL	£50?	Farnborough. 288lb. Tyres were 300-21 front, 325-19 rear
WB30 pre-production	M/C solo 350cc OHV		C7975		EX 309	EX 309	1	13/07/40 CD 16/07/40 DL	£50.3s 6d	313lb, 315-19 tyres
WB30 + BSA - Matchless	M/C solo 350cc OHV	4379578-4379627 (less 4379619) 4379619	C8330	28	WB30-101 to 139, 101A, 140, 141, 143-150. Also as part of this contract frame EX 289 fitted with AMC engine 23297	WB30-503, 505-511, 513-521, 523-527, 529-533, 535-539, 541-555, 557-560	50 + 1	09/08/40 DM 02/01/42 CD 18/12/40 DL onwards	£57.16s 7d	As contract C7975. Chilwell - 25, Canada - 2, Feltham - 19, USA - 3, and 1 to AMC
WB30	M/C solo 350cc OHV	GPO	C13683		WB30-501 to 600	WB30-501 to 600	100*	27/02/42 DM		*Possibly not delivered if BSA ledgers correct
WB30	M/C solo 350cc	RN	C/S13872		WB30-601 to 700	WB30-601 to 700	100	14/03/42 DM		
WB29	M/C solo 350cc OHV	4191834-4191854, 4191866	C7370	27			167*	28/08/40 DM 14/09/40 CD	£42.8s 3d	Colchester or Catterick. *Only 22 serial numbers, but 170 originally demanded
M24	M/C solo 500cc OHV	387078-387080	C2007	13	385, 398, 404	JM24-344, 369, and 365	3*	04/07/38 DM 30/07/38 CD 19/08/38 DL	£64	Civilian regs EOF 200, 201 and 202. *Another three also purchased by MEE Frames 362, 367, 386. Engines 345, 347, 358. Civilian regs EOG 20, 21 and 22
M24	M/C solo 500cc OHV		?		5003, 5004, 5006, 5014-5016, 5029, 5228	KM24-425-427, 429, 432, 435, 437, 439	8	September 1939 DL		

Maker's Type	Military Class	WD Serial No. Allocation	Contract Number	CAT. REF.	Frame Number	Engine Number	Qty Prod'd	Dates	Price(s)	Delivery Destination & Notes
M22	M/C solo 500cc OHV		?		4694, 4706, 4764, 4796, 4829, 4831	KM22-109, 119, 137, 172, 177, 181	6	September 1939 DL		
M21	M/C solo 600cc SV	4191485-4191553, 4191584-4191627, 4191959-4192302	C7370	25	WM20-1440, 1457, 1494, 1819, 1822, 1827, 1845, 1871, 1880, 1939, 1941, 1945, 1957, 2354, 2360, 2367, 2368, 2382, 2383, 2387, 2395-97, 2403, 2405, 2408, 2412, 2413, 2415, 2417, 2419, 2420, 2422-29, 2431-33, 2439, 2440, 2443, 2444, 2446-50, 2452, 2454, 2456, 2458-63, 2465, 2466, 2469-80, 2483-2500, 2721, 2722, 2768, 2771, 2781, 2782, 2784-93, 2796-2800, 2825-32, 2834-41, 2843, 2844, 2846, 2848-52, 2854-61, 2865, 2867, 2869-72, 2877, 2878, 2882, 2886, 2888, 2893-95, 2897, 2904, 2905, 2912, 2918-20, 2923-31, 2934, 2936-67, 2969, 2970, 2972-75, 2978-80, 2983, 2986, 2989, 2991, 2992, 2994, 2996, 3862, 3975, 3976, 3985, 3986, 3989, 3997, 3998	WM21-354, 356, 357, 360, 362-71, 373, 374, 376, 378, 379, 381-85, 393, 395, 402, 1440, 1457, 1494, 1819, 1822, 1827, 1845, 1871, 1880, 1939, 1941, 1945, 1957, 2354, 2360, 2367, 2368, 2382, 2383, 2387, 2395-97, 2403, 2405, 2408, 2412, 2413, 2415, 2417, 2419, 2420, 2422-2429, 2431-33, 2439, 2440, 2443, 2444, 2446-2450, 2452, 2454, 2456, 2458-63, 2465, 2466, 2469-80, 2483-2500, 2721, 2722, 2771, 2781, 2782, 2784-93, 2796-2800, 2825-30, 2832, 2834-41, 2843, 2844, 2846, 2848-50, 2852, 2854-57, 2859-61, 2869, 2870, 2882, 2893, 2897, 2904, 2918-20, 2923-31, 2934, 2936-67, 2969, 2970, 2972-80, 2982, 2994	212*	28/08/40 DM 14/09/40 CD 28/29/30 May DL	£48.4s 3d	Colchester or Catterick. *211 demanded, 457 serial numbers, 233 frames and engines
M21	M/C solo 600cc SV		?		4929	1382	1	04/10/39 DL		
M21	M/C solo 600cc SV				WM20-2732	WM21-288	1	23/12/40 DL		

Maker's Type	Military Class	WD Serial No. Allocation	Contract Number	CAT. REF.	Frame Number	Engine Number	Qty Prod'd	Dates	Price(s)	Delivery Destination & Notes
M21 SWD prototype	M/C comb. 600cc SV		?		EX 311	EX 311	1	11/07/40 DL		Experimental frame and engine
Prototype parallel twin	M/C solo 500cc SV		?				1?			
M20	M/C comb. 500cc SV	RAF					?			
M23	M/C solo 500cc OHV		?		KM20-4681, 4696, 4698, 4711, 4713, 4714, 4720, 4730, 4740, 4741, 4775, 4921, 4934, 4971, 5002, 5007, 5011, 5017, 5023	KM23-941, 970, 976, 977, 985, 994, 995, 998, 1004, 1005, 1009, 1013, 1015, 1017, 1019, 1021, 1023, 1025, 1027	19	September 1939		
B23	M/C solo 348cc SV				111	HB23-101		21/09/36 DL		Returned same day
B-2 or B-18 or B-3	M/C solo 249cc OHV				103	104		21/09/36 DL		Returned same day
B26	M/C solo 348cc OHV				HB24-104	HB26-106		21/09/36 DL		Returned same day
M22	M/C solo 496cc OHV				HM19-833	HM22-309		21/09/36 DL		

DOUGLAS

Maker's Type	Military Class	WD Serial No. Allocation	Contract Number	CAT. REF.	Frame Number	Engine Number	Qty Prod'd	Dates	Price(s)	Delivery Destination & Notes
L29	M/C solo 350cc SV Flat twin		C.1933	1			150	04/05/29 DM 18/06/29 CD	c. £40	

Maker's Type	Military Class	WD Serial No. Allocation	Contract Number	CAT. REF.	Frame Number	Engine Number	Qty Prod'd	Dates	Price(s)	Delivery Destination & Notes
L29/2	M/C solo 350cc SV Flat twin	20518, 20430	C.2922	2	WF 1925, 1838, ?	EN 1703, ?	27	20/07/29 DL		Civilian registration of one was MT 6461
L29/2	M/C solo 350cc SV Flat twin	21125, 21107, 21097, 21158	C.3644	3	WF 2014, 1697, 1347, 1663, ?	EN 2508, 2502, 2491, 2559, ?	70	07/04/31 DM 05/06/31 CD 10/04/31 DL	£41.7s	Farnborough. Civilian registration of one was MG 9719
L29/3	M/C solo 350cc SV Flat twin	21697, 21714, 21758, 21757, 21752, 21753, 21755, 21754, 21709, 21759	C.4259	4	FA 963, 1309, 1530, 1451, 1038, 1446, 1344, 1480, ?	EN 2331, 2320, 2332, 2203, 2212, 2330, 2171, 2222, ?	30?	15/09/31 DL		Civilian registration of one was HX 6383 HX6436 was C21759
L29/4	M/C solo 350cc SV Flat twin	22410, 22420	C.4443	5	2148 WF, ?	2820, ?	30?	1933		Civilian registration of one was MV 5267
5Y2 Blue Chief	M/C solo 500cc SV Flat twin					5/H/103	1	22/11/34 DL		Douglas property 3-speed. Civilian registration was DC 5187
5Y2 Blue Chief	M/C solo 500cc SV Flat twin					5.B/2	1	22/11/34 DL		Douglas property 4-speed
5Y2 Blue Chief	M/C solo 500cc SV Flat twin	341192	C.7122	6	FZ 135 then FZ 256	5/H/148	1	25/01/35 CD 22/11/34 DL		Civilian registration was BMM 395
A31	M/C solo 348cc SV Flat twin				FC 1141	EV 1202	1	1931 09/04/31 DL		
DV60 proto	M/C solo 600cc SV Flat twin						2	1944/45		Farnborough
Experimental	M/C solo				FH 119	35/C.101	1	04/01/32 DL		

EXCELSIOR

Maker's Type	Military Class	WD Serial No. Allocation	Contract Number	CAT. REF.	Frame Number	Engine Number	Qty Prod'd	Dates	Price(s)	Delivery Destination & Notes
Army prototype	M/C solo 98cc, 2-stroke						1			
Prototype Welbike	M/C solo 98cc, 2-stroke		?				6?	1942		
Mk.1 Welbike	M/C solo 98cc, 2-stroke	4658474-4659673	S.789	1	14-1186	XXE- ? to ?	1,183*	26/08/42 CD 15/10/42 CP	£26.18s 0d	*1,200 serial numbers issued, 24 machines/day
Mk.2 Welbike	M/C solo 98cc, 2-stroke	5152014-5153413	S.1649	2	1214-2613	XXE- ? to ?	1,400	19/11/42 CD 15/03/43 CP	£26.18s 0d	Delivery at 400/month from February 1943. 302 to be boxed for export by 6/5/43.
Mk.2 Welbike	M/C solo 98cc, 2-stroke	5153414-5154654	S.1946	3	2614-3954	XXE- ? to ?	1,340*	27/12/42 CD	£26.18s 0d	*Reduced later by 100. Delivery at 400/month from May 1943
Mk.2 Welbike Series 2	M/C solo 98cc, 2-stroke	5367454-5368694	S.3662	4	3955-5195	XXE- ? to ?	7778*	21/06/43 CD		*Amended to 1,241, later cancelled entirely in October 1943
Universal	M/C solo 125cc, 2-stroke		S.545	-			1?		£31.3s 7d	

FRANCIS BARNETT

Maker's Type	Military Class	WD Serial No. Allocation	Contract Number	CAT. REF.	Frame Number	Engine Number	Qty Prod'd	Dates	Price(s)	Delivery Destination & Notes
Exptl Military LW (Model 9)	M/C solo 172cc 2-stroke	19257			16211	TL 1391	1	15/06/28 DL		Farnborough. Civilian reg. was MP 8175
Model 12 (Modified)	M/C solo 350cc 2-stroke	20407			E1644	CZA 2959	3	04/05/29 DM 18/06/29 CD 02/09/29 DL	£38.15s	Farnborough
Plover	M/C solo 150cc 2-stroke		C12029				25	02/10/41 DM 01/11/41 CD	£33.5s 5d	

GILLET-HERSTAL

Maker's Type	Military Class	WD Serial No. Allocation	Contract Number	CAT. REF.	Frame Number	Engine Number	Qty Prod'd	Dates	Price(s)	Delivery Destination & Notes
	M/C comb. 728cc 2-stroke parallel twin						1	22/05/39 DL		Farnborough Had SWD fitted and reverse gear. Returned 24/05/39

HARLEY-DAVIDSON

Maker's Type	Military Class	WD Serial No. Allocation	Contract Number	CAT. REF.	Frame Number	Engine Number	Qty Prod'd	Dates	Price(s)	Delivery Destination & Notes
WLC	M/C solo 750cc SV V-twin	4782631, 4782632	S/M2164	-	-	42 WLC - - - -	2	1942		Received at the same time as two Indian 640Bs. Another record shows these as Indians

Maker's Type	Military Class	WD Serial No. Allocation	Contract Number	CAT. REF.	Frame Number	Engine Number	Qty Prod'd	Dates	Price(s)	Delivery Destination & Notes
WLC	M/C solo 750cc SV V-twin	RAF 157554, 157684,			-	43 WLC - - - -	?	1942/43 DL		Canadian specification. US Defence Aid supplied 8686 45cu in motorcycles to the British Empire
UA	M/C comb. 1200cc SV V-twin					42 U - - - -	?	1942/43		Fitted with left-hand sidecars. British used
ELC test comb.	M/C comb. 1000cc OHV V-twin				42 LLE.1347	42 ELC.1600	1	29/12/41		Fitted with left-hand sidecar. Ex-Canadian Army
WLC test model	M/C solo 750cc SV V-twin	C.M.D.I.			-	42 WLC.1436	1	25/09/41		Slough
US	M/C comb. 1200cc SV V-twin				42 LLE. - - - -	42 US - - - -	1,597	November 1942		Sent to South Africa via British Supply Council (no. 9259) USA contract LL-NOS-105-A. Fitted with left-hand sidecar

INDIAN

Maker's Type	Military Class	WD Serial No. Allocation	Contract Number	CAT. REF.	Frame Number	Engine Number	Qty Prod'd	Dates	Price(s)	Delivery Destination & Notes
340B	M/C comb. 1204cc SV V-twin	4369589- 4369674, 4370932-	Dds 1624 V4042	1	CAV - - - -	CAV - - - - B	325	29/07/40 12/08/40 DL		Chilwell, test model C4370969 was frame

Maker's Type	Military Class	WD Serial No. Allocation	Contract Number	CAT. REF.	Frame Number	Engine Number	Qty Prod'd	Dates	Price(s)	Delivery Destination & Notes
		4370981, 4372332-4372518, 4448086, 4448087								CAV4510 and engine CAV4510 B 4.00-18 tyres fitted. 150 to Canada
340B	M/C comb. 1204cc SV V-twin	4501466-4501601	S/M2039	2			136*	June 1940 20/02/41 30/02/41 February to April 41 DL		Possibly went to Canada (originally for France) *Total may be 150. Delivery to UK 26/7/43
340B	M/C comb. 1204cc SV	4648240-4648339	S/M2289	3	340-4275 to 4374	CDO-4275 to 4374	100	19/12/41 CD 21/04/42 October 1942 CP 1941 PL		12 to Polish, rest to British. Sidecar chassis nos were FC263010 to FC263109. US contract DA-W-398-QM-47
741B	M/C solo 500cc SV V-twin	4896842-4898825, 4953034-4955033, 5574052-5575051	S/M2404	5	741-?	GDA-101 to 5600** and GDA-5601 to 18705**	10,248*	13/02/42 CD November 1942 DL 21/2/44 20/6/44		UK 4,272, India 1,000, India Admiralty 6, Australia 1,816, West Africa Admiralty 4, Trinidad 6, Poland 67, New Zealand 1,066, Crown Agents British Honduras 2, Crown Agents Mauritius 16, Crown Agents Ceylon 25, West African Air Ministry 80, Middle East Air

Maker's Type	Military Class	WD Serial No. Allocation	Contract Number	CAT. REF.	Frame Number	Engine Number	Qty Prod'd	Dates	Price(s)	Delivery Destination & Notes
										Ministry 868, Belgian Congo 259, Jamaica 5, South Rhodesia 94, South Caribbean 8, UK (MOWT) 50. *Only 4,984 serial nos. **Details from Chilwell parts list. (C489681 relates to frame 741-26458 ??)
741B	M/C solo 500cc SV V-twin	4782691-4784490	S/M2220	6	741-?	See S/M2404	4,900*	01/10/42 19/06/43 CP		UK 1,888, New Zealand 2,500, Australia 500, Poland (Canada) 12. *Only 1,800 serial nos. Also 50 fitted with Norton handlebars. (C4784364-4784412, and C4784448)
741B	M/C solo 500cc SV V-twin	4895721-4896841	S/M2384	7	741-?	See S/M2404	2,624*	13/02/42 CD 23/08/42 26/07/43 CP		UK 1,390, Australia 1162, Admiralty of South Africa 72. *Only 1,121 serial nos. Total also noted as 2324
741B	M/C solo 500cc SV V-twin		S/M2193		741-?	See S/M2404	1,100	26/07/43 CP		Malaya 370, Australia 680, New Zealand 50

Maker's Type	Military Class	WD Serial No. Allocation	Contract Number	CAT. REF.	Frame Number	Engine Number	Qty Prod'd	Dates	Price(s)	Delivery Destination & Notes
640B	M/C solo 750cc SV V-twin	4782629 to 4782632	S/M2164	8	640-4445, 640-4446, ?, ?	FDO-4445, FDO-4446, ?, ?	4	October 1942 5/11/43		UK. USA contract DA-W-398-QM-224. Last two WD serial nos shown as Harley-Davidson by another record
?	M/C comb.		S/M2300				2,182	19/12/41 CD		Cancelled July 1942
344B ?	M/C comb. 1204cc SV	India	S/M6451		344-1001 to ?	CDD-1001 to ?	360*	21/12/44		UK. *Originally was 385. Left-hand sidecar on '344'. USA contract W-19-059-ORD-215

JAMES

Maker's Type	Military Class	WD Serial No. Allocation	Contract Number	CAT. REF.	Frame Number	Engine Number	Qty Prod'd	Dates	Price(s)	Delivery Destination & Notes
ML (prototype)	M/C solo 125cc 2-stroke	5146001	S.1718		11896	20105	1	23/01/43 CD	£39.15s 9d	ML lightweight prototype model. Possibly ended up in East Africa
K17	M/C solo 125cc 2-stroke		S.1549				2	05/02/43 CD	£34	
K15/K16	M/C solo 150cc 2-stroke		S.1698				10	30/04/43 CD	£34.10s	Exact model not known
ML (prototype)	M/C solo 125cc 2-stroke		S.1833				12	11/05/43 CD	£32.10s 6d	Further improved evaluation models

Maker's Type	Military Class	WD Serial No. Allocation	Contract Number	CAT. REF.	Frame Number	Engine Number	Qty Prod'd	Dates	Price(s)	Delivery Destination & Notes
ML	M/C solo 125cc 2-stroke	5146002-5149541	S.1972	1	ML 2-3541	AAA - - - - A -	3,540	03/43 DL November 1943 PL	£31.17s 6d	Delivery commencing March 1943 at 300 per month, May 1943 at 400 per month, after then 500. Some used by Canadians
ML	M/C solo 125cc 2-stroke	5522209-5522308	S.5571	2	ML 5209-5409	AAA - - - - A - ?	200	1943	£32.7s	Delivery of first 100 machines to Army Remainder to the Admiralty (Navy)
ML	M/C solo 125cc 2-stroke	5830501-5831400	S.6603	3	ML 6001-6900	AAA - - - - A - ?	900	1943-44	£32.6s 4d	
ML (prototype)	M/C solo 125cc 2-stroke	5146001	S.1718		11896	20105	1	23/01/43 CD	£39.15s 9d	ML lightweight prototype model. Possibly ended up in East Africa
ML	M/C solo 125cc 2-stroke	5854601-5856100	S.7113	4	ML 7001-8500	AAA - - - - A - ?	1,500	1944	£33.15s	Contract originally for 3,000 machines but cancelled after 1,500 delivered
ML	M/C solo 125cc 2-stroke		S.8236				200	05/02/45 CD	£34.6s 6d	No details known. Possible contract for Admiralty

LEVIS

Maker's Type	Military Class	WD Serial No. Allocation	Contract Number	CAT. REF.	Frame Number	Engine Number	Qty Prod'd	Dates	Price(s)	Delivery Destination & Notes
Model M	M/C solo 250cc 2-stroke		8345				1	03/10/28 DM 13/10/28 CD 23/10/28 DL	£38.10s	Farnborough

Maker's Type	Military Class	WD Serial No. Allocation	Contract Number	CAT. REF.	Frame Number	Engine Number	Qty Prod'd	Dates	Price(s)	Delivery Destination & Notes
Model 6-Port	M/C solo 250cc 2-stroke	19725, ?	8789		20079, ?	24380, ?	2	30/11/28 DM 05/12/28 CD	£38.10s	Farnborough and Feltham (for Egypt). Standard trim with electric lights. Civilian registration MT 9344
Model 6-Port	M/C solo 250cc 2-stroke		1126				10	28/08/29 DM 05/12/29 CD	£37	Feltham
Model 6-Port	M/C solo 250cc 2-stroke		3520				9	12/08/30 DM 02/09/30 CD	£37	Feltham
?	M/C solo 350cc		C10484				2,000	26/04/41 DM		Cancelled on 28/06/41

MATCHLESS

Maker's Type	Military Class	WD Serial No. Allocation	Contract Number	CAT. REF.	Frame Number	Engine Number	Qty Prod'd	Dates	Price(s)	Delivery Destination & Notes
T/4	M/C solo 350cc SV	20351, ?, ?	C1933	1	10397, ?, ?	T/4 4419, ?, ?	3	04/05/29 DM 18/06/29 CD	£42.10s	Civilian registration of one was MT 6345
Silver Arrow	M/C solo 400cc SV V-twin	20974, 20966	P.2.T. 4145	3	1390, 967, ?	1299, 1022, ?	?	1930 20/02/30 DL		Civilian registration of one was MG 9485
Silver Arrow	M/C solo 400cc SV V-twin	21821, 21813	C3644	5	2098, 2103	A1991, 1961	37	07/04/31 DM 05/06/31 CD 11/09/31 DL and into 1932	£49.7s 8d	Farnborough. Civilian registration of one was HX 6501
?	?		P.2.T. 3932	2						
?	?		P.2.T. 4219	4						

Maker's Type	Military Class	WD Serial No. Allocation	Contract Number	CAT. REF.	Frame Number	Engine Number	Qty Prod'd	Dates	Price(s)	Delivery Destination & Notes
G7	M/C solo 246cc SV	363870-364021	C9221	7	1744, ?, ?	37/G7 526, ?	152	17/08/36 DM 26/09/36 CD	£30.1s 4d	Chilwell at 13/16 per week. Civilian registration of one was EMV 635
G80, G90, G5. (All civilian specification)	M/C solo 500cc SV or OHV	4191348-4191353, 4191749-4191750, 4191752-4191755, 4191757-4191759	C7373	8			12 - G80 1 - G90 2 - G5		£50.0s 1d £53.0s 1d £44	Catterick or Stirling
Exptl LW	M/C solo 250cc OHV	4187516	C6674		550	W40/G2M 4237	1	16/04/40 DM 03/06/40 CD 19/03/40 DL	£49.19s	Farnborough
?	M/C solo 350cc	37180, 37181					2			
?	M/C solo		?		D.E.6	4247	1	10/06/40 DL		
Exptl LW	M/C solo 250cc OHV		C8019		578	4249	1	19/07/40 DM 17/08/40 CD 20/06/40 DL	£49.18s 9d	Chilwell
G3	M/C solo 350cc OHV	35795	C7641	6	617	36/G3 630	1	15/08/35 11/09/35 DL	£44.4s	Civilian reg. CMM 749. Evaluation model
G3	M/C solo 350cc OHV	36260-36270	C8968	24			11	02/07/36 DM 19/08/36 CD	£42.17s 9d	Feltham. Fitted with air cleaners
G3	M/C solo 350cc OHV	353512-353555, C8239, 354624-354689	25		1001, 990, ?	36/G3 767, 777, ?	110	22/11/35 DM 31/12/35 CD 30/03/36 CP	£38.18s	Feltham at 10 per week. C353544 had air cleaner. Civilian registration of one was DMF 42

Maker's Type	Military Class	WD Serial No. Allocation	Contract Number	CAT. REF.	Frame Number	Engine Number	Qty Prod'd	Dates	Price(s)	Delivery Destination & Notes
G3	M/C solo 350cc OHV		C422				2	13/07/37 DM 13/08/37 CD 16/10/37 CPs	£45	Feltham
G3	M/C solo 350cc OHV	3811084-3811347	C2073	21	3257-3520	39/G3-2715 to 39/G3-2978	264	30/06/38 DM 26/09/38 CD 25/11/38 CP	£42	Feltham at 50 per week. (Panel in tank) Civilian registration of one was RHX 643
G3	M/C solo 350cc OHV	3916253-3916452	C3360	18			200	27/04/39 CD	£43	Feltham at 50 per week
G3	M/C solo 350cc OHV	39515-39534	C3398	28			20	20/12/38 DM 09/08/39 CD	£45.2s 1d	
G3	M/C solo 350cc OHV	3917752-3918091	C4608	13	502-841	40-G3WO-3516 to 40-G3WO-3855	340	26/07/39 DM 02/10/39 CD		Chilwell at 50 per week. (Panel in tank) as C3360
G3	M/C solo 350cc OHV	65586-65551, 65553-65569, 65571-65583, 65586-67585, 78041, 78058, 78061, 78065, 78068, 78069, 78078	C5247	10	845-4844	40-G3WO-3862 to 40-G3WO-7861	4,000	25/10/39 DM 18/01/40 CD 23/03/40 CP	£49.18s 9d	Feltham at 200 per week from 25/11/39. (Panel in tank)
G3	M/C solo 350cc OHV	65552, 65570, 65584, 65585, 78038-78040, 78042-78057, 78059, 78060, 78062-78064, 78066, 78067, 78070-78077, 78079-80037, 80764-80766	C6094	11	5000-6999	40-G3WO-8226 to 40-G3WO-10225	2,000	25/01/40 DM 24/06/40 CD 15/11/40 CP	£49.18s 4d	Olympia at 180 per week from 01/06/40. (Panel in tank)

Maker's Type	Military Class	WD Serial No. Allocation	Contract Number	CAT. REF.	Frame Number	Engine Number	Qty Prod'd	Dates	Price(s)	Delivery Destination & Notes
G3	M/C solo 350cc OHV	92889-93358, 95889-96828, 934001-938590	C7183	17	7000-12999	40-G3WO-10226 to 40-G3WO-16225	6,000	23/05/40 DM 29/03/41 CD	£49.13s 11d	Ashchurch and Feltham. (Destined for Middle East) 150 per week rising to 450 per week. Deliveries starting from 29/03/41
G3	M/C solo 350cc OHV	4335008-4337785, 938591-938900, 938930-938940	C8078	12	13000-16399	40-G3WO-17226 to 40-G3WO-20325	3,000* *gaps in frame/ engine & serial nos	01/08/40 DM 29/07/41 CD	£49.12s 4d	321 to Slough, rest to Chilwell by April 1941. 256 have panel in tank. C4337785 had BSA WB30 engine fitted (WB30-556)
G3	M/C solo 350cc OHV	938901-938929, 938941-941911	C8934	14	16300-19299	41-G3WO-20000 to 41-G3WO-22999	3,000	15/10/40 DM 26/04/41 CD	£49.12s 11d	Feltham and Slough. Deliveries at 300 per week. 50 fitted with teles
G3	M/C solo 350cc OHV	RAF								
G3	M/C solo 350cc OHV	4191756	C7373	9			1	26/05/40	£46.5s 6d	Catterick or Stirling. Standard specification
G3L proto.	M/C solo 350cc OHV				16100, ?	20326, ?	2	21/11/40 DL	£49.18s 9d	Farnborough. 328lb. Civilian registration EED 869 and GPP 869. Frame from contract C8078
G3L	M/C solo 350cc OHV	4588175-4589424	C9506	15	19400-20649	41-G3L-23800 to 41-G3L-25049	1,250	02/01/41 DM 26/09/41 CD	£52.15s	Chilwell

Maker's Type	Military Class	WD Serial No. Allocation	Contract Number	CAT. REF.	Frame Number	Engine Number	Qty Prod'd	Dates	Price(s)	Delivery Destination & Notes
G3L	M/C solo 350cc OHV	4649425-4651174 less catalogue reference 20 941912-943911 less catalogue reference 20	C9841	16	20650-24399 including catalogue reference 20	41-G3L-25050 to 41-G3L-28799 including catalogue reference 20	3,608*	15/02/41	£52.15s	Chilwell or Liverpool. *3,643 serial numbers. Lucas lighting fitted
G3L	M/C solo 350cc OHV	4649432, 438, 466, 470, 481, 528, 719, 764, 765, 768-70, 772-75, 795, 796, 798, 805, 882, 883, 886, 891, 4650032, 056, 077, 105, 112, 115, 130, 136, 140, 142, 144, 146, 161, 162, 170, 171, 174, 177, 187, 199, 203, 204, 209, 238, 310, 464, 507, 510, 511, 610, 618, 707, 941961, 963, 988, 991-94, 997, 942000, 002-05, 007-10, 013, 015, 018-23, 026-029, 032, 033, 035, 038, 043, 044, 050, 055, 057, 060, 118-20, 254, 256, 257, 260,	C9841	20	See catalogue reference 16	See catalogue reference 16	142	15/02/41		Chilwell or Liverpool. Miller lighting fitted

Maker's Type	Military Class	WD Serial No. Allocation	Contract Number	CAT. REF.	Frame Number	Engine Number	Qty Prod'd	Dates	Price(s)	Delivery Destination & Notes
		261, 263-65, 268, 271, 273, 277, 278, 280, 282-84, 287, 289, 290, 292, 293, 295, 297, 299, 319, 326, 335, 340, 345, 356, 369, 943048, 058, 062, 065, 068, 076, 091, 092, 124, 153, 198, 206								
G3L	M/C solo 350cc OHV		C/S11462				500	12/08/41 DM 17/09/41 CD, 09/41 CP	£52.15s	
G3L	M/C solo 350cc OHV	RAF	C/S12428		25000-25199	41-G3L-40000 to 41-G3L-40199	200	10/11/41 DM 28/01/42 CD	£55.17s	To MUs throughout country at 50 per week starting in January
G3L	M/C solo 350cc OHV	RAF	C/S12800		25200-26011	41-G3LWO-40200 to 41-G3LWO-41011	812	12/12/41 DM	£55.19s	Quedgeley, Milton, Stafford, Hartlebury, Carlisle, and Haywood
G3L	M/C solo 350cc OHV	943912-945110, 155-58, 160, 161, 166-71, 173-76, 180, 182, 183, 185, 191-771, 922-41, 952-66,	C11102	30	26012-29363	41-G3L-41012 to 41-G3L-44363	3,352*	21/07/41	£56.18s 3d	Chilwell and Tewkesbury. Miller lighting fitted. *Only 3,252 serial nos

Maker's Type	Military Class	WD Serial No. Allocation	Contract Number	CAT. REF.	Frame Number	Engine Number	Qty Prod'd	Dates	Price(s)	Delivery Destination & Notes
G3L	M/C solo 350cc OHV	972-91, 946007-946041, 047-66, 072-96, 102-16, 946120-947521								
G3L	M/C solo 350cc OHV	945111-154, 159, 162-65, 172, 177-79, 181, 184, 186-90, 772-921, 942-51, 967-71, 945992-946006, 042-46, 067-71, 097-101, 117-19, 4688899, 4692898, 4777736-4778125	C11102	19	29364-34011	41-G3L-44364 to 41-G3L-49011	4,648	05/07/41 DM 11/04/42 CD	£56.18s	Chilwell and Tewkesbury. Lucas lighting fitted
G3L	M/C solo 350cc OHV	4837001-4842500	C12632	23	34012-39511	41-G3L-49012 to 41-G3L-54511	5,500	26/11/41 DM	£62.13s 10d	Lucas lighting fitted
G3L	M/C solo 350cc OHV	4842501-4844000, 947522-947921	C12633	22	39512-41011	41-G3L-54512 to 41-G3L-56011	1,500	26/11/41 DM	£65.16s	Miller lighting fitted
G3L	M/C solo 350cc OHV	4990101-4997100	C14499	27	41012-48011	41-G3L-56012 to 41-G3L-63011	7,000	01/05/42	£65.17s 10d	Chilwell
G3L	M/C solo 350cc OHV	5255460-5264459	S.1050	29	48060-57059	41-G3L-63060 to 41-G3L-72059	9,000	01/10/42	£60	Army, but some to RAF regiment
G3L	M/C solo 350cc OHV	5477370-5484369	S.2604	31	57070-64069	72070 to 79069	7,000	03/03/43	£67.15s 10d	
G3L	M/C solo 350cc OHV	5800000-5807999	S.4555	32	64070-72069	79070-87069	8,000	20/09/43	£60.15s	Delivery at 1,300 per month

Maker's Type	Military Class	WD Serial No. Allocation	Contract Number	CAT. REF.	Frame Number	Engine Number	Qty Prod'd	Dates	Price(s)	Delivery Destination & Notes
G3L	M/C solo 350cc OHV	6112000-6121999	S.6150	33	73000-79088 (was to 82999)	90000-96088 (was to 99999)	6,089 (was 10,000)	15/03/44		All fitted with air cleaners. Late deliveries had push-button head lamps (no ammeter)
Prototype	M/C solo OHV						1	1944		Rear springing fitted

MOTO-CHENILLE

Maker's Type	Military Class	WD Serial No. Allocation	Contract Number	CAT. REF.	Frame Number	Engine Number	Qty Prod'd	Dates	Price(s)	Delivery Destination & Notes
'Mercier'	M/C solo 350cc OHV		V7223				1	08/06/39 DM 07/06/39 CD 06/06/39 DL	£75	Farnborough, from W.R. Chadborn of Victoria Street, SW1

NEW HUDSON

Maker's Type	Military Class	WD Serial No. Allocation	Contract Number	CAT. REF.	Frame Number	Engine Number	Qty Prod'd	Dates	Price(s)	Delivery Destination & Notes
83 E	M/C solo 350cc SV	20374, ?, ?	C.1933		L.16631, ?, ?	H.T. 313, ?, ?	3	04/05/29 DM 18/06/29 CD 02/08/29 DL	£42	Civilian registration on one was MT 6368

NEW IMPERIAL

Maker's Type	Military Class	WD Serial No. Allocation	Contract Number	CAT. REF.	Frame Number	Engine Number	Qty Prod'd	Dates	Price(s)	Delivery Destination & Notes
Model 40	M/C solo 350cc OHV	35794	C.7641		28230	35976	1	1935 10/09/35 DL	£42	1935 evaluation model. Civilian registration was CMM 748
Model 76	M/C solo 500cc OHV	4191311-343	C.7377	1			33	07/06/40 DM 16/08/40 CD		To Stirling

NORMAN

Maker's Type	Military Class	WD Serial No. Allocation	Contract Number	CAT. REF.	Frame Number	Engine Number	Qty Prod'd	Dates	Price(s)	Delivery Destination & Notes
The Lightw't	M/C solo 125cc 2-stroke		S 1916				161	25/05/43	£32.9s 10d	
The Lightw't	M/C solo 125cc 2-stroke		S 6960				55	10/10/44	£32.9s 10d	

NORTON

Maker's Type	Military Class	WD Serial No. Allocation	Contract Number	CAT. REF.	Frame Number	Engine Number	Qty Prod'd	Dates	Price(s)	Delivery Destination & Notes
16H	M/C solo 500cc SV	Not registered			7868	54410	1	25/10/32 DL		On loan. Returned on 15/11/32

Maker's Type	Military Class	WD Serial No. Allocation	Contract Number	CAT. REF.	Frame Number	Engine Number	Qty Prod'd	Dates	Price(s)	Delivery Destination & Notes
16H	M/C solo 500cc SV	35801	C.7641	1	57283	62012	1	14/8/35 CD 16/09/35 DL	£46.12s 6d*	Model 16H evaluation machine. 'CMM 754' *Plus 12s for electric horn
16H	M/C solo 500cc SV	352836-353146	C.8245	2	61206-64510 (with gaps)	65501-65809	308	13/12/35 DM 21/01/36 or, 02/36 CD Delivered February 1936 at 50/week	£39.18s 2d	To Chilwell at 50 per week. As C.7641 but modified
16H	M/C solo 500cc SV	361206-361514	C.8496	3	63808-64108	67700-68019	309	11/03/36 DM 20/04/36 CD	£41.3s 11d	To Chilwell at 50 per week Similar to C8245, air cleaners
16H	M/C solo 500cc SV				66625	70069	1	04/09/36 DL		Odd machine. Possibly lightened 16H
16H	M/C solo 500cc SV	362679-362897	C.8753	4	64127-64199 66000-66136 66145-66153	69100-69309 70060-70068	219	08/05/36 DM 17/06/36 CD 16/09/36 CP	£41.3s 11d	To Chilwell at 50 per week. Air cleaner fitted. Civilian reg. of one was EMG 221 Similar to C8496
16H	M/C solo 500cc SV	364737-364844	C.9438	5	73301-73406	72200-72307	108	20/10/36 DM 12/11/36 CD 02/01/37 CP	£44.15s 8d	To Chilwell at 30 per week. 72308 and 72309 are spare engines. 30/week from early December 1936

Maker's Type	Military Class	WD Serial No. Allocation	Contract Number	CAT. REF.	Frame Number	Engine Number	Qty Prod'd	Dates	Price(s)	Delivery Destination & Notes
16H	M/C solo 500cc SV	373731-375334, 375336-375354, 375356-375358, 375360-375365, 375367-375369, 375371-375373, 375375-375376, 375380-375385, 375387-375388, 375391, 375395-375397, 375399-375401, 375403, 375406-375407, 375410-375411, 375415, 375417, 375419, 382717-383196, 384330-384409	C.9681	6	75149, 78000 to 79785, 87047, 88498, 91618	72829, 76410 to 76499, 76510 to 76599, 76612 to 78217, 84083, 86144, 83589	1,792*	28/12/36 DM 02/03/37 CD 19/03/38 CP	£44.15s 8d	To Chilwell at 73 per week dropping to 30. *2,223 serial numbers allocated & quantity amendment on 27/08/37
16H lightweight	M/C solo 500cc SV				66154	70869	1	15/10/36		
16H	M/C solo 500cc SV				79063	77557	1	12/10/37 DL		Fitted with twin seat
16H	M/C solo 500cc SV					73400-73535 (less 73521)	135	?/02/37 CD		India Office contract
16H	M/C solo 500cc SV				85480, 85608, 85606, 85604, 85605, 85606*, 85607	82136, 81305, 81301, 81303, 81302, 81300, 81304	7	?/11/37 CD		Delivery to NIZAM(?) – forces. Fittings incl. sand Amal carb; pillion seat; modified Vokes air cleaner & lifting-handle to front guard. *Frame 85606 quoted twice. Probable error

Maker's Type	Military Class	WD Serial No. Allocation	Contract Number	CAT. REF.	Frame Number	Engine Number	Qty Prod'd	Dates	Price(s)	Delivery Destination & Notes
16H	M/C solo 500cc SV		C.1202				200	30/12/37 DM 30/11/38 CD		Spares to Chilwell. Not confirmed if 200 spare machines or part of such to produce complete machines as required by workshops
16H	M/C comb. 500cc SV						1	1937-38		16H combination with SWD. Probable experimental machine
16H	M/C solo 500cc SV	386444-386943	C.1666	8	95000-95499	88000-88499	500	02/04/38 DM 25/05/38 CD 02/11/38 CP	£46.18s 10d	To Chilwell. Delivery due 25-50/week from end of June. Similar to those on C9681
16H	M/C solo 500cc SV	388449-388948, 3810603-3810702	A.9764	10	99000-99499	89250-89749 89800-89899	500*	19/07/38 CD 9/12/38 DL	£46	To Chilwell at 50 per week. *600 serial numbers allocated. Similar to C1666, delivery 25-50/week
16H	M/C solo 500cc SV	395732-396081	C.3139	12	101700-101949 102500-102599	93700-93799 93350-93599	350	24/02/39 CD 27/11/39 DL	£45.11s 6d	To Chilwell. 75/100/week
16H	M/C solo 500cc SV	3910768-3912368	C.3655	13	104700-106300	95100-96700	1,601	20/06/39 DL	£45.4s 6d	Similar to C3139
16H	M/C solo 500cc SV	3932709-3334708, 4101401-4105400	C.5109	15	W 1000-6999	W 1000-6999	6,000	16/03/39 CD 10/10/39 to 6/3/40 DL		

Maker's Type	Military Class	WD Serial No. Allocation	Contract Number	CAT. REF.	Frame Number	Engine Number	Qty Prod'd	Dates	Price(s)	Delivery Destination & Notes
16H	M/C solo 500cc SV	3943989, ?	C.3309				7	22/03/39 DM 24/03/39 CD	£45.11s 6d	Ex-works (?) As contract A9764
16H	M/C solo 500cc SV	4152168-4156167, 4163938-4163939	C.5612	18	W 7000-10999. W 10292 used by Sir (Capt.) Malcolm Campbell of Bluebird fame	W 7000-10999	4,000*	21/11/39 DM 24/04/40 CD 15/11/40 CP	£48.14s 6d	To Chilwell at 300 per week. *4002 serial numbers allocated. Similar to C5109
16H	M/C solo 500cc SV	4191202, 4191204, 4191206, 4191209-4191211, 4191215, 4191221-4191222, 4191226, 4191231, 4191234-39, 4191242-4191263, 4191265, 4191267-69, 4191271, 4191274-75, 4191278-80, 4191282-310	C.7371	23	W11151-W11259	W11151-W11259	78	07/06/40 DM 03/08/40 CD	£48.13s 4d	To Stirling
16H	M/C solo 500cc SV	4191203, 4191205, 4191207-08, 4191212-14, 4191216-20, 4191223-25, 4191227-30, 4191232-33, 4191240-41, 4191264, 4191266, 4191270, 4191272-73, 4191276-77, 4191281	C.7371*	23	See above	See above	31	1940 As above		*LP civilian models embraced under contract C.7371

Maker's Type	Military Class	WD Serial No. Allocation	Contract Number	CAT. REF.	Frame Number	Engine Number	Qty Prod'd	Dates	Price(s)	Delivery Destination & Notes
16H	M/C solo 500cc SV	4192303-4196302	C.6127	19	W 14001-18000	W 14001-18000	4,000	01/02/40 CD 01/02/40 CD 30/5/40 to 14/8/40 DL		Also to Canadian forces. Similar to C5612. (Noted on 31/10/40 as 73 still due)
16H	M/C solo 500cc SV	4316278-4320277	C.6653	25	W 18001-22000	W 18001-22000	4,000	10/04/40 DM 17/07/40 CP	£54.9s 10d	To Chilwell at 300 per week after contract C.6127
16H	M/C solo 500cc SV	4386027-4403026	C.7353	22	W 26001-43000	W 26001-43000	17,000	03/06/40 DM 25/07/40 CD 28/07/40 CP	£54.9s 10d	To Chilwell at 2,000 per week after contract C.6653. Many machines allocated to Egypt (Noted as still in production late 1941). 30 to Dutch forces and renumbered - see overseas allocations
16H	M/C solo 500cc SV	4490148-4492040	C.9062	27	W 43001-44893	W 43001-44893	1,893	30/10/40 DM 22/04/41 CD	£55.5s 11d	
16H	M/C solo 500cc SV	4583129-4588128	C.10217	28	W 45001-50000	W 45001-50000	5,000	26/03/41 DM 03/09/41 CD	£64.17s 2d	Chilwell
16H	M/C solo 500cc SV	4595601-4605600	C.11082	30	W 60001-70000	W 60001-70000	10,000	03/07/41 DM 19/11/41 CD	£65.6s 10d	Contract included 1,000 spare engines/frames & 250 gearboxes. Some used by Canadians

Maker's Type	Military Class	WD Serial No. Allocation	Contract Number	CAT. REF.	Frame Number	Engine Number	Qty Prod'd	Dates	Price(s)	Delivery Destination & Notes
16H	M/C solo 500cc SV	4678658-4684657	C.12426	31	W 70001-76000	W 70001-76000	6,000	10/11/41 DM 28/01/42 CD Del. from 8/42	£65.3s 1d	Contract was initially 250 x 350cc machines. Chilwell at 1,600/ month
16H lightweight	M/C solo 500cc SV	4773811-4773860	C.14274	33		LW100-LW160	50	15/04/42 DM 18/4/42 CD		Lightweight 16H. 25 to RASC, and 25 to RAOC
16H	M/C solo 500cc SV		C.12524			42399, 42418, 42420	3	18/11/41 DM 02/12/41 CD	£65.2s 1d	
16H	M/C solo 500cc SV	4671302, ?	C.12872				39	22/12/41 DM12/01/42 CD	£65.3s 1d	Royal Marines, Hayling
16H	M/C solo 500cc SV		C.13845				35	12/03/42 DM 27/03/42 CD	£61.0s 1d	
16H	M/C solo 500cc SV		C.13908				25	18/03/42 DM 02/04/42 CD	£65.3s 1d	
16H	M/C solo 500cc SV	RAF	C.9891				20	15/02/41 DM 05/06/41 CD	£51.12s 6d	
16H	M/C solo 500cc SV	RAF	S7743				1	05/10/44	£67.8s 5d	
16H	M/C solo 500cc SV		S7927				12	02/12/44	£67.8s 5d	
16H	M/C solo 500cc SV	RN	S9175				200	03/05/45	£69.3s 1d	Tropicalisation extra
16H	M/C solo 500cc SV	RAF			W 22250-22780	W 22250-22780	531			
16H	M/C solo 500cc SV	4188854-4188991					138			India

Maker's Type	Military Class	WD Serial No. Allocation	Contract Number	CAT. REF.	Frame Number	Engine Number	Qty Prod'd	Dates	Price(s)	Delivery Destination & Notes
16H	M/C solo 500cc SV	6191545-6191556	Ex-Min. OWT				12			
16H	M/C comb. 500cc SV	53288-53323	C7371	36	92046	86787	36			Converted from solo
16H			Unknown		W12001-W12045	W12001-W12045	45			Australian forces
16H			Unknown		W12154-W12403	W12154-W12403	250			Australian forces
16H	M/C comb. 500cc SV	RAF	S921				522	10/05/43	£92.2s 3d	
16H	M/C comb. 500cc SV	RAF	S3959		W88765-W88884	W88765-W88884	120	26/08/43	£93	
16H	M/C comb. 500cc SV	RAF	S4460				150	06/11/43	£93.3s 7d	
16H	M/C comb. 500cc SV	RN	S4669				75	07/01/44	£89.17s	
16H	M/C comb. 500cc SV		S2704				30	17/04/44	£88.15s 5d	
16H	M/C comb. 500cc SV	RAF	S2762		W83552-W83764	W83552-W83764	212	19/06/44	£92.2s 3d	
16H	M/C solo 500cc SV				25354	Not stamped	1	04/04/41 DL		Civilian registration was FOJ 890
16H	M/C solo 500cc SV	4183563-4183595	Ex-Can E1081/CD/817				34			
16H	M/C solo 500cc SV	4183675	BM/2783 WS 6 (d)				1			
16H	M/C solo 500cc SV	4184030-4184032	Ex-Can.				3			
16H	M/C solo 500cc SV	4473264-4473297	Ex-Can.				34			

Maker's Type	Military Class	WD Serial No. Allocation	Contract Number	CAT. REF.	Frame Number	Engine Number	Qty Prod'd	Dates	Price(s)	Delivery Destination & Notes
16H	M/C solo 500cc SV	4183951	NC				1			
16H	M/C solo 500cc SV	4858001-4859250	S.150	34	W76001-W77250	W76001-W77250	1,250	14/06/42 DM 19/12/42 CD 1943 DL	£65.12s	Chilwell
16H	M/C solo 500cc SV	4865801-4870800	C.14498	35	W 78001-83000	W 78001-83000	5,000	04/02/42 DM 01/05/42 CD 1943 DL	£66.15s 3d	First 500 fitted with leg shields, delivery at 750/month November 1943. Some issued to Canadian Provost
16H	M/C solo 500cc SV		S.1046				2	13/04/43	£66.16s 11d	
16H	M/C solo 500cc SV	RN	S.3103				150	08/08/43	£66.18s 8d	
16H	M/C solo 500cc SV	RN	S.4723				125	16/11/43	£67.15s 4d	
16H	M/C solo 500cc SV	5266965-5271964	S.2602	37	W83765-W88764	W83765-W88764	5,000	3/3/43 CD Delivered from January 1944	£67.8s 4d	Delivery/collection at 1,600/month
16H	M/C solo 500cc SV	4958019	S.2942				1	21/05/43	£66.16s 11d	To OC troops to Expl Station Porton Down, Wiltshire (Chemical Warfare Exptl. Station)
16H	M/C solo 500cc SV	5484401-5490400	S.5161	38	W 90001-96000	W 90001-96000	6,000*	27/11/43 Del from August 1944	£67.8s 4d	*Quantity reduced to 4,600. 1,200/month

Maker's Type	Military Class	WD Serial No. Allocation	Contract Number	CAT. REF.	Frame Number	Engine Number	Qty Prod'd	Dates	Price(s)	Delivery Destination & Notes
16H	M/C solo 500cc SV	RN	S.3103				150	11/08/44	£67.11s	
16H	M/C comb. 500cc SV	RAF	S7010		W96001-W96676	W96001-W96676	675*			*Quantity reduced to 560
16H	M/C comb. 500cc SV		S.7584				2	29/09/44	£67.7s 5d	
16H	M/C comb. 500cc SV		S.8048				200	18/01/45	£69.5s 11d	
16H	M/C comb. 500cc SV		S.8047				50	13/01/45	£97.16s 7d	
16H	M/C comb. 500cc SV		S.7671				1	22/11/45	£95.18s 1d	Passenger sidecar
16H	M/C comb. 500cc SV		S.7671				1	22/11/45	£90.6s 8d	Box sidecar
?	M/C comb.	4163937	A/248/16				1			
Exptl	M/C comb. 1096cc V-twin				Not marked	LTZ/P67714/S	1	1940, 19/05/41 DL		SWD. JAP engine
50	M/C solo 350cc OHV	387072–387077, 4184317, 4184318	C.2007	9	39285, ?, ?	4305, ?, ?	6	04/07/38 DM 30/07/38 CD 22/06/38 DL	£75	Likely ISDT machines. Same contract number used for BSAs
Exptl	M/C solo 350cc SV		C.6775				2	12/04/40 DM 07/11/40 CD	£231	To Chilwell as part of C.5612. Aluminium substitutes
Exptl LW	M/C solo 346cc SV	3938953	C.3585	14	LW 100	LW 100	1	04/04/39 DM 25/05/39 CD 25/08/39 CP 13/11/39 DL	£300	Farnborough

Maker's Type	Military Class	WD Serial No. Allocation	Contract Number	CAT. REF.	Frame Number	Engine Number	Qty Prod'd	Dates	Price(s)	Delivery Destination & Notes
18	M/C solo 500cc OHV	4381738-4381744 4337786-4337790	C.8461	26			12*	17/08/40 DM 09/11/43 CD	£58.19s 10d	Chilwell. *Possible quantity 7. 12 serial nos allocated (could be 16Hs)
Exptl LW	M/C solo 500cc SV		C.8031		LW 103	LW 103	1	18/07/40 DM 16/09/40 CD 26/06/40 DL	£100	Farnborough
Big 4	M/C comb. 633cc SV	385691-385705	C.1561	7	92872, 93460-93474	86558, 84876-84890	1 on 14 on	29/03/38 DM 30/04/38 CD 13/05/38 DL 21/08/38 DL	£120	Chilwell. C385691 had civilian registration JMF192 C385695 had civilian reg. JMK783 (frame 93464, engine 84880). Amended on 14/7/38 to include air cleaners
Big 4	M/C comb. 633cc SV	399012-399326	C.2925	11	103100-103199, 103700-103914	93000-93314	315	02/12/38 DM 25/01/39 CD 30/05/39 CP	£97.1s 11d*	Chilwell at 25 per week. *Also noted as £94.1s 11d
Big 4	M/C comb. 600cc		C.3309		103915-103919		4	22/03/39 DM 27/01/40 CD	£97.1s 11d	As C2925 with sidecar wheel drive
Big 4	M/C comb. 633cc SV	4112258-4112602	V.3565	16	S 1000-1344	S 1000-1344	345	28/08/39 DM 02/11/39 CD 25/03/40 CP	£97.1s 11d	Chilwell at 15/20 per week
Big 4	M/C comb. 633cc SV	4148480-4148696, 4163994	C.5333	17	S 1345-1561*	S 1345-1561*	218	21/10/39 DM 23/01/40 CD 14/06/40 DL	£98.11s 8d	Chilwell at 50 per week. Similar to contract V3565 AA box body (9ft longer). *Another record shows this as 1562

Maker's Type	Military Class	WD Serial No. Allocation	Contract Number	CAT. REF.	Frame Number	Engine Number	Qty Prod'd	Dates	Price(s)	Delivery Destination & Notes
Big 4	M/C comb. 633cc SV	4185623-4185782	C.6831	20	S 2117-2276	S 2117-2276	160	23/04/40 DM 05/09/40 CD 10/2/41 DL	£96.7s 11d	Chilwell at 25 per week from 16/09/40
Big 4	M/C comb. 633cc SV	4185069-4185622	V.3849	21	S 1563-2116	S 1563-2116	554	22/02/40 DM 29/04/40 CD 13/06/40 CP	£98.9s 11d	Chilwell at 50 per week. C 4185089/S 1582 to SAS at Netheravon. C 4185606/S 2099 sent to AMC. C 4185179/S 1672 to SAS
Big 4	M/C comb. 633cc SV	4384906-4386026 4427053-4427072	C.7576	24	S 2276-3396*, S 3397-416	S 2276-3396*, S 3397-416. S3251-61, S3264, S3267-72, S3283-85, S3287, S3298, S3300-02, S3304, S3305, S3307-09, S3311, S3314, S3315, S3319-22, S3330, S3332, S3333, S3366**	1,141	19/06/40 DM 02/05/41 CD 31/05/41 DL	£99	Chilwell at 25 per week 521 standard bodies, 600 AA type bodies (1121 with AA box body similar to C6831, 20 similar to C3849) 1941 Proprietary Parts List states 496cc. *Not fitted with standard sidecar body **To Australia
Big 4	M/C comb. 633cc SV	RN	C9298		S3417	S3417	1	2/12/40 CD		Box sidecar, but noted as 500cc. (Royal Naval Home Depot)
Big 4	M/C comb. 633cc SV	4591410-4593218	C.11297	29	S3500-5308	S3500-5308	1,809*	28/07/41 DM 25/09/41 CD	£106.3s 0d	Chilwell at 400 per month. *Contract originally for 2,238, but 429 cancelled for RAF. SWD similar to C5333

Maker's Type	Military Class	WD Serial No. Allocation	Contract Number	CAT. REF.	Frame Number	Engine Number	Qty Prod'd	Dates	Price(s)	Delivery Destination & Notes
Big 4	M/C comb. 633cc SV	RAF	S284		S5309-S5737	S5309-S5737	429			Passenger sidecar (originally part of C11297)
Big 4	M/C comb. 633cc SV	4707738-4707949	C.13056	32	S5738-S5949	S5738-S5949	212	07/01/42 DM 11/02/42 CD 01/07/41 CD		Chilwell. Fitted with box sidecar, similar to C7576. (Originally listed as frames/engines S5309-S5521)
Big 4	M/C comb. 633cc SV	RAF	C.9914				10	01/07/41 CD	£72.19s 8d	Hartlebury. No SWD
?	M/C comb. ?		C.10435				1	23/04/41 DM 22/05/41 CD	£73.14s 6d	Chislehurst, fitted box sidecar
Box s'car body and chassis for 16H			C.13158				1	16/01/42 DM 07/02/42 CD		
?	M/C solo + combs		C.9693				1,985*	14/02/39, 07/03/39 CD	£51.12s	*Some with sidecars. 12 with commercial box sidecars at £21.1s 3d and 959 sidecars at £21.7s 8d
?	M/C solo 500cc OHV				100998	91820	1	Mid 1939, 06/07/39 DL		Fitted with exptl spring frame. Civilian registration EOP 68
?	M/C solo 500cc SV				106982	98012	1	Late 1939 30/10/39 DL		Fitted with exptl spring frame
Model 19	M/C comb. 596cc OHV				25171	92866	1	Mid 1940 13/06/40 DL		Had SWD

Maker's Type	Military Class	WD Serial No. Allocation	Contract Number	CAT. REF.	Frame Number	Engine Number	Qty Prod'd	Dates	Price(s)	Delivery Destination & Notes
Prototype	M/C solo 500cc SV parallel twin						1	1944		
Norton-Matchless	M/C solo 350cc OHV	4389812			29786	23267	1	To AMC on 26/04/41		Fitted with AMC engine
Norton-BSA	M/C solo 350cc OHV	4389667			Not stamped	WB30-522	1	To BSA on 20/02/41		Fitted with BSA engine
Model 18	M/C solo 500cc OHV	Not registered			47861	54440	1	25/10/32 DL		On loan
Model 19	M/C solo 596cc OHV	Not registered			47869	54291	1	25/10/32 DL		On loan

OEC

Maker's Type	Military Class	WD Serial No. Allocation	Contract Number	CAT. REF.	Frame Number	Engine Number	Qty Prod'd	Dates	Price(s)	Delivery Destination & Notes
?	M/C solo 342cc 2-stroke	RAF	?				?	Late 1920s		
3-wheeler	M/C solo 490cc SV	19247	C886		37227	99558	1	27/04/28 DL		Aldershot. Weight 453lb. JAP engine Civilian registration was MP 8161
3-wheeler	M/C solo 350cc SV	19621	C886		DS/8/3103	FJ 4879	1	04/06/28 DM 02/07/28 CD 18/09/28 DL	£150	Farnborough. Weight 354lb. Blackburne engine. Civilian registration was MT 9186

Maker's Type	Military Class	WD Serial No. Allocation	Contract Number	CAT. REF.	Frame Number	Engine Number	Qty Prod'd	Dates	Price(s)	Delivery Destination & Notes
3-wheeler	M/C solo 250cc SV	19622		C886	DS/8/3104	JP 1255	1	18/09/28 DL		Farnborough. Weight 310lb. Blackburne engine. Civilian registration was MP 9187
?	M/C solo 350cc SV	20467, ?, ?	C1933		5DL/9/405013, ?, ?	JPE 2540, ?, ?	3	04/05/29 DM 18/06/29 CD	£54.6s 6d	Blackburne engine fitted. Farnborough. Weight 338½lb

PANTHER

Maker's Type	Military Class	WD Serial No. Allocation	Contract Number	CAT. REF.	Frame Number	Engine Number	Qty Prod'd	Dates	Price(s)	Delivery Destination & Notes
?	M/C solo and comb. 3.5hp OHV	RAF	?				?	1925 to late 1930s		
Model 100	M/C solo 598cc OHV						100	1938-39		Probably to RAF

ROYAL ENFIELD

Maker's Type	Military Class	WD Serial No. Allocation	Contract Number	CAT. REF.	Frame Number	Engine Number	Qty Prod'd	Dates	Price(s)	Delivery Destination & Notes
Model C test model	M/C solo 350cc SV	35799	C7641?		31295	15174*	1	October 1935, 10/09/35 DL		Civilian registration was CMM 751. *New cases fitted in October 1935. New number 15179
Model B text model	M/C solo 250cc SV	35800	C7641?		2833	1855	1	10/09/35 DL		Civilian registration was CMM 752
Model D	M/C solo 250cc SV	399927-399999, 3910000-3910526	C3739	1	2275-2874	D 1001-1600	600	04/05/39 DM, 10/06/39 CD, June 1939 PL	£33.8s	Chilwell. For RAF
Model D	M/C solo 250cc SV	3922045-3922944	C4452	3	3001-3900	2001-2900	900	24/07/39 DM 15/08/39 CD August 1939 PL	£33.8s	Chilwell at 100 per week
Model D	M/C solo 250cc SV	4191639-4191653, 4191802-4191883, 4303647-4303901, 4191454-4191484	C7374	5	4337, 4343, 4379, 4396, 4406, 4408, 4414, 4535, 4565, 4571, 4576, 4579, 4580, 4584, 4588-90, 4593, 4594, 4596-98, 4602, 4605, 4609, 4610, 4636, 4643, 4648, 4651, 4653, 4655, 4666, 4667, 4669-72, 4676-81, 4683-85, 4687, 4689, 4691, 4696, 4699, 4701, 4702, 4704-20, 4722, 4726, 4733, 4734,		350	07/06/40 DM 24/09/40 CD April 1941 PL	c. £40	Chilwell, Stirling or Catterick

Maker's Type	Military Class	WD Serial No. Allocation	Contract Number	CAT. REF.	Frame Number	Engine Number	Qty Prod'd	Dates	Price(s)	Delivery Destination & Notes
					4736, 4737, 4741, 4748, 4749, 4755, 4757, 4760, 4763, 4764, 4767, 4769, 4775, 4779, 4782, 4785, 4786, 4791, 4794, 4800, 4801, 4804, 4805, 4809, 4811-13, 4815-24, 4827-35, 4837-42, 4844, 4845, 4848, 4850, 4853, 4855, 4857, 4859, 4861, 4868, 4871, 4876, 4880, 4885, 4887, 4893, 4894, 4897, 4899, 4902-04, 4907, 4909, 4911, 4912, 4914, 4916, 4924, 4930, 4931, 4936, 4937, 4939, 4945, 4947-49, 4956, 4959, 4961, 4962, 4964, 4966-4969, 4971, 4973, 4977-79, 4982, 4984-4986, 4993, 4996, 4997, 5001, 5003-5005, 5007, 5011-5013, 5015, 5016, 5018-20, 5022, 5024-26, 5028-30, 5033, 5034, 5036-42, 5044-46, 5049, 5510-14, 5516, 5519, 5520, 5523, 5526, 5527, 5532, 5533, 5538, 5540-42,					

Maker's Type	Military Class	WD Serial No. Allocation	Contract Number	CAT. REF.	Frame Number	Engine Number	Qty Prod'd	Dates	Price(s)	Delivery Destination & Notes
					5550, 5551, 5554, 5556-59, 5563, 5565, 5566, 5568-70, 5576, 5578, 5579, 5581, 5585, 5590, 5595, 5603, 5605, 5606, 5609, 5611-15, 5619, 5622, 5624, 5629, 5632, 5634, 5639-52, 5654, 5656, 5658-64, 5666, 5667, 5669-85, 5688-5700, 5702-05, 5708, 5710, 5713-15, 5717, 5718, 5725, 5728, 5730-37, 5739, 5744					
Model D	M/C solo 250cc SV	4327418-4327497, 4327574-4327801, 4327924-4327935, 4327941-4327978	C7945	10	4599, 4600, 4617, 4618, 4624, 4640, 4645, 4646, 4654, 4688, 4729, 4732, 4843, 4877, 4879, 4884, 4888, 4890, 4918-20, 4925, 4928, 4932, 4942, 4960, 4999, 5006, 5008, 5014, 5021, 5027, 5031, 5032, 5043, 5047, 5051, 5053, 5056-60, 5062, 5064-66, 5068-70, 5072-77, 5079-94, 5097, 5098, 5100, 5101, 5103, 5104, 5107, 5112-160, 5162-170, 5172-78, 5180-84,		300	27/07/40 DM 07/10/40 CD April 1941 PL	£42.6s 9d	Burscough, Woking, Tidmouth and Catterick

Maker's Type	Military Class	WD Serial No. Allocation	Contract Number	CAT. REF.	Frame Number	Engine Number	Qty Prod'd	Dates	Price(s)	Delivery Destination & Notes
Model D	M/C solo 250cc SV		C8664		5186-5201, 5203-41, 5243, 5244, 5246-49, 5251-56, 5258-67, 5269-74, 5286, 5293, 5377-85, 5502, 5529, 5537, 5567, 5582, 5593, 5595-97, 5599, 5602, 5604, 5607, 5608, 5610, 5616-18, 5620, 5621, 5623, 5625-28, 5633, 5635-38, 5657, 5665, 5668, 5686, 5687, 5701, 5706-08, 5711, 5712, 5716, 5719, 5720, 5723, 5724, 5727, 5729, 5738, 5740, 5741, 5743, 5745-47, 5749, 5750		2	04/09/40 DM 22/11/40 CD	£42.6s 9d	Woolwich Arsenal
Model D	M/C solo 250cc SV		C8881				2	05/10/40 DM 19/03/41 CD	£43.11s 3d	RA Woolwich
Exptl LW (1st)	M/C solo 350cc SV	3925599	C3585	2	101	101	1	04/04/39 DM 25/05/39 CD 17/08/39 CP	£200	Farnborough
Exptl LW (2nd)	M/C solo 350cc SV	4328451	C7972		303	D.C. 303	1	13/07/40 DM 15/08/40 CD 25/06/40 DL	£48.12s 1d	Chilwell
Exptl LW	M/C solo 350cc SV		C6718				2	01/04/40 DM 01/04/40 CD	£48.12s	Feltham

Maker's Type	Military Class	WD Serial No. Allocation	Contract Number	CAT. REF.	Frame Number	Engine Number	Qty Prod'd	Dates	Price(s)	Delivery Destination & Notes
WD/C	M/C solo 350cc SV	67586-68280, 68286-68883, 68898, 68903, 68904, 68907-68927	C5107	6	101-1100	101-1100	1,000*	27/09/39 DM 12/02/40 CD November 1939 PL	£41.7s 7d	Feltham at 100/150 per week from 06/01/40. *Too many serial numbers
WD/C	M/C solo 350cc SV	4328291-4328353, 4328393, 68884-68897, 68899-68902, 68905, 68906, 68928-69585, 75250-75557, 75648, 75649, 75654-75659, 75663-75665	C5654	7	1101-2100	1101-2100	1,000*	28/11/39 DM 13/02/40 CD	£43.9s	Feltham and Olympia at 75 per week after C5107. *Too many serial numbers
WD/C	M/C solo 350cc SV	4328354-4328392, 4328394-4328398, 75558-75647, 75650-75653, 75660-75662, 75666-77567	C6125	8	3001-5000	3001-5000	2,000*	25/01/40 DM 28/03/40 CD 03/08/40 CP February 1940 PL	£45	Olympia at 150 per week from 03/05/40. *Too many serial numbers issued for frames
WD/C	M/C solo 350cc SV	4327498-4327573, 4327887-4327907	C7945	11	2176-2183, 5334, 5339, 5344, 5347-49, 5369-71, 5373, 5374, 5377, 5379-82, 5385, 5386, 5395-97, 5411, 5412, 5415, 5418-21, 5431, 5434, 5435, 5440, 5443-45, 5447-51, 5454-56, 5459-66, 5468-84, 5486-95, 5497-5512, 5514-49, 5551-59, 5567-69	2176-2183, 5334, 5339, 5344, 5347-49, 5369-71, 5373, 5374, 5377, 5379-82, 5385, 5386, 5395-97, 5411, 5412, 5415, 5418-21, 5431, 5434, 5435, 5440, 5443-45, 5447-51, 5454-56, 5459-66, 5468-84, 5486-95, 5497-5512, 5514-49, 5551-59, 5567-69	150*	27/07/40 DM August 1940 PL 07/10/40 CD	£46.9s 3d	Burscough, Woking, Tidmouth, and Catterick. *Not enough serial numbers. French specification. Some are militarised civilian models

Maker's Type	Military Class	WD Serial No. Allocation	Contract Number	CAT. REF.	Frame Number	Engine Number	Qty Prod'd	Dates	Price(s)	Delivery Destination & Notes
WD/C	M/C solo 350cc SV	984216, 984217, 984219, 984222, 984251-987400, 987426-989562, 989614-989750, 989801-989900, 989926-990402	C7182	17	5901-11900	5901-11900	6,000*	16/05/40 DM August 1940 PL 23/11/40 CD 29/08/40 CP		Olympia at 250 per week after C6125. *Too many serial numbers
WD/C	M/C solo 350cc SV	99139-99291, 984001-984215, 984218, 984220, 984221 984223-984250, 984223-984250, 987401-987425, 989751-989800, 989901-989925	C7890	20	11901-12400	11901-12400	500	10/07/40 DM 15/08/40 CD August 1940 PL	£44.12s	Slough, after C7182
WD/C	M/C solo 350cc SV	4361416-4364196, 990403-990723	C8136	9	12401-15500	12401-15500	3,100*	13/08/40	£47.18s.9d	*Too many serial numbers
WD/C	M/C solo 350cc SV	4437509-4439008, 990727-992227	C8732	15	15501-18500	15501-18500	3,000*	18/09/40 DM 23/11/40 CD May 1941 PL	£44.14s.10d	1,500 to Chilwell and 1,500 to Feltham. *Too many serial numbers Australians used 15501 to 16225
WD/C	M/C solo 350cc SV		C11463		18501-19100	18501-19100	600	12/08/41 DM August 1941 PL 30/09/41 CD 30/09/41 CP	£48.16s	
WD/C	M/C solo 350cc SV	RAF	C12429		19101-19350	19101-19350	250	10/11/41 DM 07/02/42 CD		Milton, Quedgeley, Carlisle, Stafford, Hartlebury, and Haywood

Maker's Type	Military Class	WD Serial No. Allocation	Contract Number	CAT. REF.	Frame Number	Engine Number	Qty Prod'd	Dates	Price(s)	Delivery Destination & Notes
Model L	M/C solo 570cc SV		On loan		28921	11206	1	19/04/40 04/12/39 DL		
WD/L	M/C solo 570cc SV	4191354–4191453	C7374	4	28903, 28907, 28912, 28923, 28927, 28932, 28934, 28936, 28940, 28943, 28949, 28950, 28952, 28957, 28960, 28963–28965, 28969, 28971, 28973, 29005, 29008–29085	11298, 11280, 11302, 11278, 11297, 11272, 11291, 11293, 11296, 11273, 11289, 11292, 11287, 11284, 11286, 11285, 11288, 11277, 11323, 11294, 11279, 11290, 11305, 11317, 11304, 11283, 11306, 11313, 11295, 11301, 11274, 11327, 11322, 11328, 11308, 11271, 11310, 11270, 11307, 11333, 11315, 11303, 11336, 11309, 11300, 11314, 11281, 11311, 11312, 11299, 11275, 11360, 11325, 11370, 11365, 11368, 11359, 11335, 11316, 11354, 11343, 11318, 11358, 11340, 11329, 11341, 11337, 11321, 11353, 11347, 11356, 11355, 11351, 11282, 11346, 11334, 11330, 11369, 11357, 11362, 11344, 11366, 11332, 11364, 11320, 11319, 11331, 11363, 11352, 11361, 11342, 11348, 11338, 11324, 11345, 11276, 11367, 11349, 11339, 11350	100	07/06/40 DM 24/09/40 CD April 1941 PL	c. £62	Chilwell, Stirling and Catterick
WD/L	M/C solo 570cc SV		Unknown		29806–29094, 29096–29097, 29099–29108, 29110, 29113, 29116–29119, 29125–29128, 29130–29136, 29138, 29140–29141, 29143–29165, 29195	11393, 11396, 11418, 11380, 11408, 11410, 11385, 11395, 11265, 11414, 11421, 11430, 11415, 11418, 11411, 11403, 11422, 11412, 11402, 11432, 11417, 11428, 11377, 11406, 11442, 11413, 11443, 11390, 11426, 11446, 11399, 11424,	65	Delivered 9/8/40 to 30/8/40		Impressed?

Maker's Type	Military Class	WD Serial No. Allocation	Contract Number	CAT. REF.	Frame Number	Engine Number	Qty Prod'd	Dates	Price(s)	Delivery Destination & Notes
						11400, 11429, 11434, 11398, 11445, 11440, 11405, 11433, 11397, 11384, 11420, 11373, 11435, 11439, 11407, 11438, 11425, 11379, 11409, 11423, 11437, 11374, 11372, 11383, 11391, 11381, 11386, 11375, 11427, 11419, 11431, 11436, 11394				
WD/L	M/C solo 570cc SV	4478583-4478832	C8620	13	29201-29450	29201-29450	250	29/08/40 DM Nov 40 PL 26/03/41 CD	£48.7s 6d	Chilwell. Produced from February 1942
WD/G prototypes	M/C solo 350cc OHV				G101, G102	WDG 101, 102	2	16/01/41 DL		Telescopic forks, registration DWP740
WD/G	M/C solo 350cc OHV	4327802-4327886, 4327908-4327923	C7945	12	728, 748, 750, 755, 756, 759, 760, 767, 771, 799, 819-24, 826-30, 832-37, 839-53, 855, 856, 858-73, 876-84, 886-90, 892-912, 914-36	3572, 3523, 3529, 3567, 3604, 3547, 3571, 3551, 3616, 3613, 3575 3554, 3608, 3533, 3526, 3611, 3530, 3589, 3512, 3568, 3528, 3578, 3606, 3522, 3518, 3556, 3612, 3531, 3581, 3521, 3625, 3520, 3577, 3534, 3558, 3549, 3574, 3541, 3542, 3515, 3525, 3583, 3579, 3619, 3573, 3563, 3513, 3537, 3550, 3511, 3516, 3510, 3565, 3540, 3532, 3548, 3580, 3527, 3600, 3524, 3584, 3599, 3564, 3519, 3582, 3574, 3566, 3552, 3569, 3556, 3570,	118*	22/07/40 DM 07/10/40 CD April 1941 P	£52.13s 3d	Burscough, Woking, Tidmouth, and Catterick *Not enough serial numbers

Maker's Type	Military Class	WD Serial No. Allocation	Contract Number	CAT. REF.	Frame Number	Engine Number	Qty Prod'd	Dates	Price(s)	Delivery Destination & Notes
WD/G	M/C solo 350cc OHV	4478833–4479082, 990724–990726	C8621	14	29701–29950	3576, 3545, 3598, 3559, 3514, 3553, 3517, 3546, 3560, 3593, 3535, 3562, 3536, 3544, 3561, 3579, 3591, 3601, 3592, 3605, 3585, 3586, 3595, 3622, 3594, 3588, 3607, 3603, 3590, 3597, 3596, 3587, 3543, 3539, 3610, 3609, 3617, 3538, 3621, 3602, 3623, 3618, 3614, 3615, 3624, 3620, 3557 29701–29950	250*	17/08/40 DM November 1940 PL 03/02/41 CD Delivered from May 1942	£48.13s 6d	Chilwell. *Too many serial nos
WD/G	M/C solo 350cc OHV	RN 4553327, 4553328	C9311	16	29951–30000 1042, ?	29951–30000 WB30–540, ?	50 2	22/2/41 DL 04/12/40 DM 04/12/40 CD		Allotted to RN, so C4500287 to C4500336 not used C4553327 fitted with BSA engine. C4553328 may be Matchless-engined machine
WD/G	M/C solo 350cc OHV	99389–99488	C8200	21	937–53, 955–91, 993–95, 997–99, 1003–10, 1012–14, 1016–27, 1030, 1032 1034–40, 1045–46	3682, 3681, 3632, 3661, 3676, 3664, 3626, 3637, 3642, 3698, 3666, 3648, 3662, 3663, 3638, 3633, 3639, 3636, 3635, 3688, 3670, 3658, 3631, 3630, 3656, 3634, 3629, 3674, 3660, 3679, 3699, 3675, 3650, 3672, 3659,	100	02/08/40 DM 08/11/40 CD 25/10/40 CP Del from February 1942	£52.13s 3d	Feltham

Maker's Type	Military Class	WD Serial No. Allocation	Contract Number	CAT. REF.	Frame Number	Engine Number	Qty Prod'd	Dates	Price(s)	Delivery Destination & Notes
KX	M/C comb. 1140cc SV V-twin		C11467		10305, 10307, 10395, 10399	3673, 3693, 3725, 3651, 3628, 3644, 3703, 3654, 3680, 3669, 3655, 3640, 3627, 3692, 3683, 3657, 3701, 3649, 3641, 3697, 3646, 3677, 3691, 3690, 3671, 3684, 3652, 3723, 3667, 3647, 3645, 3695, 3653, 3668, 3689, 3678, 3643, 3685, 3694, 3710, 3696, 3721, 3723, 3706, 3717, 3687, 3715, 3720, 3709, 3711, 3705, 3714, 3704, 3718, 3722, 3707, 3708, 3716, 3724				
KX	M/C comb. 1140cc SV V-twin		C11467		10305, 10307, 10395, 10399	10305, 10307, 10395, 10399	4	12/08/41 DM 10/09/41 CD 11/3/42 DL	£90	Thorp-Arch, York. Supplied without bodies
Exptl V-twin	M/C comb. 1140cc SV		?		101	EXKX101	1	1941		Had SWD
?	M/C comb.		V3609				2	26/09/39 DM		Chislehurst
WD/G	M/C solo 350cc OHV	RN	C10175		129701-129750	129701-129750	50	22/03/41 DM 24/04/41 CD 22/04/41 CP 26/4/41 DL	£50.10s 9d	Chatham, Portsmouth, Devonport, and Rosyth
WD/G	M/C solo 350cc OHV	RN	C10850		129801-129850	129801-129850	50	05/06/41 DM 15/07/41 CD 2/7/41 DL	£50.17s 6d	Chatham, Portsmouth, Devonport, and RN Store Dept at Preston, Staffs

Maker's Type	Military Class	WD Serial No. Allocation	Contract Number	CAT. REF.	Frame Number	Engine Number	Qty Prod'd	Dates	Price(s)	Delivery Destination & Notes
Unknown	M/C solo	??	C10484				2,000	2/5/41 CD		Linked to Levis (Cancelled)
WD/J2	M/C solo 500cc OHV	RAF	C10103				6	15/03/41 DM 18/06/41 CD May 1941 DL	£55.16s	MAP Pool, Horseferry Road, London
WD/CO	M/C solo 350cc OHV	4605601-4610600	C11081	18	1001-6000	1001-6000	5,000	03/07/41 DM 22/10/41 CD March 1942 PL Delivered from March 1942	£50.3s 6d*	1,055 to Tewkesbury, rest to Chilwell. *Could also be £57.16s 9d
WD/CO	M/C solo 350cc OHV	5104201-5109200	C12425	19	6001-11000	6001-11000	5,000	10/11/41 DM 07/02/42 CD	£50.3s 6d	Frame/Eng 6001 to 6491 to Republic of Ireland
WD/CO	M/C solo 350cc OHV	4940701-4943700	C13869	24	11001-14000	11001-14000	3,000	14/03/42 DM		Paisley War Office
WD/CO/B	M/C solo 350cc OHV	4847001-4850000	C13870	22	14001-17000	14001-17000	3,000	14/03/42 DM Delivered from 11/7/42 to November 1943		Burman gearbox fitted Frame/Engine 16901 to 16999 to Republic of Ireland
WD/CO	M/C solo 350cc OHV	RAF	S14219		17001-19826	17001-19826	2,826	09/04/42 DM 1944 DL		Sandtoft, Yorkshire
WD/CO	M/C solo 350cc OHV	5162167-5167166	S1546	26	19827-24826	19827-24826	5,000	14/11/42 DM Late 1944 DL November 1944 PL		Vokes filter fitted
WD/CO	M/C solo 350cc OHV		Unknown		24827-24909	24827-24909	83	3/6/44 DL		
WD/CO	M/C solo 350cc OHV		S4606		24910-25019	24910-25019	110	1944 January 1944 PL		

Maker's Type	Military Class	WD Serial No. Allocation	Contract Number	CAT. REF.	Frame Number	Engine Number	Qty Prod'd	Dates	Price(s)	Delivery Destination & Notes
WD/CO	M/C solo 350cc OHV		S5500		25023-25037	25023-25037	15	21/1/44 DL		
WD/CO	M/C solo 350cc OHV	5529038-5534037	S3357	27	25038-30037	25038-30037	5,000	21/05/43 May 1944 DL		Reduced to 1500, 1200/month. Last one del on 14/9/45
WD/CO	M/C solo 350cc OHV	RAF	S7844		30091-30540	30091-30540	450	January 1945 to 6/7/45 DL		
WD/CO	M/C solo 350cc OHV		S9635		30926-30941	30926-30941	16	10/7/45 DL	£76 1s 9d	
WD/CO	M/C solo 350cc OHV		S9669		30942-30983	30942-30983	42	31/8/45 DL		
Model RE	M/C solo 125cc 2-stroke		S831				1	06/01/43	£41 17s	Possibly prototype
WD/RE	M/C solo 125cc 2-stroke	4893237-4893256	C14775	23	2792, 2799, 2802, 2807, 2814, 2817, 2854, 2856, 2857, 2793, 2798, 2805, 2813, 2816, 2850, 2860, 2872, 2878	2792, 2799, 2802, 2807, 2814, 2817, 2854, 2856, 2857, 2793, 2798, 2805, 2813, 2816, 2850, 2860, 2872, 2878	18*	29/05/42 DM 26/06/42 CD 22/07/42 DL and 25/07/42 DL	£23	Coventry and Leicester. *Delivered in two batches of 9. Too many serial numbers
WD/RE	M/C solo 125cc 2-stroke	5111171-5115170	S1945	25	4171-8170	4171-8170	4,000	02/01/43 DM November 1943 DL into 1944	£29	
WD/RE	M/C solo 125cc 2-stroke	5816151-5816885	S6602	28	8171-8905	8171-8905	735	04/05/44, 09/44 DL November 1944 PL	£30	Delivery at 350 per month from September

Maker's Type	Military Class	WD Serial No. Allocation	Contract Number	CAT. REF.	Frame Number	Engine Number	Qty Prod'd	Dates	Price(s)	Delivery Destination & Notes
WD/RE	M/C solo 125cc 2-stroke	5859206-5862429	S7112	29	8906-12129*	8906-12129*	3,224*	10/07/44, 14/12/44 November 1945 DL	£32	*Factory ledgers show only to 11129, so last 1,000 motorcycles were probably not taken
Exptl. Twin (prototype)	M/C solo 350cc SV		?				1	February 1944		
RE/Matchless	M/C solo 350cc OHV				874	23305		29/05/41 DL to AMC		Fitted with Matchless engine

RUDGE WHITWORTH

Maker's Type	Military Class	WD Serial No. Allocation	Contract Number	CAT. REF.	Frame Number	Engine Number	Qty Prod'd	Dates	Price(s)	Delivery Destination & Notes
Rapid (modified)	M/C solo 250cc OHV	364845	W.7917	1	57906	A.477	1	09/10/36 DM 23/11/36 CD 08/07/36 DL	£44	Farnborough. Civilian reg. was EHX 707
Ulster (modified)	M/C solo 500cc OHV	364846	W.7917	2	57907	S.3006	2	09/10/36 DM 23/11/36 CD 08/07/36 DL	£52	Farnborough. Civilian reg. was EHX 708
Service model	M/C solo 250cc OHV	3810114-3810125	C.1927	3	64533-64544	1871-1882	12	11/06/38 DM 26/08/38 CD 29/10/38 CP	£45	Chilwell

STEWART-EHRLICH

Maker's Type	Military Class	WD Serial No. Allocation	Contract Number	CAT. REF.	Frame Number	Engine Number	Qty Prod'd	Dates	Price(s)	Delivery Destination & Notes
Prototype	M/C solo 350cc 2-stroke (split-single)						1	15/10/41 DL		Returned same day

S.O.S.

Maker's Type	Military Class	WD Serial No. Allocation	Contract Number	CAT. REF.	Frame Number	Engine Number	Qty Prod'd	Dates	Price(s)	Delivery Destination & Notes
?	M/C solo ???cc 2-stroke						1	1940 DL		
?	M/C solo ???cc 2-stroke						1	1942 DL		

SUNBEAM

Maker's Type	Military Class	WD Serial No. Allocation	Contract Number	CAT. REF.	Frame Number	Engine Number	Qty Prod'd	Dates	Price(s)	Delivery Destination & Notes
Model 6	M/C solo 500cc SV		?				?	1927 DL		
'Lion'	M/C solo 500cc SV				MM 774	29/238	1	09/10/36 DL		Farnborough. Civilian registration was ADA 508

Maker's Type	Military Class	WD Serial No. Allocation	Contract Number	CAT. REF.	Frame Number	Engine Number	Qty Prod'd	Dates	Price(s)	Delivery Destination & Notes
Prototype SWD combination	M/C comb. 1000cc OHV V-twin		?		Not stated	Not stated	1	27/10/41 DL		Had SWD. (Also referred to as Matchless Heavy M/C combination in some War Office literature)

TRIUMPH

Maker's Type	Military Class	WD Serial No. Allocation	Contract Number	CAT. REF.	Frame Number	Engine Number	Qty Prod'd	Dates	Price(s)	Delivery Destination & Notes
Model P	M/C solo 494cc SV		?				?	1925 to 1927		
Model P	M/C comb. 494cc SV	165??	?				?	1925 to 1927		
Model N	M/C comb. 494cc SV	19240	?		1011233	257071	?	09/06/28 DL		Farnborough. Civilian reg. was MP 8114
Model N and NP	M/C solo 494cc SV	19189, 19401, 19467, 19582, 19403	C839		1011133, 1009639, 1010754	257073, 256128, 254837	29	1927/8 01/06/27 DL		Farnborough. Used by Armed Forces Signals. 1927 N had engine 254837. 1928 NP had engines 257073, 256128
Model NL	M/C solo 494cc SV	19956	C1417		2007152	507550	30	19/12/28 DM 28/12/28 CD		Farnborough
Model NL3	M/C solo 494cc SV	19895, 19855, ?	C1417		?, 2009098, ?	?, 507472, ?	80	19/12/28 DM 28/12/28 CD 12/02/29 DL		Farnborough

Maker's Type	Military Class	WD Serial No. Allocation	Contract Number	CAT. REF.	Frame Number	Engine Number	Qty Prod'd	Dates	Price(s)	Delivery Destination & Notes
Model NP	M/C solo 494cc SV		C1412				3	30/11/28 DM 20/12/28 CD	£39.15s.	Feltham. As C839
Model P 3-wheeler	M/C solo 494cc SV	16247			931179	237951	1	09/05/28 DL		Civilian registration was MK 5625. Originally a 1926 motorcycle
?	M/C solo	33275, 33276	C5244				2	1933/34?		
Model ND	M/C solo 549cc SV	33424-33466	C5467	17			43			
Model ND	M/C solo 549cc SV	33713-33743	C5678	16			31			
Model ND	M/C solo 549cc SV	34748-34760	C6877	15			13			
3/1 (test model)	M/C solo 350cc SV	35798	C7641?		SL.3315	1.T6.1537	1	1935 18/09/35 DL		Civilian registration was CMM 799
3S (test model)	M/C solo 350cc SV	373232	C9800	3	1630	7/3S/216	1	04/02/37 DM 01/03/37 CD 25/11/36 DL	£41.7s.	Farnborough. Civilian registration was FMG 604
3SW	M/C solo 350cc SV	38614-38999, 3811000-3811039	C2073	11	TL 7773, 7893, ?	14822, 14783, ?	426	30/06/38 DM 26/09/38 CD 21/01/39 CP	£40	Feltham at 50 per week
3SW	M/C solo 350cc SV	3812675-3812715	C3398	19			41	20/12/38 DM 07/11/39 CD	£39.7s	Feltham
3SW	M/C solo 350cc SV	3916045-3916247	C3360	14			203	28/02/39 DM 27/04/39 CD	£39.13s 9d	Feltham at 25 per week
3SW	M/C solo 350cc SV	3917452-3917751	C4631	18			300	26/07/39 DM 02/10/39 CD	£39.19s	Chilwell at 50 per week. As C3360

Maker's Type	Military Class	WD Serial No. Allocation	Contract Number	CAT. REF.	Frame Number	Engine Number	Qty Prod'd	Dates	Price(s)	Delivery Destination & Notes
3SW	M/C solo 350cc SV	60788-61000, 62686-62885, 62916-63085, 63144-63585, 69586-70088, 70586-72365	C5108	10	14612, ?	27606, ?	3,300*	27/09/39 DM 19/01/40 CD 07/11/40 DL	£43.16s 6d	Feltham at 150 per week from 28/10/39. *27/9/39 for 300, 21/10/39 for 3,000
3SW	M/C solo 350cc SV		C5334				??			
3SW	M/C solo 350cc SV	72366-72585, 80038-80763, 4359296	C6128	6	TL 17300 to 18299	40-3SW-34401 to 35400	1,000	25/01/40 DM 28/03/40 CD 13/08/40 CP	£43.16s 6d	Olympia at 300 per week. After C5108. Not enough serial numbers. 17366 was converted to carry Bren gun. 11/7/40
3SW	M/C solo 350cc SV	4358641-4359295	C8079	7	See contract C7162	See contract C7162	3,000*	27/07/40 DM 28/09/40 CD	£47.18s.11d	Feltham and Slough at 150 per week. *Reduced to 649
3SW	M/C solo 350cc SV	80889-81274, 83889-84230, 84786-84829, 884001-886686	C7162	13	TL 18300 to 18329, 20834-24812, 24814-29997, 29999, 30001-30265, 30416-30700. With gaps	3SW-35401 to 44500. With gaps	5,000*	20/05/40 DM 07/08/40 CD 08/01/41 CP		3,000 to Slough at 300 per week, and 2,000 to Feltham at 75 per week. As C6128. *Further quantity added, all sent to Ashchurch
3SW	M/C solo 350cc SV	RAF	C11465		TL 30266 to 30415	3SW-40266 to 40415	150	12/08/41 DM 18/09/41 CD August 1941 to September 1941 DL	£55	Quedgeley, Carlisle and Stafford. From temporary factory at Cape Warwick
?	M/C solo 350cc		C12177				1	16/10/41 DM		From Cape Warwick

Maker's Type	Military Class	WD Serial No. Allocation	Contract Number	CAT. REF.	Frame Number	Engine Number	Qty Prod'd	Dates	Price(s)	Delivery Destination & Notes
?	M/C solo	4133005–4133011	?				7			
?	M/C solo	4187767	C5247				1			
5SW	M/C solo 500cc SV	4320278–4321625	C7828	5	TL 18330 to 20833. With gaps	5SW-31897 to 34400. With gaps	1,322*	18/07/40		*1,655 ordered
5SW	M/C solo 500cc SV		C7827				9	18/07/40 DM 21/02/41 CD		
5SW	M/C solo 500cc SV	4403027–4403171	C8575	8			145	27/08/40 DM 26/11/40 CD	£48.18s 6d	Chilwell
Speed twin	M/C solo 500cc OHV parallel twin	4133940–4133941	C5819				2	18/12/39 DM 22/01/40 CD 22/12/39 DL	£57.1s 4d	Chilwell
5TW (prototype)	M/C solo 500cc SV parallel twin		?				1	1942		
?	M/C comb.		?				1	1940/1		Had SWD
3TW (prototype)	M/C solo 350cc OHV parallel twin	3937042	C3585	4	?	3TW EXP 1	1	04/04/39 DM 25/05/39 CD 27/07/39 DL	£250	Farnborough. First prototype. Both GLU 653 and ERW 784 accredited to this motorcycle!
3TW (2nd version)	M/C solo 350cc OHV parallel twin		C6523		F.1083, ?	3TW EXP 5, ?	2	09/03/40 DM 17/06/40 CD 13/06/40 DL	£238.10s	Feltham, incorporating aluminium substitutes
3TW (3rd version)	M/C solo 350cc OHV parallel twin		C8020		F.1965, ?	E 1742, ?	2	September/October 1940 11/09/40 DL		

Maker's Type	Military Class	WD Serial No. Allocation	Contract Number	CAT. REF.	Frame Number	Engine Number	Qty Prod'd	Dates	Price(s)	Delivery Destination & Notes
3TW (prod. version)	M/C solo 350cc OHV parallel twin	4854130-4854179	C8331	9	LT 101 to 150	3TW-41401-41450	50*	09/08/40 DM		As C8020 with modifications. *Possible only 10 taken
3H	M/C solo 350cc OHV	See C7162 of 3SW	C7162	13	TL 24813, 29998, 30000, 30701-30840	3H 37899	143	20/05/40 DM 07/08/40 CD		EWTDD, Feltham and Ashchurch
3HW	M/C solo 350cc OHV	RAF	C12492		TL 30841-30922	3HW-30841-30875, 40876-40922	82	14/11/41 DM		Hartlebury. From Cape Warwick
3HW	M/C solo 350cc OHV	886687-890052, 4852001-4854129	C13948	20	TL 30923-36417	3HW-40923-46417	5,495	21/05/42 DM 03/04/42 to June 1943 DL		Tewkesbury, Slough, Ashchurch and No. 7. VRD Glasgow
3HW	M/C solo 350cc OHV	5205018-5207517	S1246	22	TL 36418-38917	3HW-46418-48917	2,500	June 1943 to September 1943 DL		Littlewoods at Liverpool, Vauxhall Motors at Hendon, and R.A. Brand Co.
3HW	M/C solo 350cc OHV	5271968-5274467	S2114	23	TL 38918-41417	3HW-48918-51417	2,500	September 1943 to December 1943 DL		As above
3HW	M/C solo 350cc OHV	5423418-5428417	S2956	24	TL 41418-46417	3HW-51418-56417	5,000	December 1943 to June 1944 DL		Littlewoods at Liverpool, Mars factory at Slough and VRDs
3HW	M/C solo 350cc OHV	5566918-5570917	S5340	25	TL 46418-50417	3HW-56418-60417	4,000	15/12/43, June 1944 to October 44 DL		As above

Maker's Type	Military Class	WD Serial No. Allocation	Contract Number	CAT. REF.	Frame Number	Engine Number	Qty Prod'd	Dates	Price(s)	Delivery Destination & Notes
3HW	M/C solo 350cc OHV	4854180–4857179	C8886	21	TL 50418-50431, 50439-53417	3HW-60418-60431, 60439-63417	3,000	07/10/40 DM*. October 1944 to February 1945 DL	£63.14s 10d	*Original demand not delivered. Pearson's Garage and Littlewoods in Liverpool, and Morris Motors in Wales
3HW	M/C solo 350cc OHV	6101418–6109417	S6680	26	TL 53418-58617	3HW-63418-68617	8,000*	15/05/44, February 1945 to September 1945 DL	£63.9s 8d	S.G.B. (Dudley) Ltd and ?. Some supplied without tyres. *Reduced to 5,200

VELOCETTE

Maker's Type	Military Class	WD Serial No. Allocation	Contract Number	CAT. REF.	Frame Number	Engine Number	Qty Prod'd	Dates	Price(s)	Delivery Destination & Notes
MAC	M/C solo 350cc OHV				MDD 10430	MAC 6476	1	25/10/39, 23/10/39 DL	£67.10s	MAC evaluation model
MSS	M/C solo 500cc OHV				Not stated	MSS 4447	1	20/10/39, 23/10/39 DL	£77	MSS evaluation model
MAC (WD)	M/C solo 350cc OHV	4321935–4323134	C.7974	1	MDD 11001-12200	MDD 11001-12200	1,200	29/06/40 or 10/41 CD August 1940 PL	£50.15s	Ex-French government contract. 100 to York (ROD), remainder to Chilwell

Maker's Type	Military Class	WD Serial No. Allocation	Contract Number	CAT. REF.	Frame Number	Engine Number	Qty Prod'd	Dates	Price(s)	Delivery Destination & Notes
MAC (WD)	M/C solo 350cc OHV	4323135-4323334					200	22/07/40 CD		To Chilwell Central Ordnance Depot. This not confirmed, as serial number block not noted as allocated. Possible cancelled contract or for Air Ministry?
MAF	M/C solo 350cc OHV	4653101-4654048	C.10973	2	MAF 1001-1948 09/42 CP	MAF 1001-1948	947	21/06/41 CD, 03/42 DL	£68	Contract originally for 2,000 machines but cancelled after 947 produced

SIDECARS

Maker's Type	Military Class	WD Serial No. Allocation	Contract Number	CAT. REF.	Frame Number	Engine Number	Qty Prod'd	Dates	Price(s)	Delivery Destination & Notes
Swallow box	Sidecar		B/S9413				2	12/09/41 DM 24/10/41 CD	£20.14s 11d	For BSAs
Norton box	Sidecar and chassis		C/S13158				1	16/01/42 DM 07/02/42 CD		For Norton 16H
Watsonian	Chassis		C/S14583				300	12/05/42 DM		For Indian 500cc
Swallow Model 8 bodies	Sidecar		C/S14585				100	12/05/42 DM 14/05/42 CD		Passenger carrying (standard)
Swallow box	Sidecar		C/S14584				200	12/05/42 DM		For Indian M/Cs. standard WD type

LOCAL PURCHASE, IMPRESSED, OVERSEAS ALLOCATIONS, REBUILT AND CAPTURED

Maker's Type	Military Class	WD Serial No. Allocation	Contract Number	CAT. REF.	Frame Number	Engine Number	Qty Prod'd	Dates	Price(s)	Delivery Destination & Notes
Various makes	M/C solo	46001–47551	Impressed				1,551			
Various makes	M/C solo	47801–48081	Impressed				281			
Various makes	M/C solo	48301–53287	Impressed				4,987			
Various makes	M/C solo	53324–58301	Impressed				1,978			
Various makes	M/C solo	58322–60787	Impressed				2,466			AJS and ??
Various makes	M/C solo	61001–62360	Impressed				1,361			AJS and ??
Various makes	M/C solo	62415–62685	Impressed				271			
Various makes	M/C solo	63086–63143	Impressed				58			
All AJS	M/C solo. 350cc	72586–72639	Impressed				54			
Various makes	M/C solo	73586–73603	Impressed				18			R. Enfield 250cc
Various makes	M/C solo	73686–73986	Impressed				301			
R. Enfield	M/C solo. 500cc	78037	Impressed				1			
Various makes	M/C solo	99489–99490	Impressed				2			
Various makes	M/C solo	1400000–1499999	Rebuilt				100,000*			*Reserved numbers
Velocette MAC	M/C solo	4123209–4123231	LP				23	1940		
Various makes	M/C solo	4138882	NC (?)				1			
Various makes	M/C solo	4191203, 4191205, 4191207, 4191208, 4191212–4191214, 4191216–4191220, 4191223–4191225, 4191227–4191230, 4191232, 4191233, 4191240, 4191241, 4191264, 4191266, 4191270, 4191272, 4191273, 4191276, 4191277, 4191281	LP				32			

Maker's Type	Military Class	WD Serial No. Allocation	Contract Number	CAT. REF.	Frame Number	Engine Number	Qty Prod'd	Dates	Price(s)	Delivery Destination & Notes
Various makes	M/C solo	4191855-4191865, 4191867-4191957	LP				102			
Various makes	M/C solo	4333316-4333653	LP				338			
Various makes	M/C solo	4657352-4657369	Ex-RAF				18			
Various makes	M/C solo	6000000-6009999	Captured				10,000*			*Reserved numbers
Various makes & types	Some motorcycles	5307001-5327000	Captured?							All serials used and issued in North Africa
Various types possibly including motorcycles		1-5208, 5931, 5953, 6609-7426, 8001-15000, 150001-166709*, 166749-166770, 166911-166917, 166927-167049, 167061-167074, 167091-167268, 167281-167356, 167361-167442, 167551-167555, 167607-167754, 167779-167781, 167791-167801, 167845-168009, 168093-168156, 168501-168911, 168948-169112, 169174-169203, 169297-169324, 170601-172893, 173401-173781, 173801-174200, 174401-177006, 182601-185600, 18587-186608, 222645-222646, 239535-239547, 239577-239600, 242746-242804, 242834-242900, 242917-242932, 252953-252956, 1347798-1348106	Impressed							*Noted as impressed in Census but seemed to be used by RAF

Maker's Type	Military Class	WD Serial No. Allocation	Contract Number	CAT. REF.	Frame Number	Engine Number	Qty Prod'd	Dates	Price(s)	Delivery Destination & Notes
Various types including motorcycles		15001-23000, 4657536-4657629, 4459206-4459217, 4657150-4657351, 4657536-4657629, 5873482-5878511, 6246200-6246299	N.K. Misc							AJS, BSA, Douglas, Francis Bsarnett, Levis, New Hudson, Matchless, OEC and Triumph
Various types including motorcycles		25001-25249, 74000-75249, 195000-199579, 219234-219283, 232501-232600, 773680-773979, 1037501-1038300, 1039802-1041801, 1164421-1164620, 1165320-1166319, 1352207-1353206, 4200000-4299999, 4425317-4426316, 4647001-4647524, 5700001-5799999	Canadian Forces							CC75155 is a Royal Enfield WD/C. CC74624 is a side-valve Triumph
Various types possibly including motorcycles		25653-25701, 77937-78036, 202306-203055	M.E.E. (MoS)							
Various types possibly including motorcycles		26330-26335, 203056-203075	B.E.F.							
Various types possibly including motorcycles		35268-35271, 3811954-3811958, 3812119-3812121, 4614237-4614386, 5873482-5878511	Unknown							
Various types possibly including motorcycles		100586-101585, 185851-185852	Q.M.G.3 for M.E.							Some captured
Various types possibly including motorcycles		185853	C.I.M.							

Maker's Type	Military Class	WD Serial No. Allocation	Contract Number	CAT. REF.	Frame Number	Engine Number	Qty Prod'd	Dates	Price(s)	Delivery Destination & Notes
Various types possibly including motorcycles		200305	Engine i/c Woolwich							
Various types possibly including motorcycles		206550-206649, 224251-226250, 1263030-1268529, 1303831-1312330, 1324215-1334214, 1334961-1340960, 1353211-1363210, 1441561-1441960, 4462042-4446604, 4513313-4528313, 4618400-4632194, 4633221-4633263, 4634018-4635000, 4711701-4750700, 4817001-4837000, 4970101-4990100, 5171201-5191200, 5221501-5241500, 5371000-5390999, 5600001-5700000, 5900000-5999999	M/E (Middle East)							
Various types possibly including motorcycles		4339543-4341542, 4403708-4406707	C in C. M/E							Early serial numbers were issued for L.P.
Various types possibly including motorcycles		209496-209499, 211500-211501, 242947-252946, 252957-258956,	R.E.							
Various types possibly including motorcycles		150001-166709*, 216202-216336	RAF							*Seems to be used by RAF but listed as impressed
Various types possibly including motorcycles		229265-229266	R.S.A.F. Enfield							
Various types possibly including motorcycles		236349-236384	V.R.D.							For trade plates

Maker's Type	Military Class	WD Serial No. Allocation	Contract Number	CAT. REF.	Frame Number	Engine Number	Qty Prod'd	Dates	Price(s)	Delivery Destination & Notes
Various types possibly including motorcycles		1250001-1260000, 1318534-1323533, 1340971-1347940, 5141001-5146001, 5510001-5513200	East Africa							
Various types possibly including motorcycles		1268563-1278562	Free French							
Various types possibly including motorcycles		1278563-1283562	Czech Forces							
Various types possibly including motorcycles		1283563-1283782	Dutch Forces							
Norton 16H		1283811, 1283810, 1283809, 1283808, 1283782, 1283784, 1283785, 1283795, 1283793, 1283798, 1283800, 1283804, 1283799, 1283797, 1283796, 1283794, 1283792, 1283791, 1283790, 1283789, 1283788, 1283787, 1283786, 1283783, 1283807, 1283806, 1283805, 1283803, 1283802, 1283801	Dutch Forces		W29494, 29482, 29457, 29413, 29501, 29509, 29520, 30433, 30428, 30456, 30459, 30490, 30457, 30448, 30440, 30432, 30354, 30281, 30150, 30104, 30073, 29613, 29525, 29503, 29395, 29300, 30553, 30488, 30485, 30461	W29492, 29482, 29457, 29413, 29501, 29509, 29520, 30433, 30428, 30456, 30459, 30490, 30457, 30448, 30440, 30432, 30354, 30281, 30150, 30104, 30073, 29613, 29525, 29503, 29395, 29300, 30553, 30488, 30485, 30461				30 Norton 16Hs from contract C7353 renumbered 1283782-1283811
Various types possibly including motorcycles		1283812-1288562	Dutch Forces							
Various types possibly including motorcycles		1288563-1293562, 1312335-1312340, 1312357, 1312608, 1363211-1368210	Polish Forces							
Various types possibly including motorcycles		1293563-1298562	Norwegian Forces							

Maker's Type	Military Class	WD Serial No. Allocation	Contract Number	CAT. REF.	Frame Number	Engine Number	Qty Prod'd	Dates	Price(s)	Delivery Destination & Notes
Various types possibly including motorcycles		1298563-1303562	Belgian Forces							
Various types possibly including motorcycles		1313330-1315829, 1315834-1318533, 1348107-1352206	West Africa							
Various types possible including motorcycles		1323715-1324214, 1334226-1334925, 4425217-4425316, 4473460-4473659, 4485575-4485674	Malaya							
Various types possible including motorcycles		4146551-4146758, 4156168-4156667, 4162610-4162909, 4185849-4185948	India							
Various types possibly including motorcycles		4786500-4811499	10th Indian Army							
Various types possibly including motorcycles		4183559-4183562	Iceland							
Various types possibly including motorcycles		4184052-4184101, 4473995-4474144	Malta							Early serial numbers were issued for L.P.
Various types possibly including motorcycles		4315608-4315657	China							
Various types including motorcycles		4448036-4448085	Egypt							
Various types including motorcycles		4138822-4138834, 4481678-4481727	Gibraltar							Some were L.P.

Maker's Type	Military Class	WD Serial No. Allocation	Contract Number	CAT. REF.	Frame Number	Engine Number	Qty Prod'd	Dates	Price(s)	Delivery Destination & Notes
Various types possibly including motorcycles		4481766-4481776	Colombo							
Various types possibly including motorcycles		4484805-4484954	Singapore							
Various types possibly including motorcycles		5131001-5141000	P/Iraq							
Various types possibly including motorcycles		5203207-5204206, 5307001-5327000	North Africa							
Various types possibly including motorcycles		5529000-5529035	Bermuda							
Various types possibly including motorcycles		5544959-5545058	Jamaica							
Various types possibly including motorcycles		4615000-4617055, 4617501-4618241	USA							
Various types possibly including motorcycles		4633323-4633393	Captured							
Various types possibly including motorcycles		185601-185708, 242936-242940, 3811366-3811371, 3931484-3931489, 3332696-3932708, 3935710-3936735, 3936819-3937041, 3937543-3938087,	L.P.							Matchless Model X combination - C4330174 AJS 39/22 - C4330614

Maker's Type	Military Class	WD Serial No. Allocation	Contract Number	CAT. REF.	Frame Number	Engine Number	Qty Prod'd	Dates	Price(s)	Delivery Destination & Notes
		3938276-3938500, 3938504-3938795, 3938954-3943988, 4118357-4118606, 4120607-4123208, 4123232-4123606, 4123673-4123772, 4125996-4126095, 4130198-4130499, 4133012-4133311, 4137142-4137436, 4138740-4138799, 4138889-4138938, 4148053-4148250, 4163910-4163936, 4183901-4183950, 4190996-4191001, 4196303-4196508, 4304293-4304301, 4325725-4326084, 4328006-4328025, 4328466-4328503, 4328558-4332565, 4333953-4334029, 4334083-4334882, 4368889-4369588, 4370982-4371242, 4378928-4379577, 4384564-4384762, 4408652-4409707, 4411061-4411560, 4426317-4426416, 4434615-4434868, 4484955-4485334, 4553313-4553512, 4558144-4558243, 4581365-4582364, 4688613-4688805								
Various types possibly including motorcycles		1260001-1263027, 1312609-1313329, 1315830-1315833, 1334215-1334225, 1334926-1334960, 1347941-1347978, 1340961-1340970	Impressed/ L.P./Gifts							

Maker's Type	Military Class	WD Serial No. Allocation	Contract Number	CAT. REF.	Frame Number	Engine Number	Qty Prod'd	Dates	Price(s)	Delivery Destination & Notes
Various types possibly including motorcycles		4419561-4421774	L.P. & Req							
Various types possibly including motorcycles		4321626-4321785, 4326418-4327417, 4381745-4382213, 4422121-4423020, 4427110-4427209, 4436209-4436327, 4436509-4437508, 4448258-4448757, 4461742-4462041, 4477583-4478582, 4482151-4482351, 4494020-4494413, 4473808-4473857, 4687317-4687320	Req							
Various types possibly including motorcycles		4328243-4328265, 4328399-4328450, 4328538-4328557, 4328460-4328465	N.C.							
Various types possibly including motorcycles		4456472-4456814, 4576885-4576913, 4686512-4686520, 4771581-4771611, 5109201-5109700, 5149542-5152013	Acquired							
Various types possibly including motorcycles		4671780-4671836, 4671881-4671885, 5494401-5494900	Ex-RAF							
Various types possibly including motorcycles		5575052-5575558	Non accounting vehicles							

Maker's Type	Military Class	WD Serial No. Allocation	Contract Number	CAT. REF.	Frame Number	Engine Number	Qty Prod'd	Dates	Price(s)	Delivery Destination & Notes
Various types possibly including motorcycles		5586901-5587100, 6173811-6174310	Allied Forces							
Various types possibly including motorcycles		6257438-6258437	Allied Land Forces, Norway							
Various types possibly including motorcycles		5828983-5829235, 5899729-5899899	Ex-US Forces							
Various types possibly including motorcycles		6050000-6099999	Reserved for?							
AJS 40/16M					2702-2790, 2792-3011, 3013-3017, 3019-3020, 3022-3026, 3028-3032, 3034, 3036-3037, 3053, 3487, 3491-3497, 3499, 3501-3505, 3507-3513, 3513-3521, 3523-3527, 3529-3587, 3592-3596, 3598, 3600-3601, 3603-3606, 3611, 3614-3615, 3618, 3622, 3625-3629, 3632, 3634, 3637-3640, 3642-3652, 3654-3671, 3673-3686, 3688-3691, 3693-3695, 3697-3699, 3701, 3703, 3705, 3711-3712, 3715, 3718	9125, 9127, 9132, 9134, 9145-9146, 9150-9151, 9154, 9180, 9187, 9196, 9198-9238, 9240-9271, 9273-9370, 9372-9438, 9440, 9442-9443, 9446-9448, 9450, 9454-9455, 9878, 9885, 9906, 9912, 9914-9916, 9918-9925, 9927, 9929-9930, 9932, 9934, 9936-9938, 9941-10012, 10014-10015, 10017-10021, 10023, 10031, 10038, 10044, 10046, 10048, 10052-10058, 10062-10068, 10070-10078, 10080-10083, 10085-10100, 10102-10111, 10113-10124, 10126-10132	502 frames 449 engines			

Maker's Type	Military Class	WD Serial No. Allocation	Contract Number	CAT. REF.	Frame Number	Engine Number	Qty Prod'd	Dates	Price(s)	Delivery Destination & Notes
AJS Model 26					2032, 2119, 2548, 2644, 2650-52, 2683-2721, 2723-25, 2727-53, 2755-64, 2766-67, 2769-71, 2774-2777, 2279-2781, 2784, 3012, 3018, 3021, 3018, 3021, 3027, 3033, 3035, 3038-52, 3054-3182, 3184-3349, 3353-54, 3366, 3376, 3419-86, 3488-90, 3498, 3500, 3506, 3514, 3522, 3528, 3589-91, 3597, 3599, 3602, 3607-10, 3612-13, 3615, 3617-21, 3623-24, 3630-31, 3633, 3635-36, 3641, 3646, 3672, 3676, 3687, 3692, 3696, 3700, 3702, 3704, 3706-10, 3713-14, 3716-17, 3719-67	8642, 9045, 9064, 9083-85, 9087, 9089-96, 9098-100, 9105-19, 9121-24, 9126, 9128-31, 9133, 9135-44, 9147-49, 9152-53, 9155-79, 9181-86, 9188-95, 9197, 9439, 9441, 9444-45, 9449, 9453, 9456-694, 9696, 9699, 9701-20, 9722-9670, 9762-65, 9767-68, 9770-74, 9777, 9779, 9781, 9783-85, 9788, 9795-96, 9835-39, 9842, 9844, 9847-52, 9854-56, 9859-77, 9879-84, 9886-905, 9907-09, 9911, 9913, 9917, 9926, 9928, 9931, 9933, 9935, 9939-40, 10022, 10024-37, 10039-43, 10045, 10047, 10049, 10051, 10059-61, 10069, 10079, 10084, 10101, 10125, 10133-82, 10184-92	589			
AJS Model 40/26L					2481-83, 2487, 2490, 2508, 2512, 2538, 2542, 2544, 2626, 2654-82	965, 9697-9700, 9721, 9761, 9766, 9769, 9775-76, 9778, 9780, 9782, 9786-87, 9789-94, 9797-9821, 9823-34, 9840-41, 9843, 9846, 9853, 9857-58	65 frames 65 engines			
AJS Model 8					815, 822, 826-912, 914-924	621-25, 627-34, 636-48, 659-71, 673-86, 688, 690-94, 696-97, 699-719, 721-35, 739, 746, 759	100			

You may also be interested in …

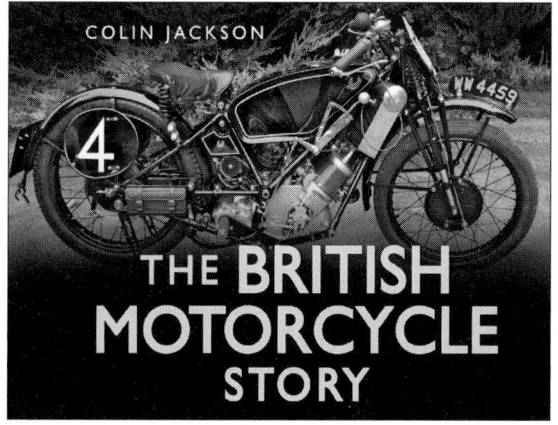

9780 7524 8735 9

Tells the story of these incredible machines and the men who rode them, charting the 'golden age' of British motorcycles from its earliest beginnings as little more than a bicycle with a tiny engine, to the fast, powerful machines we recognise today.